Peter Doig

Peter Doig

Edited by Judith Nesbitt
With an essay by Richard Shiff

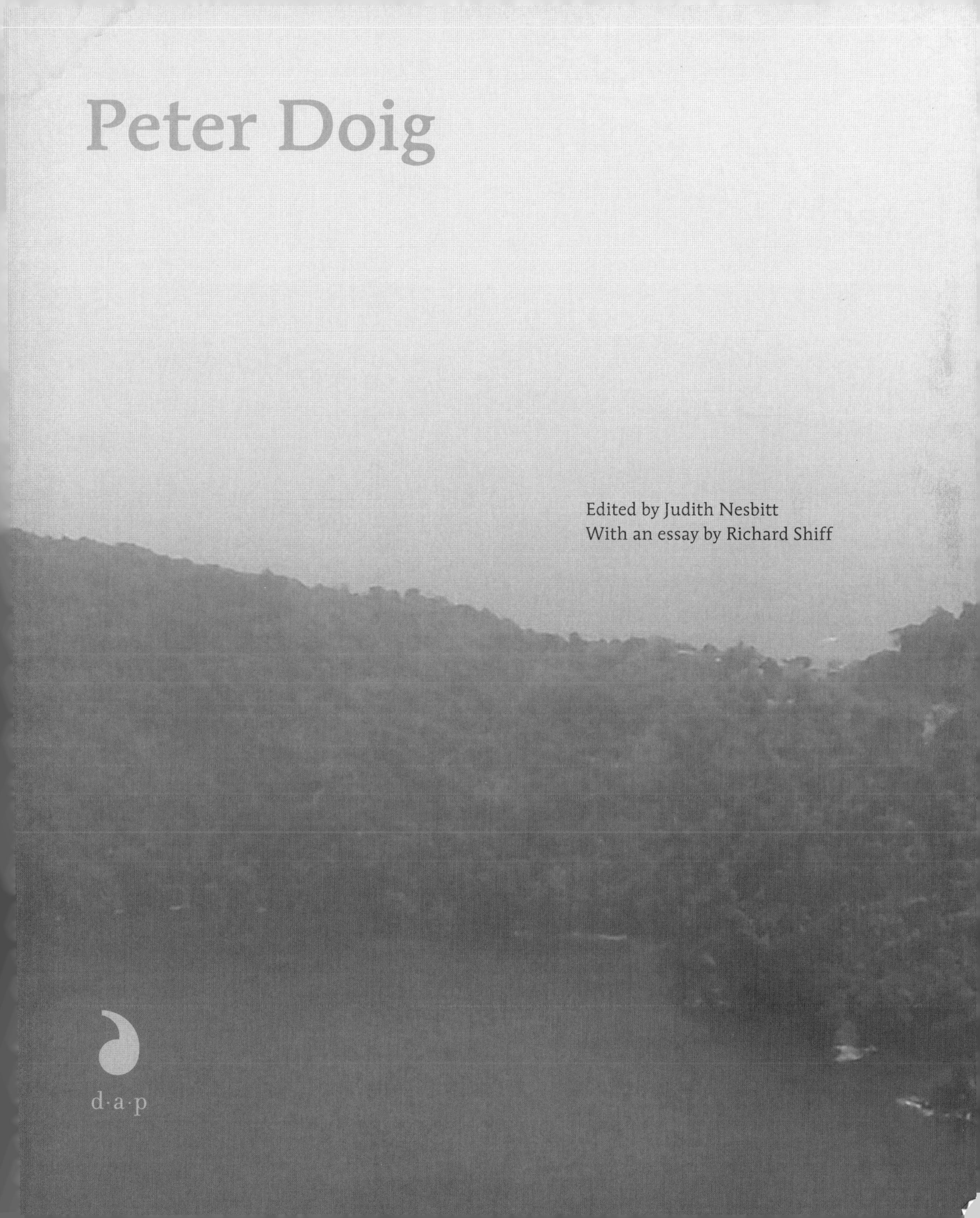

d·a·p

First published 2008 by order of the
Tate Trustees by Tate Publishing,
a division of Tate Enterprises Ltd,
Millbank, London SW1P 4RG
www.tate.org.uk/publishing

on the occasion of the exhibition
at Tate Britain, London
5 February – 27 April 2008

ARC/Musée d'Art moderne
de la Ville de Paris
21 May – 14 September 2008

Schirn Kunsthalle Frankfurt
9 October – 11 January 2009

Published in North America by
D.A.P./Distributed Art Publishers, Inc.
155 6th Avenue, 2nd Floor
New York, NY 100013
www.artbook.com

A CIP record for this book is available
from the Library of Congress

ISBN 978-1-933045-84-9

Designed by Peter B. Willberg at
Clarendon Road Studio, London
Printed and bound in Belgium by
Die Keure

Cover: Peter Doig, *Country Rock* 1998–9
(detail) (p. 84)

*Measurements of artworks are given in
centimetres, height before width.*

Contents

Foreword

Tate Britain is proud to present this survey exhibition of the art and career, to date, of Peter Doig. He is, of course, one of the most important painters of his generation at work anywhere in the world, and indeed though this show will inevitably reveal his distinctive place in the history of British art, his roots and impact extend far beyond these shores. Born in Scotland, raised in Trinidad and Canada, trained in London and now based principally in Trinidad, his work draws from and in some measure articulates his experiences of those many cultures. His subject matter is, invariably, richly described and wholly specific, yet its mesmeric ambiguity – that persistent air of a puzzle not yet quite solved – endows it with an emotional charge whose potential far exceeds the formal confines of the canvas.

Peter Doig's influence on his contemporaries and on the young artists he has taught in London and (currently) Düsseldorf has been profound. He seems to inspire the fierce loyalty of all who are touched by his work, not least a number of collectors who have followed and supported his career with unusual conviction. We have prevailed upon many of them to support this show through the loan of their possessions to its venues in London, Paris and Frankfurt. It constitutes the most searching overview of his work since the revelatory exhibition at the Whitechapel in 1998, and it promises to bring the range and significance of his work to the attention of a new, wide public. This is an exciting moment.

We are very grateful to our tour partners – the Musée d'Art moderne de la Ville de Paris and its director Fabrice Hergott, and the Schirn Kunsthalle Frankfurt and its director Max Hollein – for working with us to reach a broad European audience, and to the Exhibition Supporters Group, whose financial support was vital. Tate is indebted to the Museums Libraries and Archives Council for arranging indemnity cover on behalf of Her Majesty's Government.

The catalogue benefits greatly from the contributions of Richard Shiff, Rachel Tant, Chris Ofili and, above all, Judith Nesbitt, Tate Britain's Chief Curator, who has led and delivered the whole project in close collaboration with Peter.

Peter's own commitment to the selection, preparation and installation of the exhibition has been unfailingly generous – indeed absolute. It has been a privilege to work with him, and a pleasure.

Stephen Deuchar
Director, Tate Britain

Peter Doig Exhibition Supporters Group

Mr and Mrs Baz; Mr Charles Booth-Clibborn and The Paragon Press; Mr and Mrs Ben Brown; Ole Faarup, Copenhagen; Carolyn and Leslie Goldbart; Stan and Gail Hollander; Agnès and Edward Lee; William H. Neukom; Helen and Ken Rowe; The Glasshouse Trust; Speyer Family Foundation; David Teiger; James van Damme and Dean Johnson; American Patrons of Tate and those who wish to remain anonymous.

A Suitable Distance *Judith Nesbitt*

Peter Doig's paintings take us to strange places. They might be ordinary enough places in many respects, but an odd quiescence hangs over them – not calm, but dead stillness, with an undertow of disturbance. Viewing his paintings in an exhibition such as this, selected from two decades of work, is a disorientating experience of perpetual scene-shifting; we find ourselves circling across different terrains and domains, where locations and situations seem to recur, at once familiar and strange. What is this seemingly obsessive act of distraction that the artist practices on his viewers, on himself, on his paintings?

Doig has himself circled around the world to a remarkable degree, following a more individual route than most of his artist friends and peers. His biography is much repeated in texts on his work, and it remains a substratum within the paintings, a back-story that will out. Born in Edinburgh in 1959, Doig moved with his family to Trinidad two years later, where they lived until he was seven. His father's work for a shipping company led to another relocation in 1966 – this time to the suburbs of Montreal – and later to Foster, Quebec, and then to rural Ontario. At the age of nineteen, Doig took himself to London, drawn by the idea of going to art school in the city that produced much of the music he was listening to. He thought theatre design might be a way to earn a living, and won a place on the foundation course at Wimbledon School of Art in 1979.

At St Martins School of Art from 1980–83, Doig made his first forays into a brash kind of figurative painting, with cartoon-like story boards and characterisation. (fig.1) Hyper-charged and bursting with narrative, these urban pop scenarios (frequently observed by a lone-ranger character) were far adrift from the mainstream. Doig recalls that 'At St Martins in the early 1980s, we had the tyranny of post-American Abstract Expressionism via British Abstract Expressionism.'[1] It provided something for him to react against, and he also had helpful provocation from his tutors there (John Stezaker, Rosetta Brooks, Tim Hyman, Tim Allen and Adrian Searle), as well as the influential exhibitions that opened up a recent history of painting in Europe and North America and whetted the appetite of similar minded students.[2]

On leaving St Martins, Doig occupied a semi-squatted studio in Rosebery Avenue (which he would keep for over a decade), and worked as a dresser at English National Opera. After a couple of solo shows in 1984 and 1986, he returned to

Canada, uncertain of his relationship to London and his relationship to art. 'I wanted to experience a new city, a new place', he recalls.[3] He chose Montreal, not having previously lived in the city itself, and worked as a scene painter in the film industry. Meanwhile, he struggled on with his own painting in the evenings and weekends. 'When I went back to Canada, I was trying to find a new subject. Of course, at the time, I didn't really think of it in that way. I was just trying to make paintings. But I was making paintings about my memories of London. I couldn't get it out of my head really.'[4] Then, as now, his subjects came through chance encounters. One evening, he happened to see on video a part of the cult horror movie *Friday the 13th* and took a photo of an image that caught his attention – the dream sequence of a girl passed out in a canoe on a placid lake at dawn. When he got his snaps developed, the image prompted him to paint it. He had used photographs as a trigger for his paintings for some time, but this was an image to which he would return many times over the course of the next decade, and photographs have continued to serve as the compositional starting point in his practice. At this stage, although Doig was still inclined to pursue painting, he was as yet uncertain what he was doing with it.

Returning to London in 1989 to concentrate in earnest on his painting, Doig took an MA painting course at Chelsea. 'Since I had just come back from Canada and was again searching for a subject, I started making these quite homely paintings, paintings of quite modest subjects.'[5] This is where the current exhibition begins, for during these first few years back in London, Doig produced a large number of

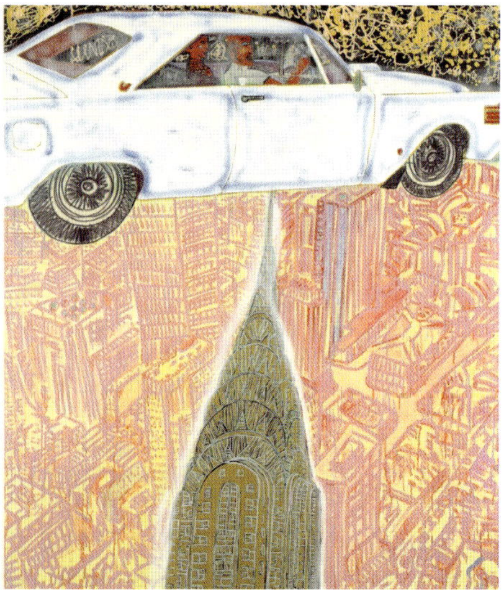

Fig.1 Boom Boom Boom (The Sublime) 1982
Oil on canvas, 180 × 151

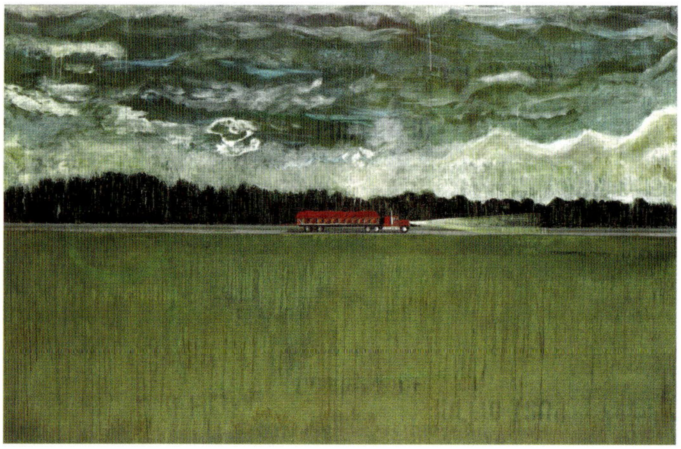

Fig.2 Hitch Hiker 1989–90
Oil on postal bags, 152 × 226

paintings that teemed with a weird individuality. Just a year after graduating from Chelsea, he won the Whitechapel Artists Award, attracted some favourable comment, and at the age of thirty had arrived at a point where his painting properly began. A feature article in the young but already influential *frieze* magazine in 1992 marked his emergence, and soon afterwards he was signed up by one of London's most prestigious contemporary art galleries.

At the time, his subjects were readily interpreted as vestiges of his Canadian upbringing, and regarded with some puzzlement by those who viewed his work as a recherché journey into the genre of landscape. Reflecting later on these over-simplified readings of this work, he comments: 'They weren't paintings of Canada (though some were) but paintings of an idea of something that was maybe folk – bringing a sort of "homeliness" into art.'[6] Even at the time he commented, 'So many of the paintings are of Canada, but in a way I want it to be more of an imaginary place – a place that's somehow a wilderness',[7] emphasising his aim to go beyond the specifics of place and time. It was as if he had deliberately, and perversely, assumed some sort of outmoded bohemian disguise – a charity shop outfit – with which to make an entrance. Appearing on the London art scene in the early nineties, when all eyes were on the cool, processed aesthetic emanating from Goldsmiths College, his subjects looked, by comparison, both romantic and banal. His choice of oil paint, the visceral, heavily worked surfaces and unflinching use of colour, all marked out a practice that was on a trajectory of its own.

His photographic sources were eclectic, found in books, newspaper images and magazines. A few would come from his own archive of snapshots, reflecting a teenage world of concerts, skiing and ball games. What was already evident in his paintings was the importance Doig attached to subject – not as narrative, but as the threshold of the viewer's experience. *Hitch Hiker* 1989–90 (fig.2) takes the viewer on a truck-ride heading west, with all the promise of an uncertain adventure. The cursory line of the open road is folded into a turbulent sky; the washed foreground falls away, drained of detail. Similarly bold, *Milky Way* 1989–90 (p.47) reconfigures the nocturnal landscape via the canoe scene of *Friday the 13th*. It is painted with startling unselfconsciousness – a stylised constellation set amid a stage-like starry sky, its inky blue-black darkness mirrored in the glassy surface of a lake. A lone figure sinks into the canoe, succumbing, it seems, to the evacuation of animate life.

* * *

Doig's notion of 'bringing a sort of homeliness into art' is a curious one. No doubt, his use of the word implied an art that was wrought from human experience, made by hand, perhaps sentimental, and even bordering on kitsch. It's notable, however, that his early landscapes include specific depictions of dwellings, both vernacular and architect-designed, executive homes and rooming houses, log cabins and farmsteads. Yet all appear uninhabited, with darkened windows like chasms, more frightening than inviting. These are, paradoxically, the most *unheimlich* of homes. Doig has often referred to his formative search for the 'atmosphere' of each painting. Given his particular treatment of homes and homeliness, there is a suggestive parallel with Freud's classic text, *The 'Uncanny'*, which pushes the idea of the '*heimlich*' to a point where it becomes identified with its opposite, '*unheimlich*'.[8] Whereas previous writers had related the uncanny to the unfamiliar, Freud exposes a paradoxical double meaning: 'We are reminded that the word "*heimlich*" is not unambiguous, but belongs to two sets of ideas, which, without being contradictory, are yet very different: on the one hand it means what is familiar and agreeable, and on the other, what is concealed and kept out of sight.'[9] He notes a similar ambiguity in the *Oxford English Dictionary* definition of the English word 'canny', 'which may mean not only "cosy" but also "endowed with occult or magical powers".'[10] Freud registers the intellectual uncertainty this engenders: 'Thus *heimlich* is a word the meaning of which develops in the direction of ambivalence, until it finally coincides with its opposite, *unheimlich*.'[11]

Intellectual uncertainty, ambivalence and contradiction are directions often taken in Doig's paintings, and embodied in their make-up. *Pine House (Rooms for Rent)* 1994 (fig.3) was a house for transient workers that Doig photographed following a bad fire; returning a few years later, he found it had been replaced by a set of new condominiums, which prompted him to paint the picture. A ramrod tree trunk slices the upper half of the picture in two, and skeins of paint cut into the surface like barbed wire. Apparition and negation are dynamically related in the formation of these paintings. *Jetty* 1994 (fig.4), Doig imagined as a kind of postcard image that one of the residents in *Pine House* might have pinned to his bedroom wall, a picture to be gazed at before drifting into sleep. In the painting, a lone figure surveys a lakeside mountain, but the drama of the image comes from the optical darkness that invades the surface – an occult disturbance that threatens to eliminate the vista. This visual dialectic is enacted in many ways within the imagery and

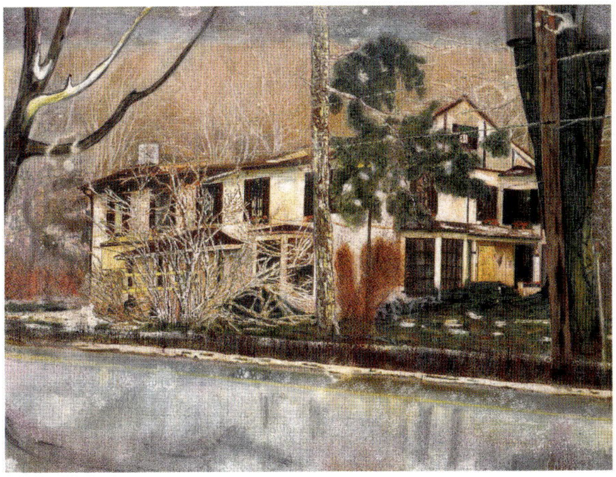

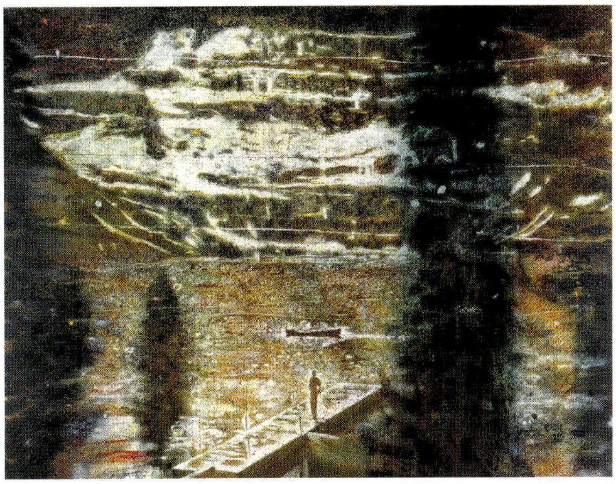

materiality of Doig's paintings, not least in the relationship between the photographic source and its painterly transformation into an imagined subject. Thus Doig creates a tension that he experiences as being 'nearly always torn between retaining the motif and undermining it'.[12]

The *Concrete Cabin* series (pp.58–65) is a sustained performance of this positive/negative dynamic: a modernist apartment block is approached from different vantage points.[13] The building is l'Unité d'Habitation, the last of Le Corbusier's series to be built, and intended to house itinerant workers. After falling into disrepair, it had been saved by a campaign from being knocked down, and one floor was occupied by an architects' and artists' cooperative. Doig himself did some of the renovation work that ensued. In his paintings, the white façade is only half glimpsed through, and lost amidst, the darkening thicket of trees and floating mists of paint. The utopian dream of the modern home dissolves into the disturbing unknown of the enclosing forest. Establishing himself as every bit a formalist as much as a representational painter, Doig was deliberately dissolving hierarchy within the painting:

> Instead of painting the façade of a building and then shrouding it in trees I would pick the architecture through the foliage, so that the picture would push itself up to your eye. I thought that was a much more real way of looking at things, because that is the way the eye looks: you are constantly looking through things, seeing the foreground and the background at the same time.[14]

Fig.3 **Pine Houses (Rooms for Rent)** 1994
Oil on canvas, 200 × 253

Fig.4 **Jetty** 1994
Oil on canvas, 200 × 248

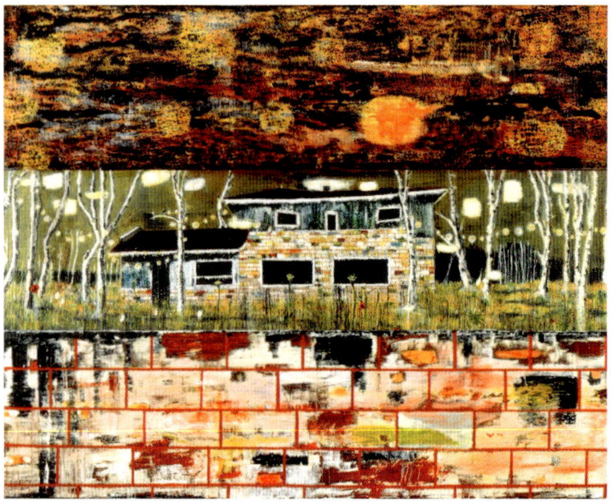

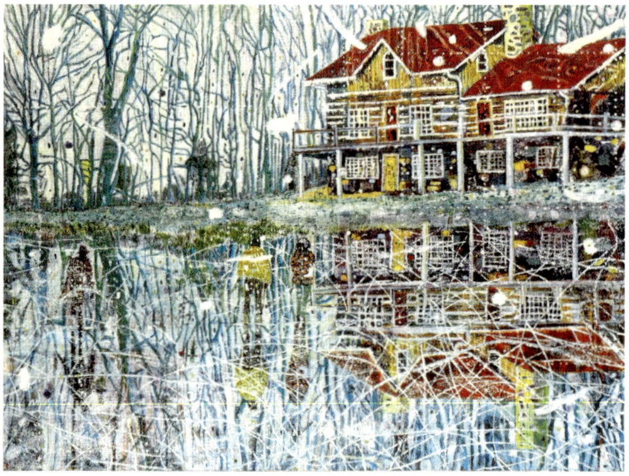

In other works, the structure of the painting – frequently a three-tier composition – denies the space of the represented image. In *The House that Jacques Built* 1992 (fig.5), the bleak house itself is sectioned between a brick wall foreground and an abstracted upper level, which serves to suppress rather than erase: 'I did like the idea that maybe these sections which had opened up to reveal a strip of existence could just as easily close down again.'[15]

Parallel to this phenomenon of uncertainty engendered by the internal contradiction of the image is Doig's predilection for doubling or mirroring the subject. Sometimes a painting actually generates its opposite, or companion, piece. *Young Bean Farmer* 1991 (p.57), Doig described as being 'about someone leaving somewhere. A small person, a shadow of a person really. It looks like he's going and he's not coming back.'[16] A year later, he completed *Night Bean Farmer* 1993, in which the boy has long since vanished. (In this trope, home is a condition that leads to exile.) Sometimes, a painting contains its own double, as in *Pond Life* 1993 (fig.6); Doig had been working on it for three months before adding the reflections of the figures: '...the mirroring opened up another world. It went from being something like a recognisable reality to something more magical.'[17] The formal resolution of the painting comes through the inversion of the represented image. This mirroring complicates the reading of the subject, which becomes a mirage – a deceptive tracery of paint. On top of all this representation lies a grid of dotted lines across the paint surface, suggestive of a sizing-up transfer process by which another image might follow.

Fig.5 **The House that Jacques Built** 1992
Oil on canvas, 200 × 250

Fig.6 **Pond Life** 1993
Oil on canvas, 185 × 240

In *Blotter* 1993 (p.66), Doig took the idea of visual disorientation still further. In this instance, he and his brother deliberately flooded a frozen pond to create a better reflection off the water on top of the ice. He photographed his brother standing amidst this 'incredible reflection' and used it to produce the painting. From a high viewpoint, the spectator's gaze drops down from the minimal screen of trees to the transfixed figure, whose orange headband becomes the pressured 'brain' of the picture. Within this mental maelstrom, there is no grip on rational space, and the eye swirls down into the refracted ripples and daubs of paint. Not for nothing do we learn that the titles of *Blotter* and its companion picture, *Window Pane* 1993 (p.67), refer to brands of LSD, the mind-altering substances of an earlier generation.[18]

These strategies of disorientation continue within the work of the mid-to-late 1990s, and take an extreme form in *Ski Jacket* 1994 (fig.7), which literally doubled into a two-panel painting. This picture, the artist recalls, 'was based on a photograph from a Toronto newspaper of a Japanese ski resort. It reminded me of a black and white oriental scroll painting. The original photograph was tall and narrow. I started by making one panel, but the scale was wrong – it seemed too narrow. So I made another panel the same size that both mirrored and distorted the original panel.'[19] In works such as *Figure in Mountain Landscape* 1997–8 (fig.8), Doig positions the viewer just behind the peculiarly hooded artist perched on a mountain top, so that we view the *plein-air* painting as well as the view itself – scale and vantage point pulling the viewer into the hallucinogenic vision.

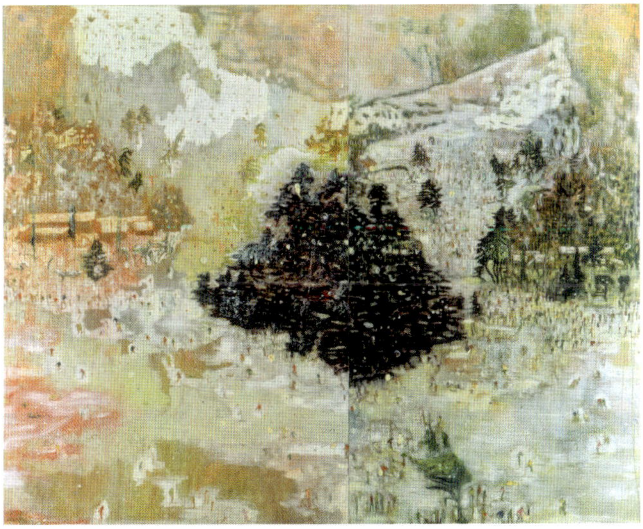

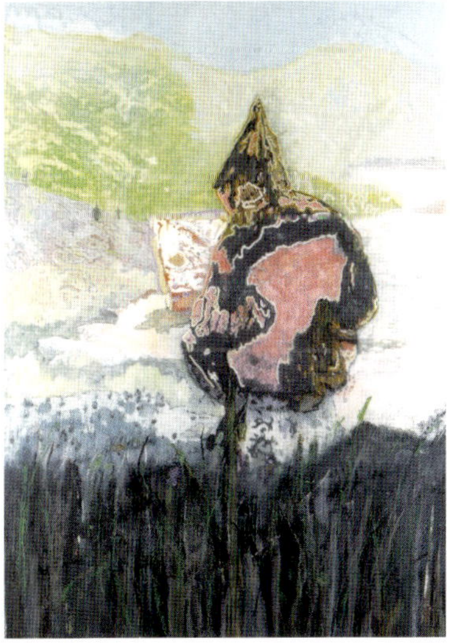

Fig.7 **Ski Jacket** 1994
Oil on canvas
(left) 295 × 190
(right) 295.3 × 160.4

Fig.8 **Figure in Mountain Landscape** 1997–8
Oil on canvas, 289 × 199.5

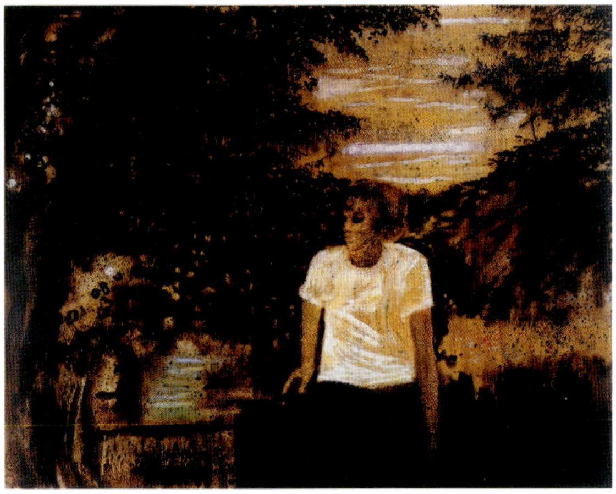

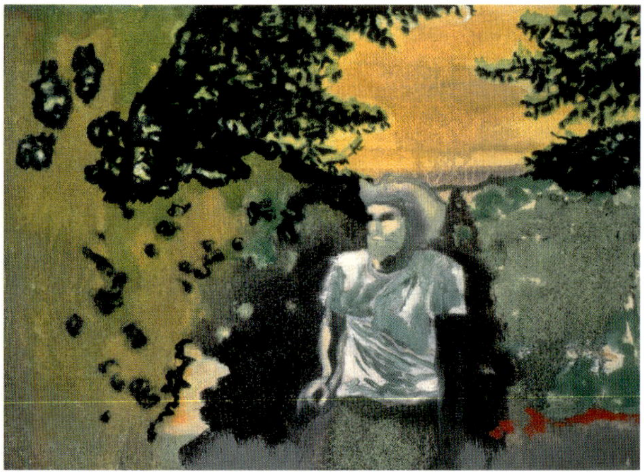

Besides this doubling and mirroring of the motif, there is a sense in which Doig has on occasions created a proxy for himself within the paintings, as if experimenting with being both author and subject, both outside and inside the work. In *The 'Uncanny'*, Freud moves from his analysis of the '*unheimlich*' to the phenomenon of the 'double' in literature:

> Thus we have characters who are to be considered identical because they look alike ... the subject identifies himself with someone else, so that he is in doubt as to which his self is, or substitutes the extraneous self for his own. In other words, there is a doubling, dividing and interchanging of the self. And finally there is the constant recurrence of the same thing – the repetition of the same features or character-traits or vicissitudes, of the same crimes, or even the same names through several consecutive generations.[20]

That Doig has used photos of himself may be incidental, or perhaps suggestive, or maybe both. *Corn Cob* 1994 (fig.9) is one such example. Perched on a fence, the figure has a youthful gaucheness, his awkwardness inscribed in the stiff painting of the T-shirt, which scarcely defines his angular frame, his left arm hanging uselessly. Another painting, *Drifter* 1999 (fig.10), derived from the same photograph, shows the young man wearing a cowboy hat, with an air of dreamy nonchalance. Neither picture could properly be considered a self-portrait, but whatever the impetus behind these paintings, the artist's persona, or his proxy, hovers not far away.

Fig.9 **Corn Cob** 1994
Oil on canvas, 121.9 × 152.4

Fig.10 **Drifter** 1999
Oil on linen, 30.5 × 41.5

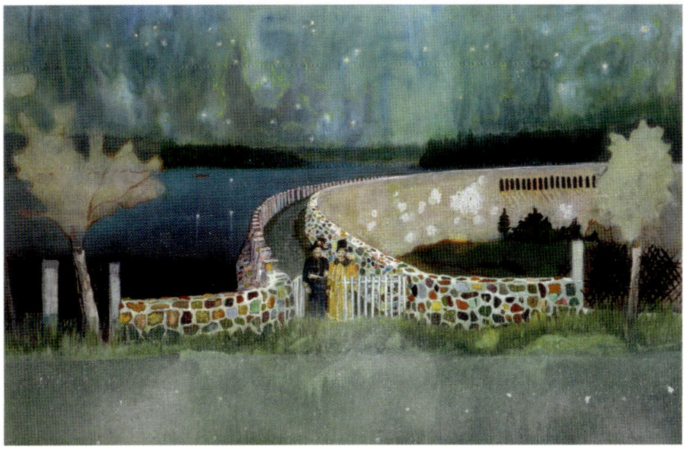

Doig dresses up for real in the bizarre, dream-like fantasy of *Gasthof Zur Muldentalsperre* 2000–2 (fig.12). The pair of figures is derived from a snapshot taken when Doig worked as a dresser at the Opera House, in which he stands with an artist friend, both got up in the costumes from a production of Stravinsky's ballet *Petrouchka*. Their matching stage moustaches make it impossible, or irrelevant, to know who is who. The painting sets up its own terms of reference, and precipitates its own drama – resulting from the merging of the photograph with a nineteenth-century postcard to create one of Doig's most surreal apparitions. But our knowledge of the artist's presence at the heart of the painting adds another layer of psychological complexity. A lark behind the scenes at the Opera House becomes enshrined in a landscape of entrancement within which the artist stands, disguised.

A similarly moustachioed character appears in a painting made a few years later. *Metropolitain (House of Pictures)* 2004 (fig.11) is a conundrum of a painting that makes a game out of identification and attribution, a core activity of the art world. Based on a Daumier painting that Doig saw in Chicago, this character is described

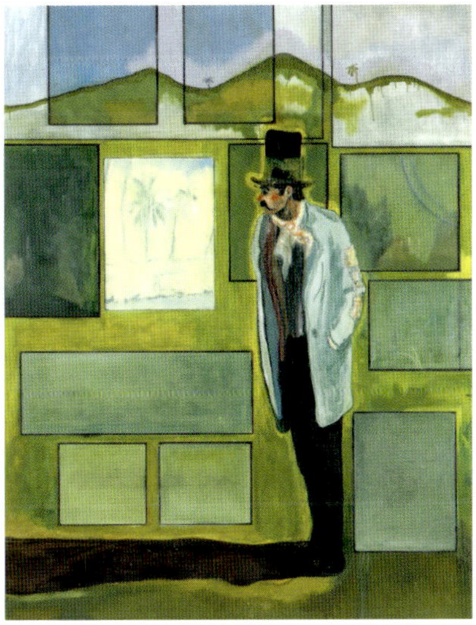

Fig.11 **Metropolitain (House of Pictures)** 2004
Oil on canvas
275.3 × 200

Fig.12 **Gasthof zur Muldentalsperre** 2000–2
Oil on canvas, 196 × 296

by Doig as 'obviously bourgeois. I wanted him to be a bourgeois but sort of beatnik bourgeois in his own time, more of an artist than a collector ... [T]here was an expression that developed through painting and painting and changing. It was quite strange, like making your own person that was almost life size.'[21] The desultory landscape forms a background for a transparent wall of paintings towards which the man leans uncertainly. Though most are rendered blank, they are attributable to Doig's own oeuvre, for each reproduced one of his own works before he over-painted most of them, except for the recognisable rainbow arc of *Purple Jesus (Black Rainbow)* 2004 (p. 112) and the one the man is staring at, easily identified as *Pelican* 2004 (fig.13).

One of the enigmas at the heart of Doig's work is the positioning of the artist in relation to his subject. His search for his subject has been curiously linked to his periodic geographical displacement, whereby the visual stimulus of his immediate environment becomes released only with distance. A month-long residency in Trinidad in 2000 offered Doig the chance to return to a place remembered from his childhood, and his decision to move there with his family two years later was an indication of the hold it had, or would have, for him as an artist. Only when he was in Trinidad did he fully recognise that:

> I'd been painting landscape – or an idea of landscape – in London, via my experiences in Canada, but that didn't come for a long, long time. I didn't start doing that until I'd been in London for almost ten years. And it was never really that kind of real experience; it was like filtering through things ... [It] was always a kind of escape to make these paintings in the studio, because what was outside the door was so different really. The work became a different world ... That was the excitement in a way: trying to find this other place in my studio, in my urban studio, in my head.[22]

It is as if a critical distance is required to enable a relationship to form between the artist and his subject, between found or recollected image and imaginatively transformed image. For Doig, it seems the real search has often been for this distance from which to approach a subject that would otherwise be too close. His personal journey – re-entering his own experience by returning to Canada, returning to London, returning to Trinidad – effects the displacement through which the familiar appears estranged. Equally, the slippage between what is real, remembered

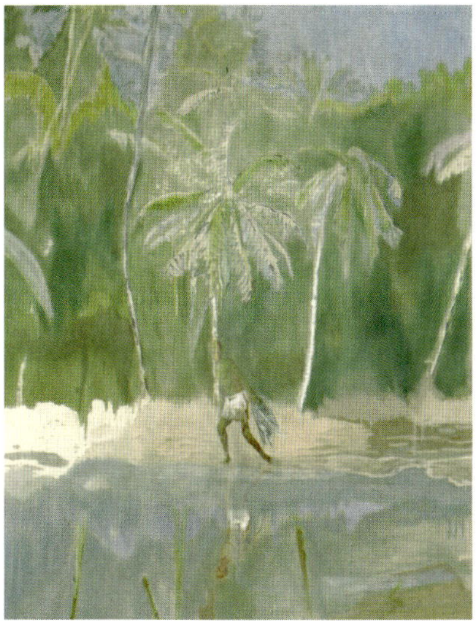

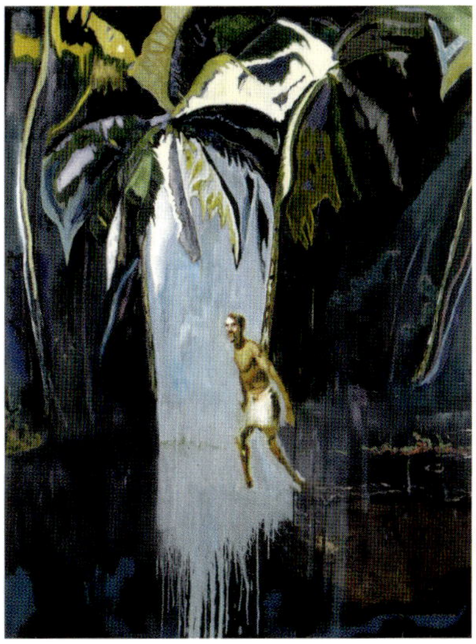

or imagined creates fertile territory for the artist. Freud recognised this 'uncanny' phenomenon 'when the distinction between imagination and reality is effaced, as when something that we have hitherto regarded as imaginary appears before us in reality'.[23]

Doig has been wary of appropriating Trinidadian subjects, but photographs taken during the month-long residency subsequently emerged as paintings back in his studio in London.[24] Amongst them are a number of his most important works of the last few years, begun in London, but completed in Trinidad: *Driftwood* 2001–2; *Grande Riviere* 2001–2 (p.86); *100 Years Ago (Carrera)* 2001 (p.82); *Pelican* (fig.13); *Pelican (Stag)* 2004 (fig.14). When he first went there, the landscape was 'so present and powerful',[25] and he circled it like an aircraft waiting for the right moment to land. Unsurprisingly, five years on, Trinidad has re-entered the work, not only figuring in his imagination, but informing his approach to the subject. He talks now of a search to make 'pure paintings, which evolve into a type of abstraction'.[26] In the work made since 2002, colour plays an increasingly important part, creating or retaining a quality of expansiveness within the canvas. Memory or visual impression may even come to dislodge the primary role of the photographic image. Doig has recently experimented with taking photographs through a telescope – simultaneously extending and shrinking the distance between the artist and the subject.

Fig.13 **Pelican** 2004
Oil on canvas
275 × 200

Fig.14 **Pelican (Stag)** 2004
Oil on canvas
276 × 200

Eliminating the context, he can isolate the motif from the landscape vista, and allow a strangeness of form to dominate the painting. He has taken to kayaking around the wild north coast of the island, offering another means of getting a physical and conceptual distance on his subject. This 'suitable' distance can be equivocal; it can be a slender threshold, breached when the unexceptional momentarily becomes the remarkable, and the unseen becomes visible.

* * *

In a recent conversation, Doig and Ofili recall an incident they witnessed when they went to Trinidad in 2000. From a remote beach, they saw a man in the sea, bobbing up and down in a swell of deep water, and wrestling, bizarrely, with a pelican:

> Doig: At first I thought he was rescuing the pelican or it had broken its wing. Then it became clear he was trying to drown it. And then he came onto the beach, and ... that's when you could see that he was just wearing his underwear, and swinging the pelican around by its neck. And by the way the pelican was looping and looping and looping, [you could see he was] obviously wringing its neck ... And at one point, I can't remember when exactly it was, he glared at us as if to say, 'You shouldn't be watching this' ... I felt [it was] a voyeuristic act watching him, but also something incredibly exciting to see ... I don't think we would have taken a photograph of it. It was too ...
>
> Ofili: It was too uncomfortable; but it was ... special in that I'd never seen anything like that before. It was also strangely quiet.[27]

In *Pelican*, a painting inspired by this moment, the bird is visible, the man's face partially obliterated by the white of the tree trunk that he walks past, as though fading into another realm. In a second version, *Pelican (Stag)*, the bird is erased, but a sudden downpour of light-infused paint isolates the subject, who stares back accusingly at his observer. It is that which 'ought to have remained secret and hidden but has come to light'.[28] Such is the excitement of the harbinger image, the quicksilver moment that brings paintings to light.

Incidents *Richard Shiff*

> My experience is just the spark ... which makes me think about things that are a part of other people's experience. Peter Doig, 1994[1]

Accident, incident

People suffer accidents, and they suffer incidents. The masonry cornice of a building loses a stone; it falls on a pedestrian below: an accident. That person loses consciousness: an incident. Two types of misfortune, two different losses – transitive and intransitive, accident and incident. Both categories accommodate unforeseen events and unintended consequences, but their connotations differ. Only when an event can be attributed to someone's action or failure to act is an accident distinguished from an incident that merely happens. To ask why of an incident is pointless, like demanding of cows why they should be bovine, or of sloths why they should be slothful: they act as they do; it happens. Paradoxically, incidental qualities prove to be the essential ones, for they animate the moment. Otherwise – lacking incident – a moment is nothing.[2]

An accidents-do-happen attitude allows events to be remembered as incidents with all their blurry edges, without being fixed by a logical order of cause and effect. As an incident, the event enters an ever expanding world of fluid insignificance. The insignificance of incidents derives from the potential of incidental events to signify too much – and to everyone. An incident that strikes the senses as clear and concrete becomes vague and ambiguous when the mind attempts to analyse and interpret it; its putative causes multiply, straining the observer's imagination. People argue over accidents, seeking resolution. But they wonder over incidents, dream over them. An incident is an accident that befalls both the intellect and the emotions.

Virtual memory

> People have confused my paintings with being just about my own memories. Of course we cannot escape these. But I am more interested in the *idea* of memory.
> Peter Doig, 2007[3]

Peter Doig suffers incidents. He observes people, situations, objects, materials, the atmosphere, his own mind. A sensory wonderer, he opens himself to situations likely to alter his emotions.[4] Regarding his practice, he speaks neither of accidents nor incidents, raising instead the related issue of 'mistakes'. Some artists would regard a mistake as an accident, fortunate or unfortunate for the progress of a work. Doig's mistakes remain neutral incidents to be exploited – experiments in feeling: 'In the late 1980s and early 1990s most art had a clean, contemporary, slick look ... I purposely made works that were handmade and homely looking ... I didn't want the surfaces to be beautiful but slightly repellent on close inspection.'[5] As he was leaving the institutional fold, he must have been aware of an aesthetic irony that was likely to benefit the reception of his work: modern viewers appreciate eccentric invention, to the extent that they often find incidental visual mistakes (but not programmatic ones) more attractive than regularity. Douanier Rousseau interests us far more than the academic artists he sought to imitate.

Doig's attitude is extreme: 'Mistakes are an essential part of everything I make. Many of the paintings are essentially mistake upon mistake upon mistake. That's how they evolve.'[6] He is Darwinian, then; his paintings thrive when left to a process of natural selection – survival of the most perceptually and emotionally evocative mutations (the mistakes, the genetic accidents). Were he to paint without mistakes, each work would come to its resolution without emotional stretch. A painting would begin with a mood and end with the same mood, detached from the immediacy of its own making, faithful to the type of fixed photographic image that Doig likes to use as a source to ground his memory and imagination. But, as he says, 'a painting [is] not fixed, still, like a photograph'.[7] So he draws from his sources loosely, subjecting them to shifts in focus, often in violation of the apparent significance of the original perspective – even when he himself is the photographer responsible for the image that guides, or misguides, his work.[8] When the photographic print itself suffers material accidents in the studio, the incidental changes only increase the initial value: 'Paint gets spilled or sprayed on it, and [this] adds an unexpected layer that you can then refer to. The reality of the original feels less constricting, and this provides an opening.' (fig.1)[9]

Every incident is an opening: the spill or spray that alters the image; technical anomalies already present in the photographic print – irregular resolution, blur, solarisation, lens flare (luminous circles and streaks of light unrelated to

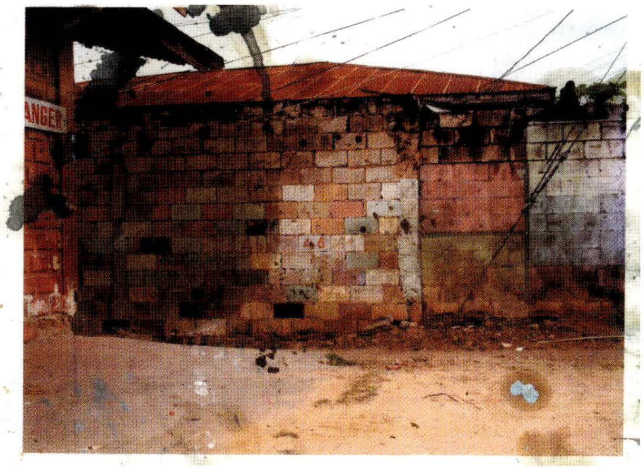

the image).[10] 'Sometimes I spend a lot of time [in the studio] just looking at things', Doig says.[11] Much of his focus is on the materials deployed this way or that. The visual incidents are well worth pondering. He realises that he need only seize the moment's perception. The object of his attention can be an eccentric stroke of paint on a canvas as much as an odd posture or other detail observed in a source photograph or illustration. Each incident contributes to the number of thematic, stylistic and technical features that remain incongruent as Doig combines them within his large surfaces, oversized to accommodate excesses of painterly caprice and pictorial tension.

As an example, take *The House that Jacques Built* 1992 (p.49).[12] Doig regarded his subject, a house in Quebec, as suitably 'homely'. He saw that the configuration of its windows gave it an anthropomorphic presence, 'that kind of mad Jack Palance face that looked like it had been carved'; here, he characteristically relates his observation of everyday situations to memorable images from the cinema.[13] He divided this painting into three horizontal zones, reserving the middle register for a view of the house while patterning the upper and lower registers as if they were details or close-ups of specific features. The lower zone, a kind of ground plane, depicts masonry; the upper zone, a kind of sky, seems to repeat the motif of the fairy lights hung through the trees around the house. The breaks are distinct, as in a film strip; but Doig had other analogies in mind. He was thinking of 'those [Barnett] Newman paintings with the "zips" – the ones with the little seemingly organic section',

Fig.1 Photograph of a multicolored masonry wall,
Port of Spain, 2002, with stains added by studio activity

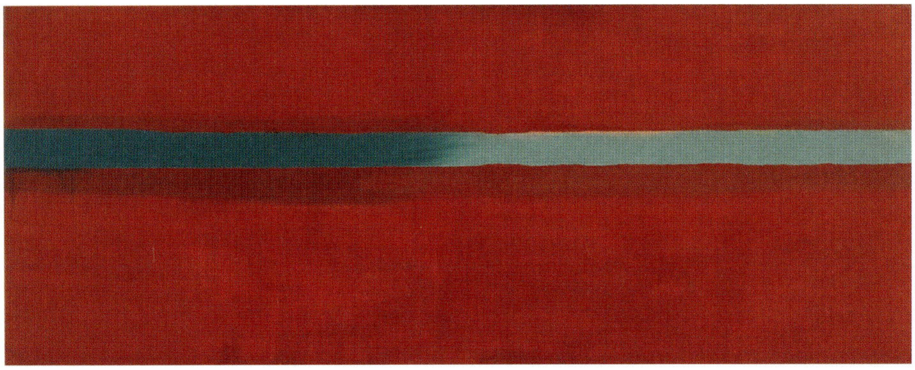

particularly those in a horizontal format, like *Horizon Light* 1949 (fig.2), with its organically brushy 'zip'. To this, he added a complicating reference, inspired by a vivid nineteenth-century description of the Canadian prairie, quoted in a book on ice hockey: 'Man is a grasshopper here, a mere insect making its way between the enormous discs of heaven and earth.'[14] He explains: 'I thought I could literally expand upon [the Newman effect] and have two abstract-organic sections and a middle that was somehow the "grasshopper".'[15]

Doig's imagination is capacious; within the frame of a single image, he can include aspects of Newman, hockey, insects of the prairie, and a Jack Palance look. The same imagination is capricious, generating odd details of visual humour or bits of whimsy. In the 'grasshopper' zone at the centre of *The House that Jacques Built*, Doig isolated a few flowers on long stalks, projecting them against dark surrounds, each flower set before an otherwise blank window. Once noticed, this incidental detail sticks in the memory; each window becomes a little puppet theatre for the performance of its flower. The effect has a comic touch; but the comedy is black, for the flowers are poppies – drug flowers – sinister like Jack Palance. Doig chose poppies because, in a metaphorical sense, they belonged to his own neighbourhood at the time: the King's Cross area of central London. This type of transfer is typical of him. He represents one locale by giving it the properties of another, introducing London drugs to a suburban garden in Quebec: 'Poppies ... deathliness, dead eyes, junkies' eyes.'[16] Somewhere, Doig may have observed flowers framed by windows – perhaps in a third location, neither Quebec nor London, possibly even in a film. Just as likely, he invented the situation during the evolution of his picture, knowing

Fig.2 Barnett Newman **Horizon Light** 1949
Oil on canvas, 77.5 × 184.2 × 5.2
Sheldon Memorial Art Gallery and Sculpture Garden, University of Nebraska-Lincoln, UNL-Gift of Mr. and Mrs. Thomas Sills

that it was a plausible visual relationship of a type he would have remembered, had he ever seen it.

A memorable motif is already a memory. With his window-flower, Doig encountered a virtual memory, either creating or perpetuating it. Such a distinction is never certain. Having created something that feels new, a person sees how much it resembles things already known, not only to that person but also to others. Doig's virtual memory became actual as he brought imagery from London and Quebec into association, and this same configured memory had the immediate potential to be actualised elsewhere, anywhere. Doig's configuration echoes remotely in the way that a parasol 'flowers' above the level of the coping stones of *Lapeyrouse Wall* 2004 (p.90). This image is at once strange and ordinary – a man walking in the sun beside a cemetery wall in Trinidad. Any number of whimsical elements enhance it. For one, pictorial features belonging to the far side of the wall – the tips of exhaust stacks from a power station beyond the cemetery, the top fronds of three palm trees, the upper part of a nearby structure – seem to peer back surreptitiously, returning the viewer's curiosity in kind. For another, the bold pink and grey pattern of the parasol. Doig had captured it in a closely related photograph. The parasol is an objective fact memorable enough to seem like a subjective invention. In contrast to *The House that Jacques Built*, nothing sinister emerges from the imagination at work in *Lapeyrouse Wall*. The pale blue of a tropical sky, itself enhanced by whimsical painterly variation, surrounds the projected form of the man and his parasol – no darkness, only light. Doig attributes the subtle shifts in blueness that he built into the upper expanse of his picture to the advice of an older artist in Trinidad, who suggested that he should 'look at the [real] sky'.[17] So he did. Whatever his observation revealed was necessarily both personal and impersonal, particular to him and common to everyone: another case of virtual memory being actualised. Painting the sky allowed memories of skies to grow into the present on the template provided by the moment's observation.

Doig's paintings create memories from mazes of disorientating detail. They show something familiar that nevertheless looks unsettlingly weird, or something weird that looks familiar.[18] *Hitch Hiker* 1989–90 (p.45) is one of his most straightforward paintings, but it too builds 'mistake upon mistake upon mistake'. The simplicity of the composition deflects its potential to confuse, which also has an emotional side, probably unavoidable: the painting is ominous. By conventional standards, the bright red truck at the centre is too small for the expanse of dull green it occupies. On the depicted highway, it seems lost in perpetual twilight. Its precise detailing, epitomised by the crisp, yet inexplicably wobbly headlamp beam, is inconsistent with the loosely rendered landscape that the viewer, as much as the truck, has been called to traverse. Potentially dizzying, the picture sets the position of the viewer too far back to establish a comfortable psychological relation to the implied action. 'Everything in Canada', the location of the scene as Doig imagines it, 'is on the edge of the wilderness'.[19] As both a pictorial and a psychological construction, *Hitch Hiker* threatens to lose its form. From foreground field to roadway to background forest to atmospheric sky, each of Doig's elements remains a separate incident with its own distinct character, barely co-ordinated. The atmospheric sky ought to recede from the land, but reveals sufficient material presence to push itself forwards, in front of the loosely detailed forest that should be occupying the closer position. This is a mistake in atmospheric perspective, an incident that the viewer cannot fail to notice. Doig consciously allows the qualities of paint to overrule the logical requirements of representation, indulging his curiosity as to what paints and solvents can do.

The materials lead Doig along novel courses of action that push his theme this way and that. His studio is itself a wilderness: 'I often find that I am unable to really paint unless I have a lot of paint out in open containers on my studio table and floor. This is part of the decision process for me – as well as chance.'[20] He depicts his human subjects, architectural views and landscape scenes with sets of oddly disjunctive technical effects: garish, psychedelic colour; jumps in scale; a roving focus; abrupt shifts in illumination and surface texture; arbitrary outlining of forms; severe geometric divisions.[21] In combination, these pictorial qualities put the image in flux, like the vagaries of memory, transient and shifting. Doig's effects are more than incidents of private fantasy. As they organise the image in their eccentric way, they also belong to a more public visual environment, whether natural or a product of the media. Either in advance of or after the fact, Doig notes parallels to his effects: the pinkish glow of snow in fading sunlight, the colour reversals of photographic solarisation, the voyeuristic angles of cinema, even the painterly leaching of minerals from masonry.[22]

In 2005, Doig photographed a leaching wall in Port of Spain; it was decidedly Doig-like (fig.3). He recognised that he had already painted the effect: during the preceding years, he had made a number of works, including *Hitch Hiker*, in which

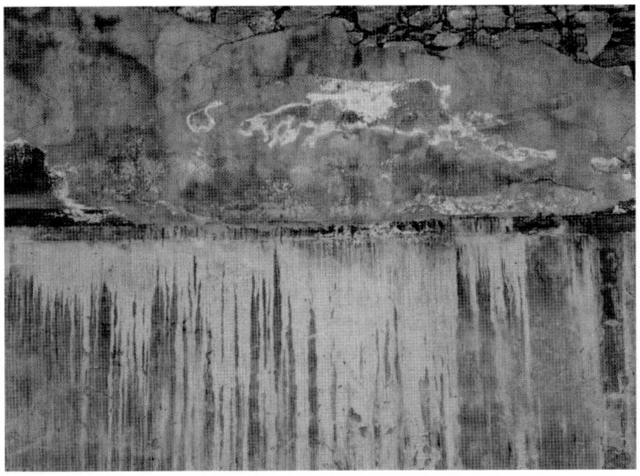

vertical runs of fluid paint or medium extend down from a horizontal division. This was a virtual memory that he would actively remember wherever it materialised – 'the way painting flows and bleeds on canvas'.[23] The vision need not be restricted to paint, nor to stains on stone or cement. Virtual memory is dreamlike, without fixed identity. Its temporality is fluid. Such memory operates forwards and back – a link, an image in formation. Often, to the contrary, we assign too much stability to memory, as if it were inalterable, its effects constant. Memory must move: 'Essentially virtual, [our past experience] cannot be known as something past unless we follow and adopt the movement by which it expands into a present image.'[24] Like the image in *Hitch Hiker*, a memory in the process of its incidental appearance or reappearance – we cannot tell which – is haunting.

Snowy effects

> I often paint scenes with snow because snow somehow has this effect of drawing you inwards. Peter Doig, 1994 [25]

The relation of Doig's subjects to their manner of rendering converts both sides of this equation into a mix that only gradually settles. The condition of his art can be discomforting, appearing either too expected or too unexpected, perhaps like Pop art in New York around 1962 (but Doig's work is not Pop). 'The paintings [shown in

Fig.3 Photograph of a masonry wall, Port of Spain 2005

2002] were full of boats, water, weather, people copied from photos, sweetie colours and snowy effects', wrote a recent observer, registering – with irreverent comic intention – a certain frustration that he believed must surely be felt by others. The critic continued: 'He does this but he is accepted as a contemporary guy. No writer has yet explained it.'[26] The implication is that Doig limits his subjects to tasteful cliché ('boats, water') and decorates his surfaces, aiming only to please and amuse ('sweetie colours and snowy effects'). Even if it were true that no writer has explained why Doig has been accepted within the contemporary canon despite these attributes, Doig himself has done so. His comments indicate that he depicts commonplace situations while perceiving the tensions, ironies and emotional edginess in these ordinary views. He leads his banalities towards a sensory and psychological precipice, over which he barely keeps from falling into kitsch. Kitsch would be a safe haven, because we feel comfortable there (until we become self-conscious about it). Doig risks the approach without the benefits of arrival, exploring incidental moments of life certain to lack resolution. A moody reflection in a pond – *Reflection (What does your soul look like)* 1996 (p.69) – becomes a speculation on the substance behind the image, perhaps what lies behind all images. We wonder; we do not know; we are not going to know. The memorable gait of a man passing by a cemetery wall – against which he seems to flow along, light-footed and lost in himself (*Lapeyrouse Wall*) – causes the viewer to muse over what kind of person this not so remarkable man could be. We have met him already: in this essay, but surely also in life. Doig photographed the figure and the wall separately, then combined them in painted studies that featured not only the man's gait but also his patterned parasol (*Lapeyrouse Umbrella* 2004) (p.110) and the patterned stones of the wall (*Cemetery Wall* 2003) (p.146). A fire hydrant entered the scene; Doig removed it, then brought it back.[27] Its blunt, matter-of-fact presence in the definitive version of *Lapeyrouse Wall* exposes by contrast the etherealness of the umbrella-man, who seems emotionally evasive and all the more mysterious.[28] His mystery is that of human existence.

Inconclusive incidents and their images rarely receive such scrutiny except when a serious accident has occurred or a crime has been committed – then, the incidental becomes evidence. Doig avoids the dramatic resolution typical of the cinematic mysteries and romances that often inspire him: 'I'm interested in [situations where] you can find something romantic ... but somehow give it a certain poignancy – without just falling into pieces of sickliness.'[29] The emotional force of the poignant moment extends beyond entertainment. It goes to the edge. To get there, Doig has studied the methods of his modernist predecessors, and marshals any number of technical conceits drawn from their work, reinvigorating and extending their potential within a contemporary representational practice.[30] He is eclectic: Cézanne, Gauguin, Munch, Matisse, Bonnard, Hopper, Beckmann, and still others are among those he enlists. To an equal extent he draws from the present visual environment – its imagery of professional and amateur photography, popular and experimental cinema, commercial television and home video. The first double-page spread in the exhibition catalogue *Peter Doig Blizzard seventy-seven* 1998 is a photographic capture of a video monitor showing a cinematic image that Doig used for a number of his paintings, including *Swamped* 1990 (p.51). It seems to condense his diversified media interests into a single pictorial moment.

Yes, the vision that informs Doig's art includes 'people copied from photos, sweetie colours and snowy effects', as in his numerous pictures of skiers and other winter scenes, such as *Ski Jacket* 1994 (p.70) and *Figure in Mountain Landscape* 1997–8 (p.73). But the situation is not as straightforward as the critic's description suggests. All is complicated by the artist's sensitivity to an environment of images and effects drawn not only from the art traditions, but also from the broad range of popular culture that relates to those traditions (cinema, record sleeves, postcards) and from the electronic imagery that generates still newer forms of popular culture – including all the technological malfunctions and electronic 'mistakes' that may form an aspect of them. There is a 'homely' side to video, too, not just to painting. The 'snowy effects' may be Doig's allusion to his youthful experience of Canada and to Canadian artists who painted the North American wilderness (Group of Seven or David Milne, for example). Snow also refers to the example of Bruegel the Elder's *Adoration of the Magi in the Snow* 1563 (fig.4), a work that Doig admires, as well as to the 'snow' that sometimes dances across a video monitor, the incidental result of internal electronic interference.[31] The snows of Bruegel and video converge: 'When you look at [Bruegel's painting,] the snow is almost all the same size, it's not perspectival, it's this notion of the "idea" of snow, which I like. It becomes like a screen, making you look through it.'[32] Doig notes that Bruegel produced long ago the condition that the video monitor produces now – it 'keeps you back [yet] looking through and into [the] picture within'. The screen effect also provides what Doig calls 'dimension', perhaps applying the term to now-and-then time as well as here-and-

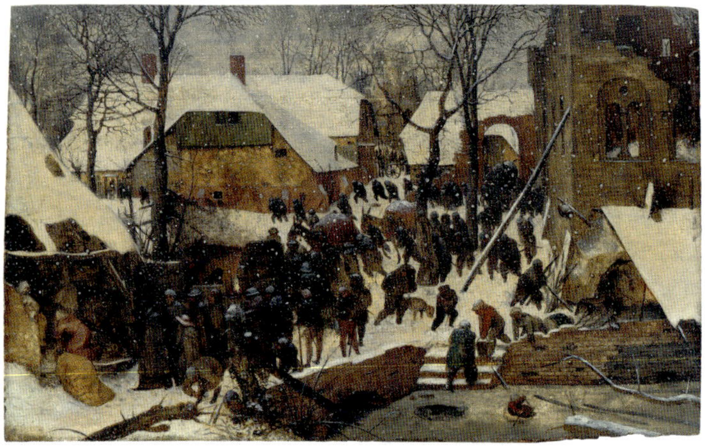

there space.[33] If certain representations of snow do capture the more general notion of 'snow' as a screen with its sensory and psychological functions, then 'snow' rises to a higher level of significance within Doig's memory project. More than a phenomenon to be remembered like any other memory, it becomes a candidate for the 'idea of memory' (alternatively, this could be called the 'memory effect' or even 'metamemory'). This may be why, as Doig remarks, snow has the 'effect of drawing you inwards'.[34] It induces introspection, as if, through it, you were remembering yourself, looking into your soul.

A screen can be actual, a physical material, like the substance of falling snow, Bruegel's flecks of white pigment, or even the very ground of the painting, the panel or canvas. In pictorial terms, it can be any screen-like formation: Doig has painted screens of trees (*Boiler House* 1994) (p.65) and overhanging branches (*Young Bean Farmer* 1991) (p.57). A screen can also be virtual, like a cinematic or electronic projection into indeterminate space. Doig uses the term 'snow' in a literal sense (the weather) as well as in its metaphorical extensions (forms of photographic and electronic interference). In every instance, snow creates the effect of a screen, whether materially perceptible or not, and perhaps also the effect of a screen over a screen – as in cases of material or electronic interference that affect a projected image located in the same visual field. Doig's painting on plywood panel, *Snowballed Boy* 1995 (p. 109), renders the equivalence of visual interference and physical substance particularly tangible. Its 'screen' of snowballs includes (fictive) linear traces of the move-

Fig.4 Pieter Bruegel the Elder
The Adoration of the Magi in the Snow 1563
Wood panel, 35 × 55
Collection Oskar Reinhart "Am Romerholz",
Winterthur, Switzerland

ment and impact of the blobs of white – all projected onto the second screen of the plywood support, with which the blobs must have interacted in order to have taken their form.[35] An illusion presents itself: the plywood panel must be transparent; it holds the snowballs to its front side while screening off the image of the boy on its back side (a painter's wonder).

Lost

> By making a painting or by looking at a painting, we [try] to get away from the ordinary. Peter Doig, 1994[36]

> People look at paintings [in a] very different way [from how] they look at just about anything else ... It's a sort of strange, lost scrutiny. Peter Doig, 2007[37]

Doig wonders at the incidents of his world – our world – with the 'lost scrutiny' appropriate to painting. He follows through by painting with the same sense of wonder. Witness the many variants he makes of a single theme over a period of years: his *Friday 13th* 1987, *Swamped* 1990 (p.51), *Canoe Lake* 1997–8 (p.18), *Echo Lake* 1998 (p.80), and *100 Years Ago* 2000 all derive (to varying degrees) from the concluding moments of the Sean Cunningham horror film *Friday the 13th*.[38] Doig treats his subjects offhandedly to allow their incidental qualities to enter deep into consciousness; he escapes the self-censorship that comes from categorising an experience too readily and too definitively in terms of a comfortable familiarity. In conversation with his former tutor and friend, the critic Adrian Searle, he remarked, regarding the fisherman depicted in *Lunker* 1995 (fig.5), that he could 'tell what kind of guy he is'.[39] It was a question of reading the projected body language: 'melancholic but not without some tragic humour'.[40] The description is probing yet unlikely to evoke this image when not conjoined with the picture; words may classify but do not translate the specificity of the painting, which has the force of a virtual memory becoming actual. On this, Marcel Proust is acute: 'As Habit [or familiarity] weakens every impression, what a person recalls to us most vividly is precisely what we had forgotten, because it was of no importance, and [we] had therefore left [it] in full possession of its strength.'[41]

An 'incident' is 'of no importance' – and therefore, deeply affecting. *Lunker* is an incident or group of incidents. If Doig were to invent a more elaborate verbal

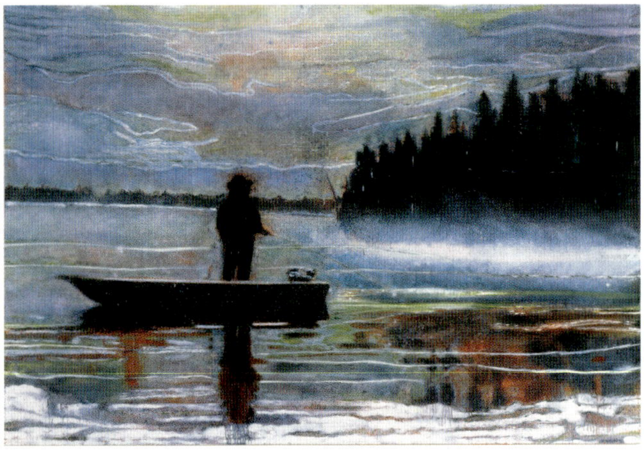

account of the fisherman, it would still not exhaust the image, which is a hybrid of what he found in a photograph and the transformation that occurred while painting. He adjusted the form of *Lunker*, letting it evolve into active memory, by using a techno kind of colour, 'like taking a photograph with a Van Gogh film in the camera'.[42] Others may not agree to a 'melancholic' characterisation of the man or perceive a 'Van Gogh' appearance in the painting. Incidental images retain their ambiguity, which is why we so easily lose ourselves among and within them. Doig chose the *Lunker* theme because he felt 'empathy' for this figure (as for others he investigates).[43] Painting it strengthened his emotional connection to it, while simultaneously altering that connection – as happens when we remember a memory.

The empathy may be Doig's feeling, but in his art it becomes public; it disseminates. Despite its peculiarities, viewers feel as if they have already experienced what they see in Doig's art because the moments he depicts feel like others' memories. Fellow painter Daniel Richter noticed this: 'Doig's simulated memories [select] the kind of approximated and casual "moments" that immediately click with everybody.'[44] In this sense, Doig's art is like the commercial cinema to which critics often compare it and to which the artist himself alludes. Cinema does not alienate its viewers; it seduces them, draws them within – like a screen of snow. Cinema is empathetic. The experience it projects is communal, as is the world Doig seeks to reach: 'I feel that my [personal] experience is just the spark ... which makes me think about things that are a part of other people's experience.' The sentiment, the

Fig.5 **Lunker** 1995
Oil on canvas
200 × 266
Courtesy Contemporary Fine Arts, Berlin

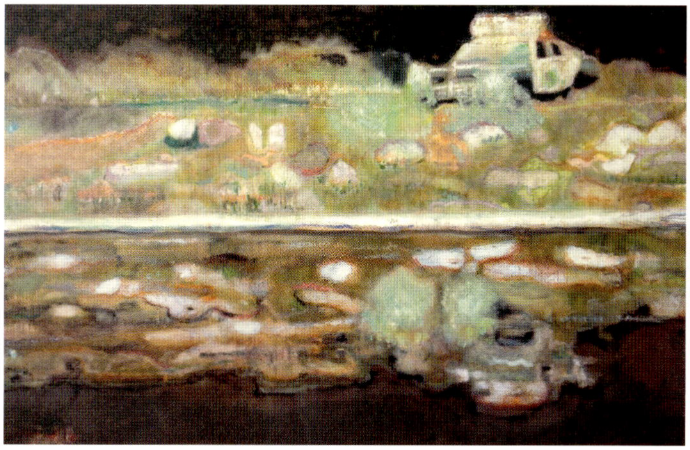

memory, is returned: he recalls a Japanese woman who, on seeing his paintings, 'felt like she had been to some of these places herself even though she had never visited North America'.[45]

'Getting lost', 'losing yourself', 'going beyond yourself' – these are colloquial expressions to which Doig resorts as he offers an experiential, as opposed to a theoretical, account of his art. 'Painting is about working your way across the surface, getting lost in it ... [The size of paintings] is about the idea of getting absorbed into them, so you physically get lost.'[46] Yet, size may not matter in the context of psychedelic experience, which, as Doig puts it, involves 'looking in a different way, and losing oneself in the looking'.[47] This psychedelia shows in the strange glow of *Lunker* as well as in the rings of colour he often sets around forms, whether large or small. In *Echo Lake* 1998 (p.80), he edged whitish rocks and their watery reflections with rose pink, acid green, magenta and violet (see the detail, fig.6).[48] Something else of a disorientating, lose-yourself nature occurs in this large painting: bits of form and colour, primarily in the central band of brightness, project forwards from the surrounding darkness to form a screen of pulsating colour and light. There is spatial depth, but without spatial logic. This condition is as real as it is the painter's fictive creation, for a scene looks this way when a person is uncertain of the situation or the terrain: all is incidental. The viewer's focus roams without a definite aim – it knows little of what it looks for – until it discerns some compelling order. The order, however, may prove less interesting than the sensation of roaming. Some of Doig's

Fig.6 Detail of rocks with police car, from **Echo Lake** 1998
Oil on canvas, 230.5 × 360.5

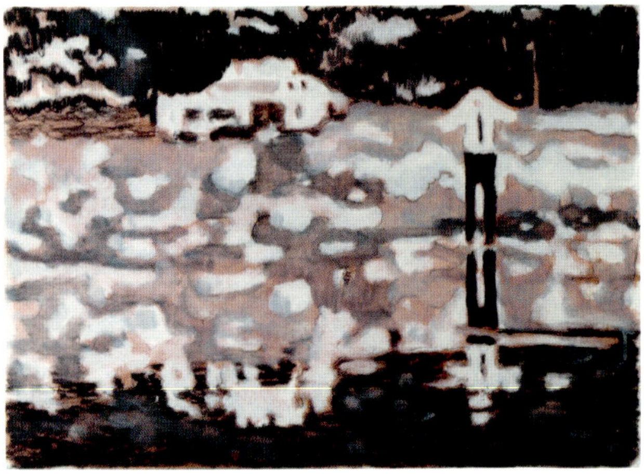

roaming occurs from one work to the next. He followed *Echo Lake* with a number of oil on paper studies, including one that exaggerates the screen-like, snow-like effect of the illuminated rocks. In this reduced version of the theme – *Echo Lake* 2000 (fig.7) – the rocks and their reflections, as well as similarly illuminated elements of the picture, seem suspended in a plane, like water droplets on a pane of glass. This and many of Doig's other works on paper are exercises in low-resolution vision, where forms join with neighbouring forms, losing their identifying distinctions in the blur that results from an ever-widening focus. Within the obscurity of blur, new locations of focus and light emerge as incidents to lure the viewer.

Some examples of Doig's Lapeyrouse Wall theme introduce analogous snow-screen effects in the stucco and stone patterning of the wall. This is relatively obvious in small paintings such as *Cemetery Wall* and *Lapeyrouse P.O.S. Pink Umbrella* 2003 (p.110), as well as in a schematic pencil rendering that isolates and abstracts this feature (*Untitled (Lapeyrouse Wall)* 2003) (fig.8). The effect is far less obvious in the large-scale *Lapeyrouse Wall*, where Doig weakened the pattern, wary that it would otherwise become too much of an attraction in itself and lessen the productive tension of the painting as a whole.[49] What remains of the detailed articulation of this wall surface nevertheless seems to lift up from its proper pictorial location, becoming (once again) a screen-like motif. Each detail is a study in painterly technique: in some parts, the additive gesture of brushing dominates; in other parts, the subtractive gesture of rubbing or wiping dominates; in still other areas, there may be

Fig.7 **Echo Lake** 2000
Oil on paper
65 × 79
Private Collection

a play of thick and thin texturing, of pure hues and blended colours, and so on. The diversity of techniques is remarkable. Even as these accentuated bits of articulation frame the implied movement of the striding figure, they detach from this central focus and from each other, maintaining an independent visual interest. In terms of conventional representation, this is a 'mistake' because the various descriptive elements lose the hierarchy of significance that would support the implied narrative content. To show a figure walking beside a wall, the conventional artist reduces the visual impact of the wall, subordinating it to the figure. On the contrary, Doig keeps all visual tensions going, deflecting a viewer's attempt to impose order. *Lapeyrouse Wall* nevertheless maintains coherence, perhaps because its dramatic spatial perspective and the emotional force of its isolated figure can at no moment be ignored. The painter brings fantasy to his realism and realism to his fantasy. Adapted for the cinema, we might call this absorbing picture 'Lost in Lapeyrouse'.

Viewers become lost in Doig's paintings because of their many incidents, which introduce material tensions and ambiguities to a general theme otherwise commonplace – a suburban house, a fisherman in the wilderness, a pedestrian in the city. Not long ago, Doig witnessed an unusual, somewhat horrific event: a man wading offshore on a remote beach in Trinidad, killing a large pelican. The scene piqued Doig's curiosity even as his sensibilities recoiled. He chose to represent what he had come upon, perhaps as a means of processing it for his own relief. The fact that this bizarre incident occurred in Trinidad – which, like Quebec and London, has meant home to Doig – gave the scene an emotional complexity suited to his art. But he had

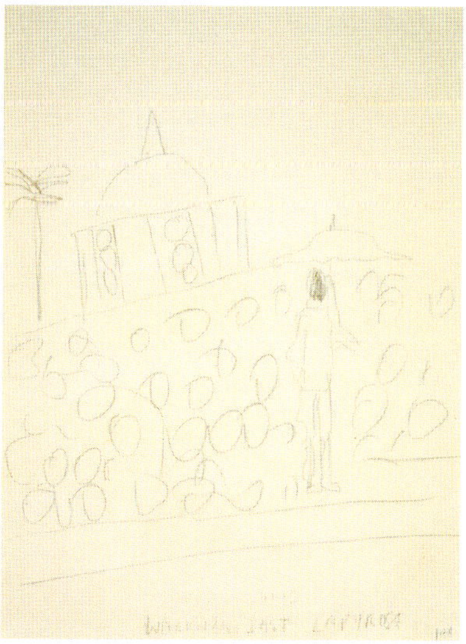

Fig.8 **Untitled (Lapeyrouse Wall)** 2003
Pencil on paper
35.5 x 25.4
Michael Werner Gallery, New York and Cologne

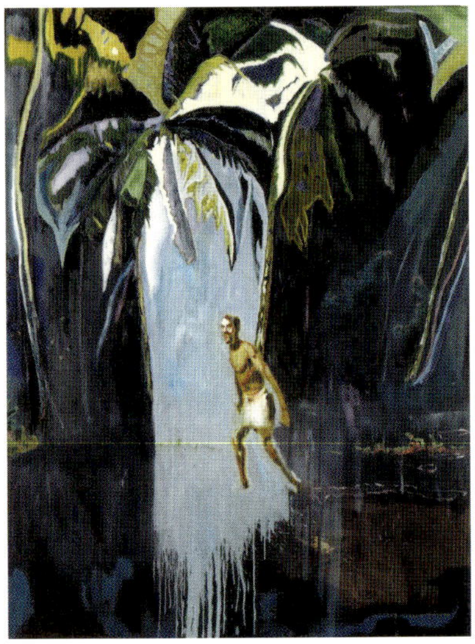

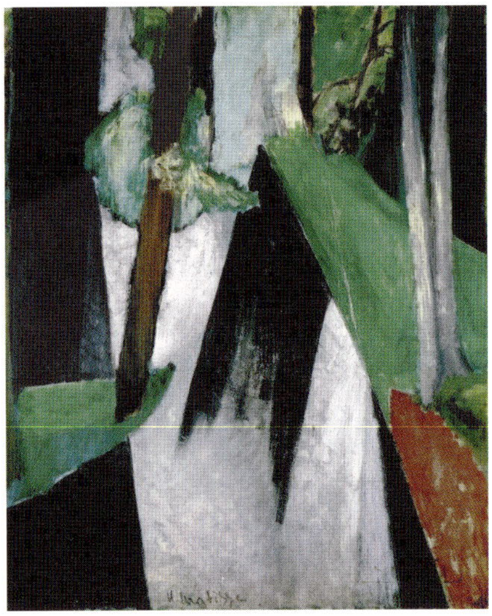

no photograph to recall it, and his attempts to work from imagination 'looked way too comic'. He solved the problem by turning to some postcards discovered in a London shop; they were scenes of south India, including a fisherman dragging a net as he walked along a beach, much as the man in Trinidad had dragged the pelican. The substitution had a hidden appropriateness because the postcard images dated back to the nineteenth century, when people from south India emigrated to Trinidad as labourers – information that Doig acquired only later. 'So the postcard was the ideal stand-in ... It now seems like this is what I witnessed.'[50] A virtual memory, sparked by a photograph, had become actual.

The photograph, however, formed only part of the configured or reconfigured memory. The paintings that resulted, *Pelican* 2004 (p 93) and *Pelican (Stag)* 2004 (fig.9), assumed much of their form from what paint can do when independent of the image.[51] Doig's friend, the artist Chris Ofili, identified in *Pelican (Stag)* a 'flash of paint', referring to a central, vertical wash of pale but luminous blue, which he might equally have described as a 'flash of light'.[52] As image, it was light; as material, it was paint. Ofili instinctively characterised the effect in material terms, recognising that Doig had set his paint free. Runny drips at the bottom of the column of blue produce a paint-incident with no requirement to signify more than itself – a washy surface of stains, not unlike the lower register of *Hitch Hiker*, another example of the

Fig.9 **Pelican (Stag)** 2003
Oil on canvas
275.6 × 200

Fig.10 Henri Matisse
Shaft of Sunlight, the Woods of Trivaux 1917
Oil on canvas, 91 × 74
Private Collection

effect. Yet Doig states that he 'always strive[s] to prevent the paint itself becoming overly prioritized'.[53] He has it both ways. In 2002, an analogous play of image and material impressed him: Henri Matisse's *Shaft of Sunlight, the Woods of Trivaux* 1917 (fig.10).[54] It too caused the immaterial presence of light and the base matter of paint to converge in perception. Facing either work, Doig's or Matisse's, a viewer traces the light, only to become lost in fluid or viscous paint. Then, drawn to the light once again, the viewer sees that it can be bright and clear, while also thin and thick and even dark – a thickening, darkening light.

Blur: the light of architecture glimpsed

> I can remember the terror of ... the pitch black, with the densest trees around. When you do finally see the light of a house it's incredibly welcoming.
> Peter Doig, 1998 [55]

> The image of the Corbusier building ... deathly looking and skull-like, vacant holes. Peter Doig, 2007 [56]

Everyone recalls feeling anxious on being immersed in darkness, relief coming with an inviting light. Doig experienced an incident when the light in the distance, to the contrary, gave him a mild fright – a building that turned skull-like on his approach. This was one facet of his complex emotional relationship to an apartment block at Briey, France, a version of Le Corbusier's Unité d'Habitation. It opened to occupancy in 1961, but was abandoned and derelict by 1973, a victim, depending on one's sympathy with Le Corbusier's aesthetic, either of economic accident – an unexpected downturn in the local economy – or of inherent design failings.[57]

During the 1990s, when Doig was involved with the building, it was undergoing restoration; he himself did some of the work.[58] The exterior, originally unfinished concrete, had been painted white by the time he first visited the site. Seen through the darkness of the surrounding forest, this whiteness reflected a welcoming light. But the surface had its own areas of darkness, its outer continuity broken by the recessed angles of the individual apartments – the 'concrete cabins' within the larger structure, as Doig regards them.[59] Resembling the voids within a bone-white skull, these 'vacant holes' lacked any living presence. As Doig's experience of the building shifted from welcoming to threatening, it may have seemed that the dramatic play of light and dark was altering his mood. Perhaps instead, the play of light responded to the painter's subtle emotional shifts, in tacit dialogue with his evolving perception – the momentary image of the building growing from an incidental seed of virtual memory. In a situation of this kind – which everyone experiences – we cannot determine whether the visual environment induces our emotional response or, on the contrary, if our response corresponds to our pre-existing inclinations. Because the Unité evoked such a broad range of emotion in Doig, it became a select site for his study of perception and feeling.

Doig first represented Briey in 1991 (*Concrete Cabin* 1991–2) (p.60) and continued the theme through 1999 (*Briey (Interior)* 1999) (p.63). The series extended his interest in features of the material environment that screen off elements of vision, obscuring things beyond, yet also (as Doig has insisted) drawing perception inwards towards this beyond. The majority of his images of Briey feature trees with dark trunks and tangles of foliage that screen the building – *Concrete Cabin*, *Concrete Cabin II* 1992 (p.61) and *Cabin Essence* 1993–4 (p.58) are examples. There is more. To *Concrete Cabin* Doig added extra layers of screening – pale green, blob-like 'leaves', as well as coarse white 'reflections', the latter seen also in *Concrete Cabin II*. These distinctive features screen the trees themselves, even while being a part of them. Likewise, the mass of flowering grasses at the base of the forest in *Concrete Cabin* floats free above its associated ground – another screen. The light reflections in the Briey series parallel the snow in some of Doig's paintings of the 1990s; so, too, do glimpses of the white architectural skin of the building. These diverse screen effects are part of a larger aim: 'I had intended these paintings to be about the act of looking through ... to find focus.' Looking through is hardly simple: 'I purposely painted the manmade buildings through the trees rather than paint them first, then paint a screen of trees [or] nature on top. I had seen Cézanne do this a lot – the light of architecture glimpsed.'[60] Cézanne allowed the white of architecture and the green of trees to interweave (fig.11). He superimposed one colour over the other, helter-skelter, regardless of the actual position of the represented objects, leaving the spatial order ambiguous. Doig adopted a similar technique, concerned with representing the process of perception and its feel, rather than with illustrating reality. Accordingly, he distinguished his conscious, functional memory – a limited store of pictorial knowledge – from an open and speculative 'idea of memory'.[61] Doig's understanding provides a fruitful view of his predecessor: Cézanne combined foliage

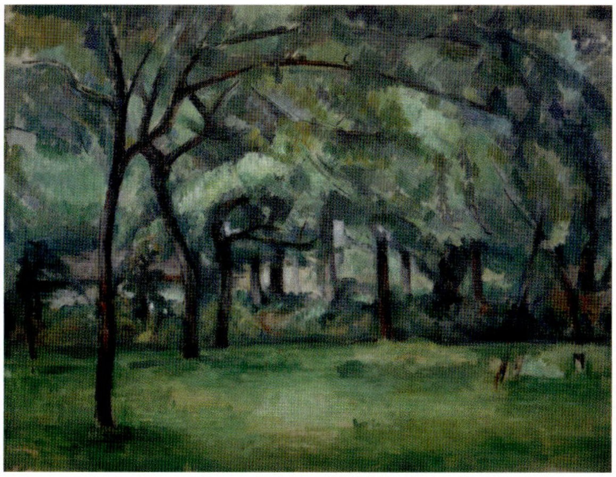

with 'the light of architecture glimpsed' to capture an 'idea of memory', not a specific memory. From Cézanne's virtual matrix, memories are still emerging. Doig himself now experiences them.

Unfixed, floating, and screen-like, memory necessarily involves movement and change: 'With the Corbusier/Briey paintings, I was trying to depict the movement of eye – not to paint a still. The eye never sees a "still".'[62] In *Study for Concrete Cabin* 1992 (p. 126), Doig wrestled with the perceptual ambiguities of three sets of colours disposed in a screen-like manner, overriden by dark blackish strokes – violet for tree trunks, greens for foliage, whites and reds for the architecture – each set in defiance of the others, each capable of thrusting forward to occupy the eye. 'The eye never sees a "still"': yet Doig took still photographs of the Unité as slides to be projected in the studio, sometimes traced onto canvas or paper as a basis for rendering. The varying angles and distances of the camera position in relation to the building added a sense of movement to the stills.

Walking with a video camera was a second way in which Doig appoached the Unité through its screen of trees. Having derived stills from the video, he realised that they were too wavy and blurred to be useful. To compensate, he hand-held the video camera in a single position for about two minutes before advancing his position; this method provided moving images in a technological sense, representing a pattern of trees, architecture and light that was hardly moving. Here technology

Fig.11 Paul Cézanne, **Farm in Normandy, Summer** 1882
Oil on canvas, 49.5 × 65.7
Private Collection, on extended loan to the
Courtauld Institute of Art Gallery, London

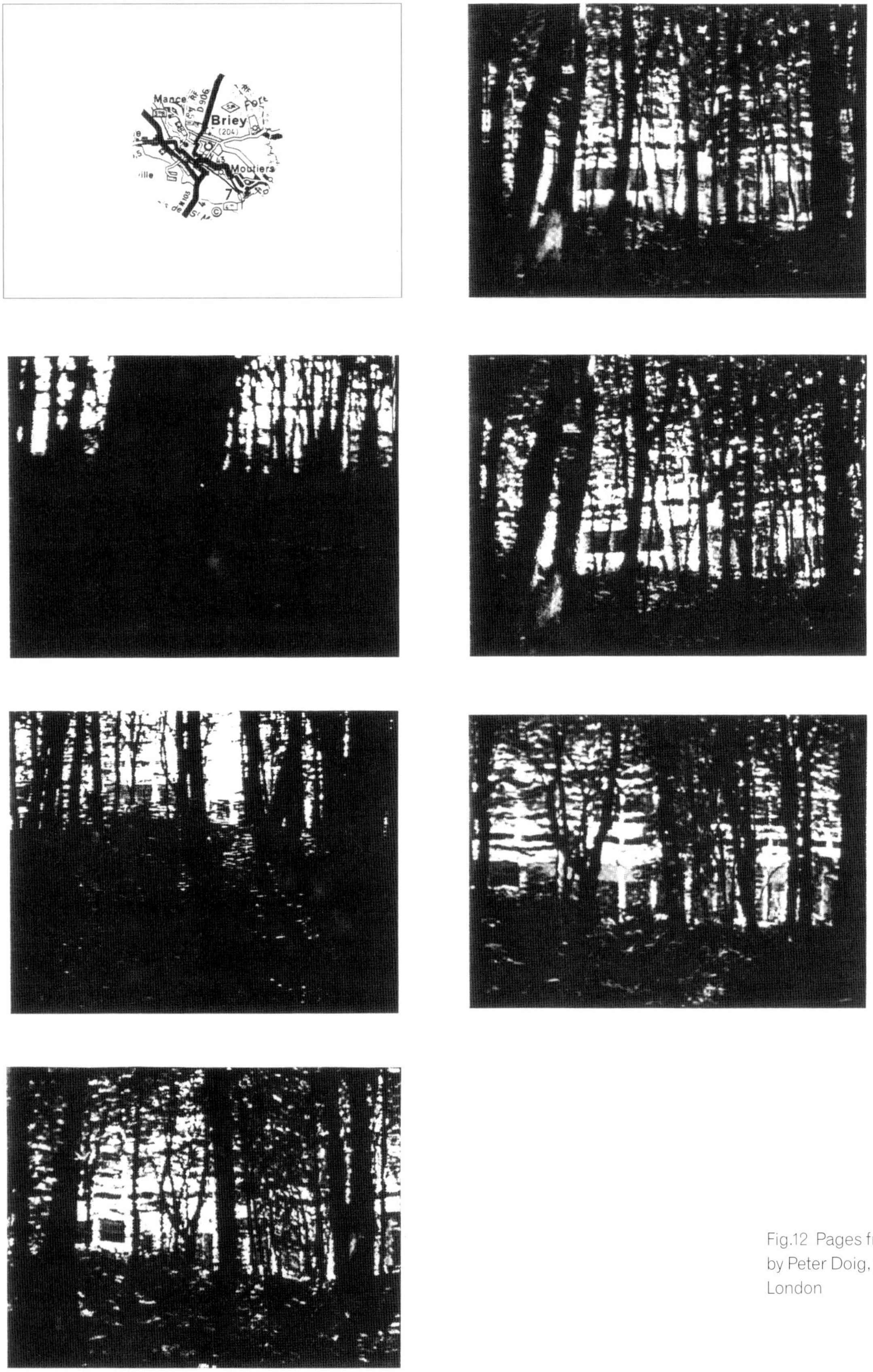

Fig.12 Pages from *Briey*, an artist's book by Peter Doig, published by Imprint 93, London

and nature colluded in assuring that although nothing much was moving, nothing stood still: 'From these films I got the stills I wanted – a suggestion of the *eye* moving.'[63] Doig used these images, especially their areas of blur, as a guide to representing the instability of his experience of the Unité and its surroundings. He 'liked to glance at the photos rather than study or try to copy them'.[64] The method alerted his disciplined eye to all the incidental moments and their potential movement. He captured this movement within his canvas, merging incidents of photographic vision with those of paint handling – 'handmade and homely looking', 'beautiful but slightly repellent', is how he described his effect.[65]

In 1993, at the instigation of a friend, Doig converted six of his video stills into a small book of photocopied images (fig.12). Each image shows the building through the trees. These blurry, black and white, low-tech products of a high-tech process capture the ambiguities of perception.[66] Individual spots of white light sometimes correspond to the building in the distance, but may also appear as light reflections in the trees close by. The effect is both beautiful and eerie, perhaps like that of the painting *Echo Lake*, a day scene in its original film still, recreated by Doig as a night scene – night-like, at least. With his Briey stills, Doig wanted to suggest the sensation of walking through trees towards a mysterious source of light – in this instance, a cross between welcoming and threatening, day-like and night-like. Through severely reduced means, the six images of his photocopy book induce the emotional edginess that might be associated with *Hitch Hiker*, *The House that Jacques Built*, *Echo Lake*, and any number of his other major works. 'Edgy' is the word, because Doig positions his works at the edge or divide between two or more conflicting feelings – like the thin line between sweet and acid colour in his snow pictures, such as *Figure in Mountain Landscape*, or between effects of welcome-light and skull-white at Briey. His set of incidental appearances presents Briey as an evocative virtual memory captured in an ambiguous perceptual movement – an intellectual and emotional blur.

Doig's art leaves too few generalised elements in its wake to have a 'style'. Despite the anecdotes and identifications that he readily offers in conversation – the story of the pelican man, his parents' use of a cabin at Echo Lake, Ontario – his imagery remains in many ways as opaque and mystifying as the screen of white patches characteristic of the Briey series. But here, too, there is a story: in a Toronto bar, Doig observed a hunting scene painted onto a plastered wall, which had flaked away in places. As a quick fix, the missing elements had been filled with unpainted plaster,

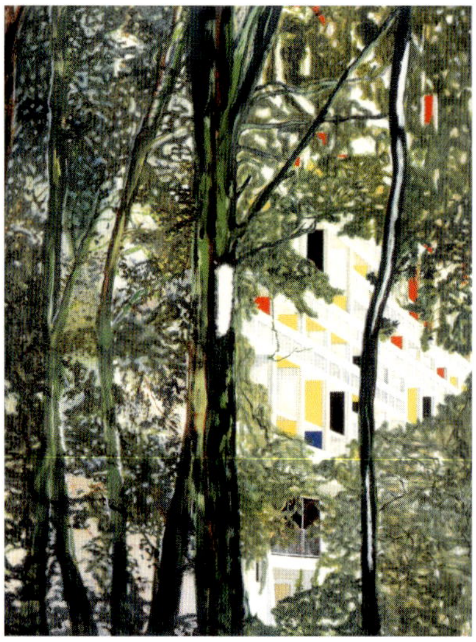

creating pictorial gaps, blanks. 'So you had this enormous semi-realist scene cut across with these white voids ... In quoting from that, I want to suggest that what you are looking at in my work is not at all real.'[67]

Doig's art may be 'not at all real' or all too real, depending on where we locate it. His illusions fail to correspond with reality, but his materiality is undeniably present: 'Those areas which feature blobs of [white paint] are what the rest of the painting is made out of.' Near the very centre of one of the Briey series, *Briey (Concrete Cabin)* 1994–6 (fig.13), a large 'blob' adheres to the vertical of a tree trunk; by Doig's reasoning, it signifies both light and white. The whiteness is of the paint itself, which in turn becomes both 'essence' and 'void' (his terms).[68] Just beside this patch is a similarly opaque white, there to render the Unité façade. Perhaps one white is real to sight, because it advances the architectural rendering, whereas the other white is real to touch, because it remains in such a surface-oriented, material state. Both whites would correspond to elements of lightness in one of Doig's black and white, photocopied video stills. The two whites create a conflict of incidents, which results in a conceptual blur, if not a perceptual one. The number of critical interpretations that will sort out the contrasts and differences that Doig builds into his paintings may be as great as there are interpreters. The conceptual blur is likely to persist, for no explanation will capture the emotional edge of these works of art.

Fig.13 **Briey (Concrete Cabin)** 1994–6
Oil on canvas
275 × 200

A simple patch of white proves the undoing of critical analysis. The incident has too many meanings, too many feelings.

This may be the key to Doig's art. We feel his painting before we know his painting (if we ever know it). His art consists of perceptual incidents, not circumscribed events. The significance of a Doig painting is neither a site (Lapeyrouse wall) nor a story (The House that Jacques Built) but a feeling. Everyone recognises his or her own feeling in Doig's painting, for he uses his 'experience [to] think about things that are a part of other people's experience'.[69] Doig leaves each incident open enough for every person, in no matter what emotional state, to appropriate and remember it. The nature of the emotional encounter – comforting, discomforting – he does not determine.

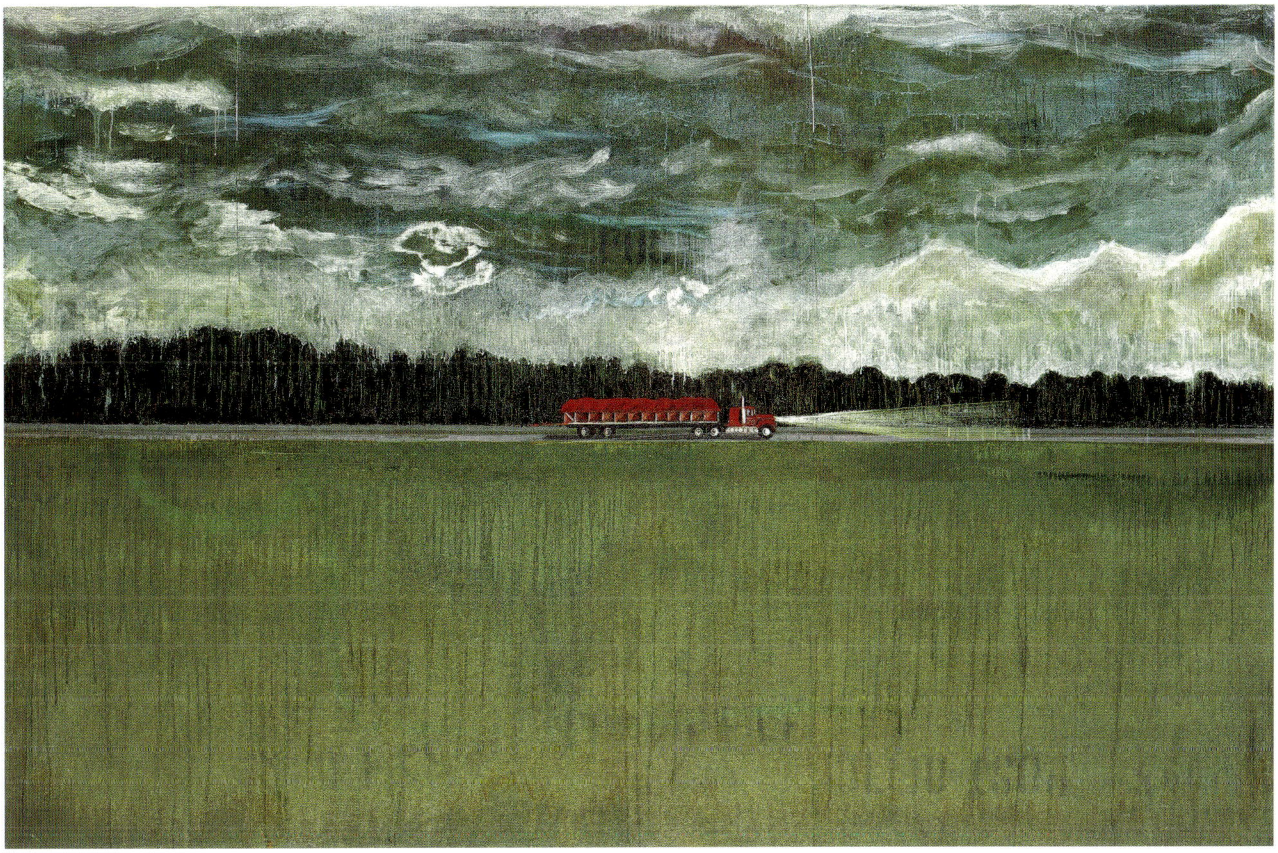

Hitch Hiker 1989–90, oil on postal bags, 152 × 226

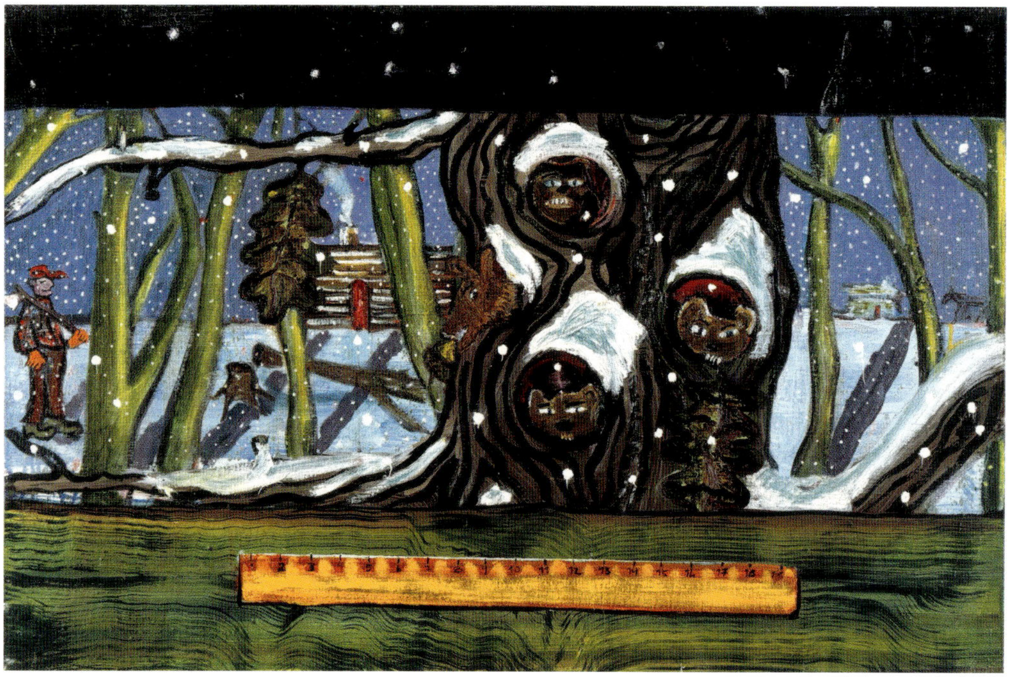

Art School 1990, oil on canvas, 58.5 × 86.5

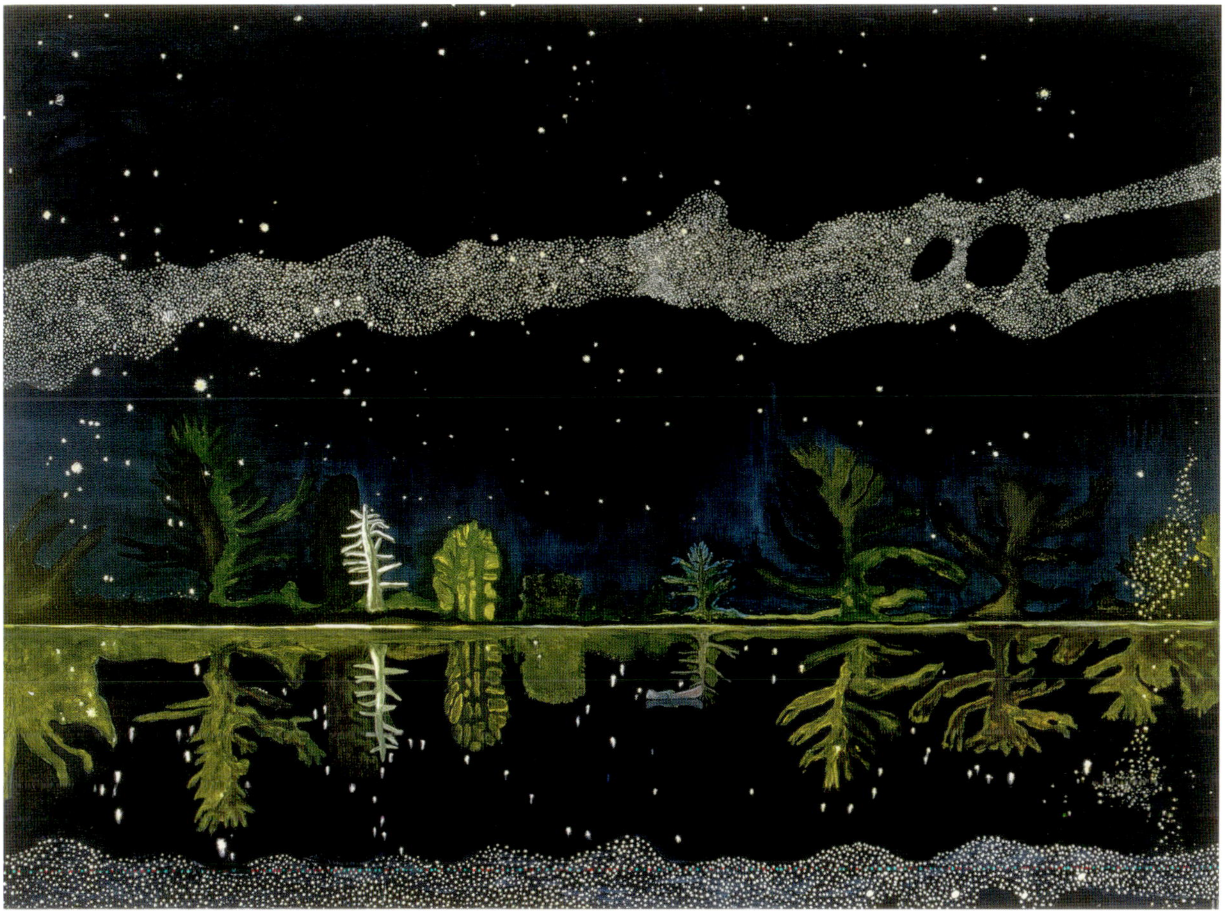

Milky Way 1989–90, oil on canvas, 152 × 203.5

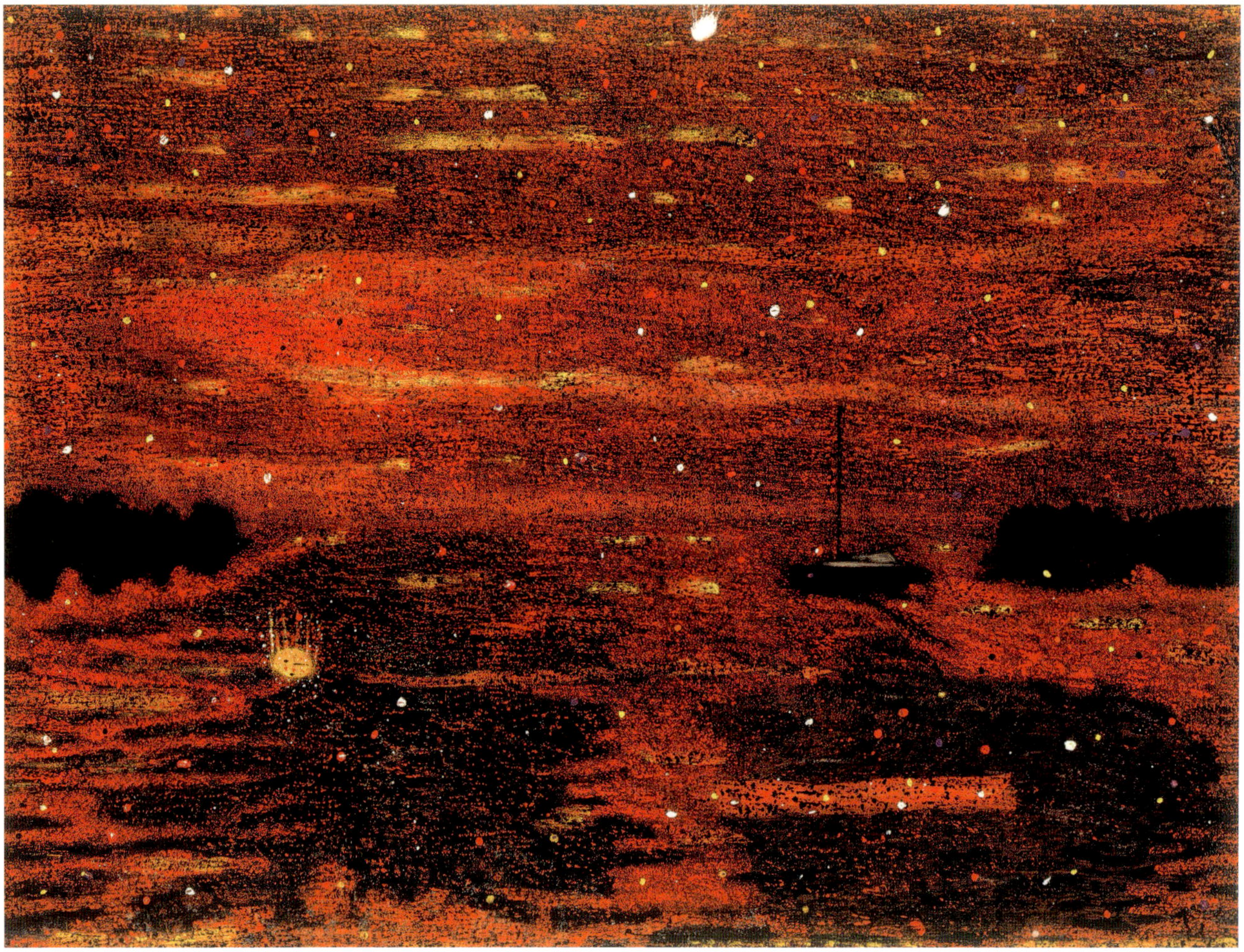

Baked 1990 oil on canvas, 182 × 235

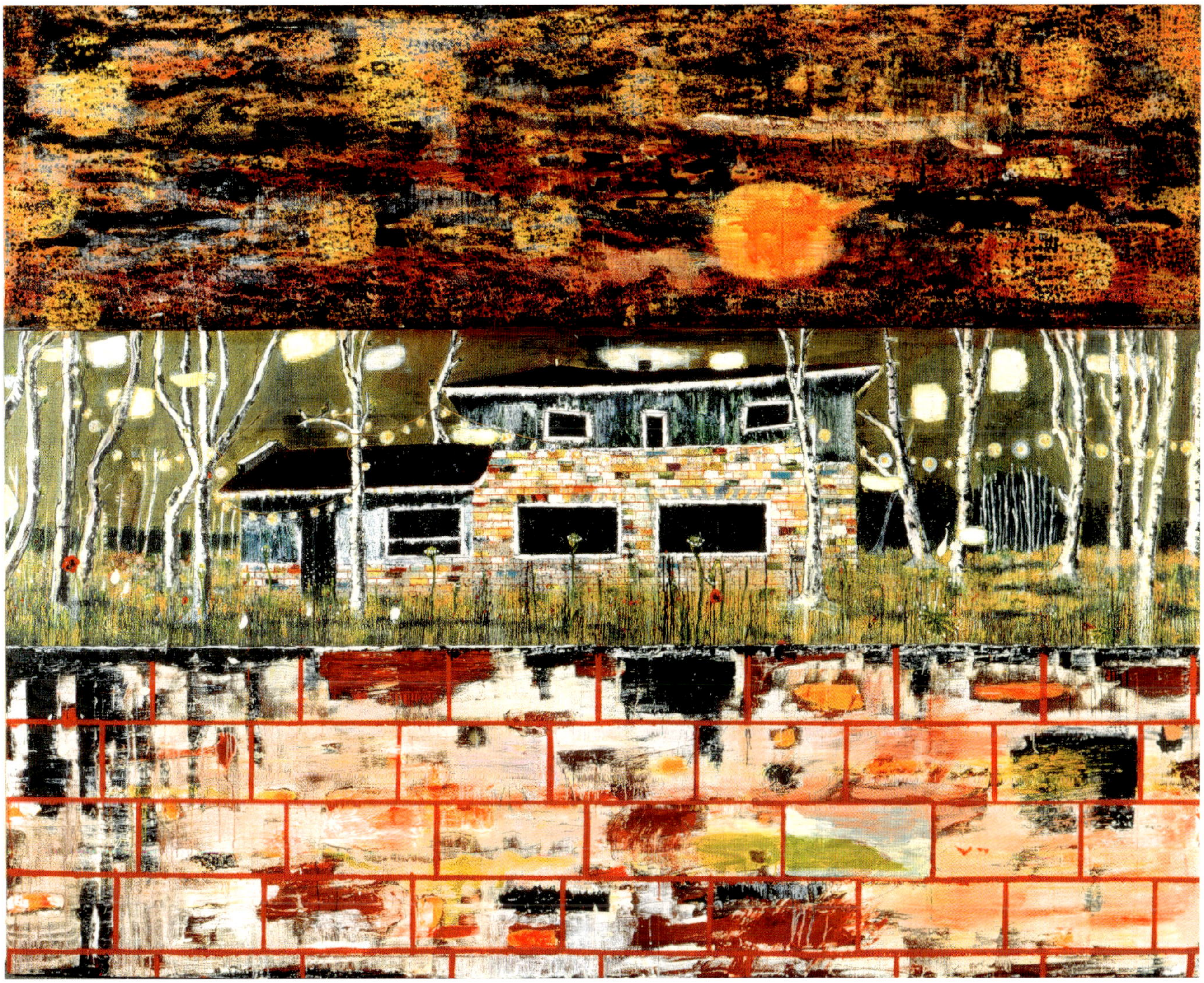

The House that Jacques Built 1992, oil on canvas, 200 × 250

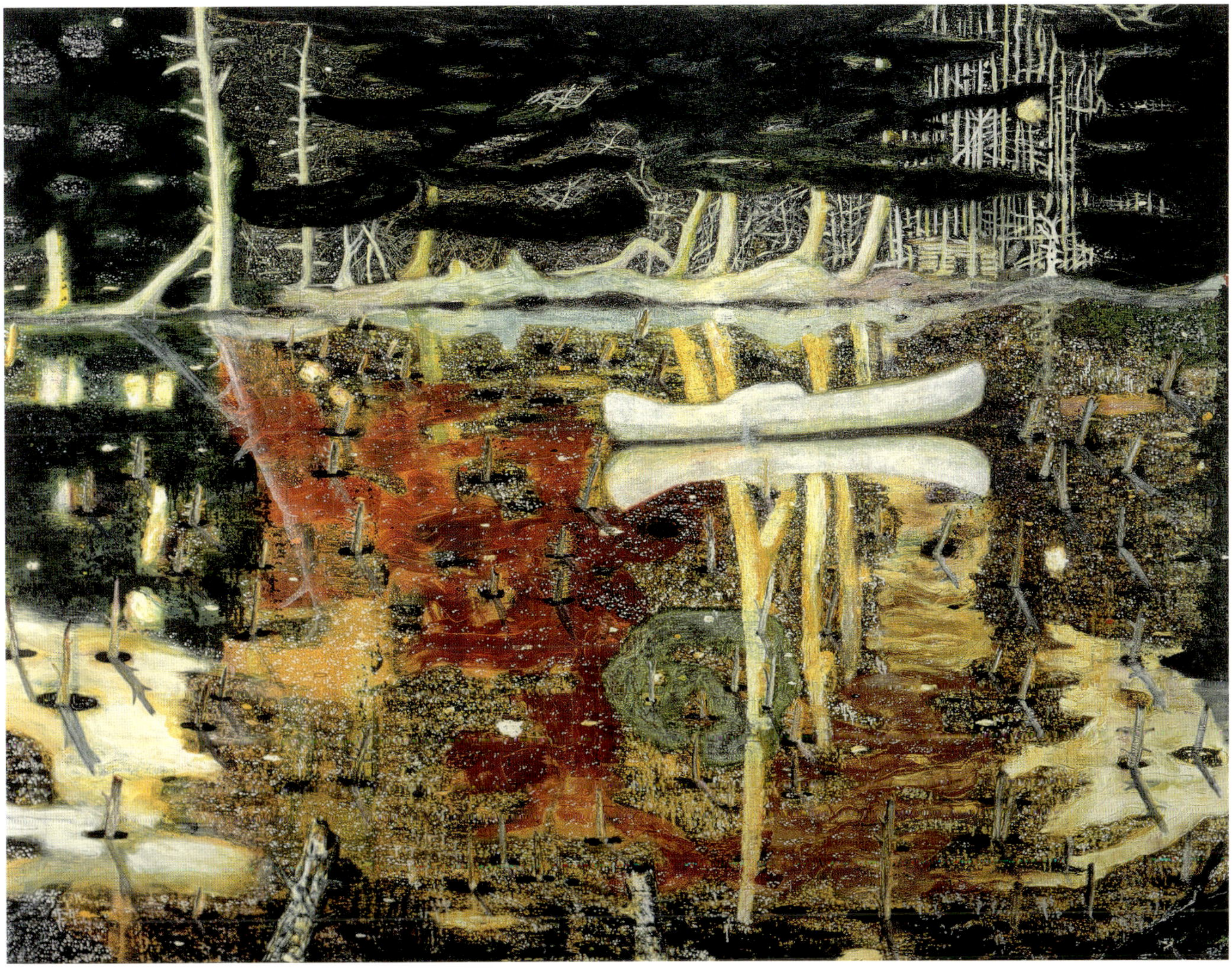

Swamped 1990, oil on canvas, 197 × 241

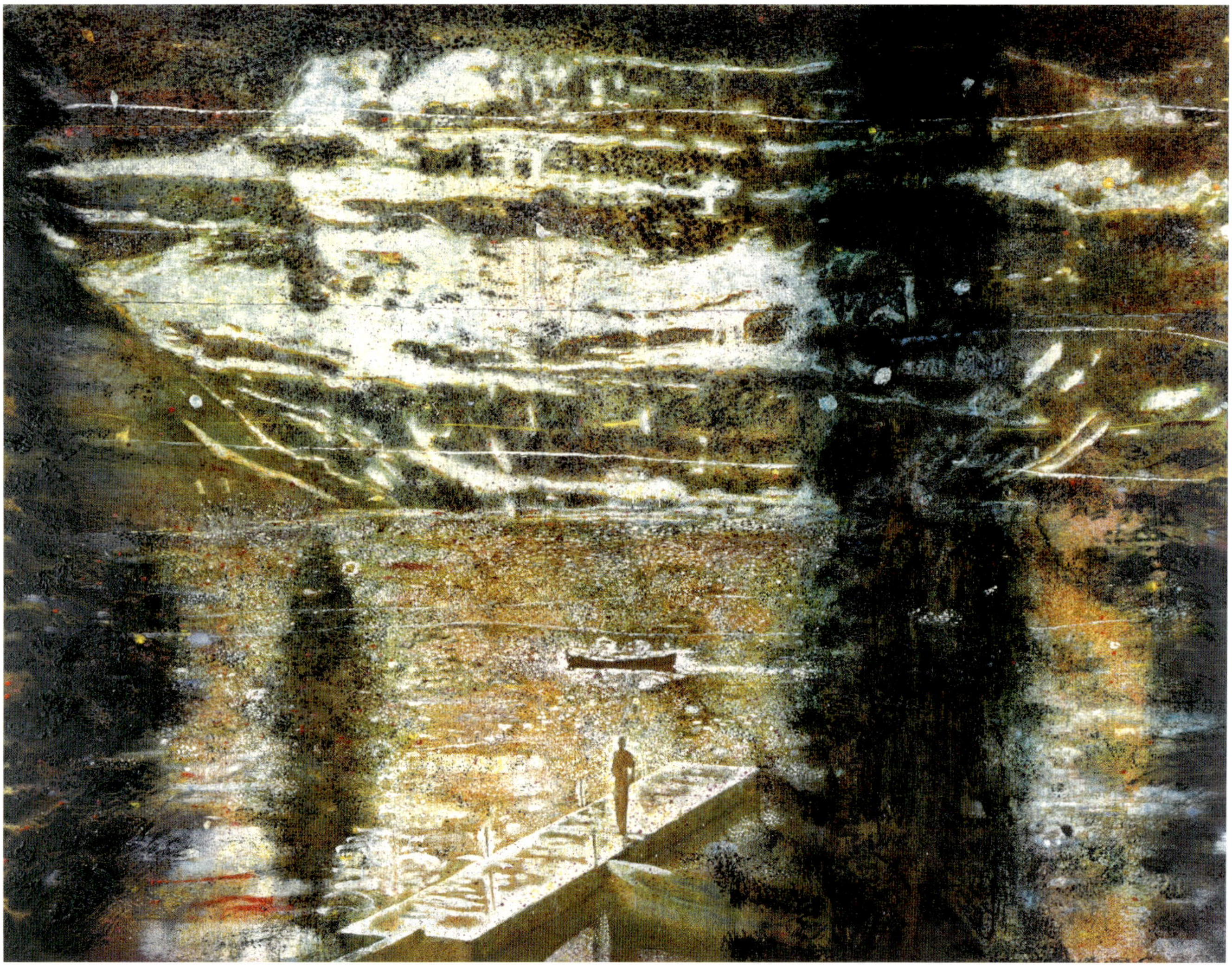

Jetty 1994, oil on canvas, 200 × 248

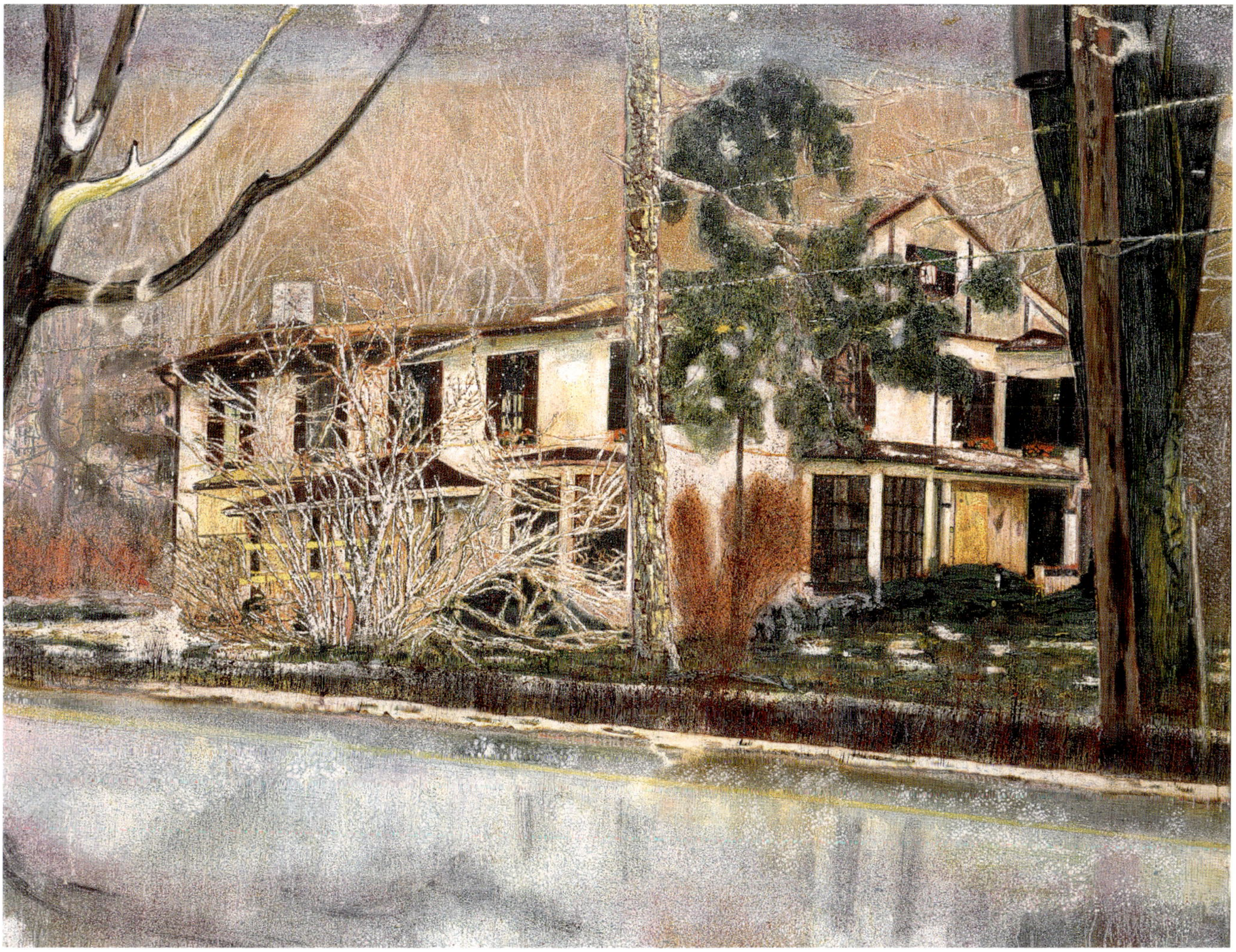

Pine Houses (Rooms for Rent) 1994, oil on canvas, 200 × 253

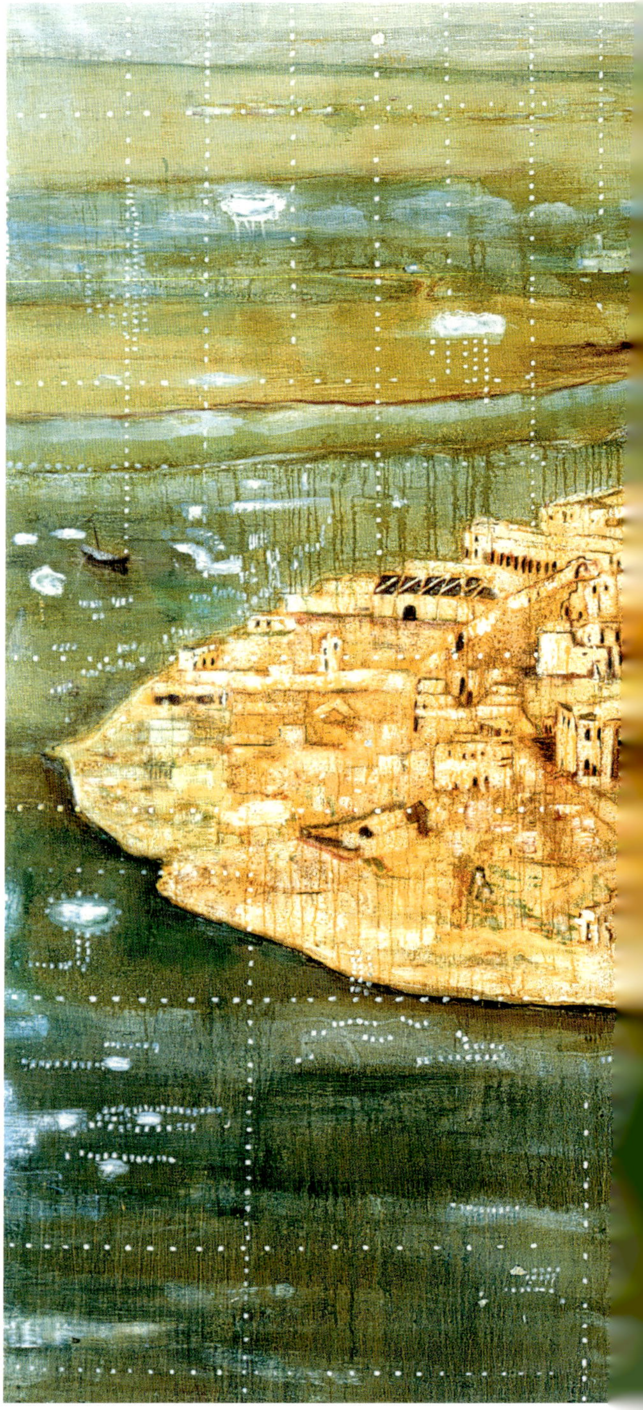

Bomb Island 1991, oil on canvas, 200 × 300

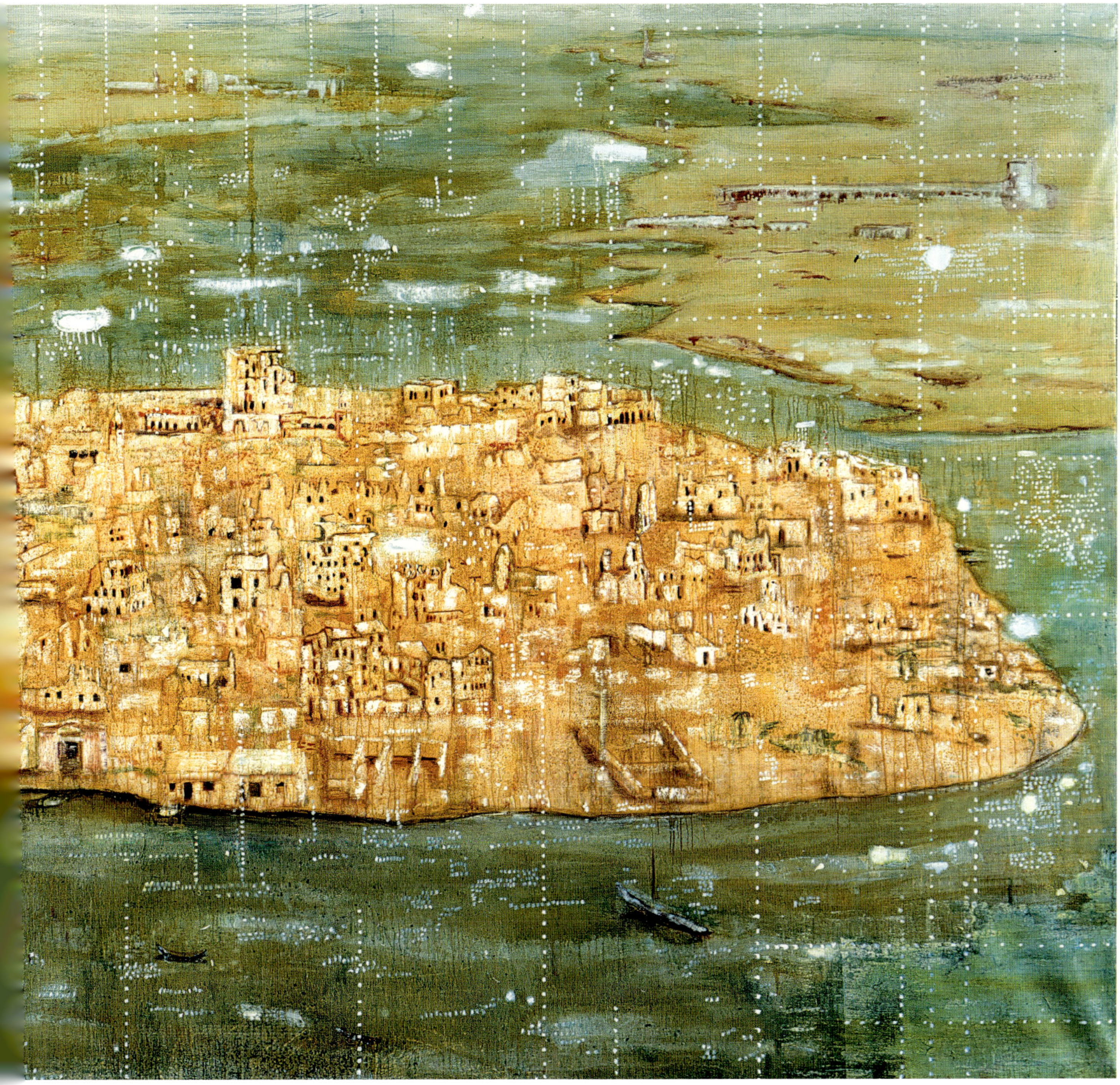

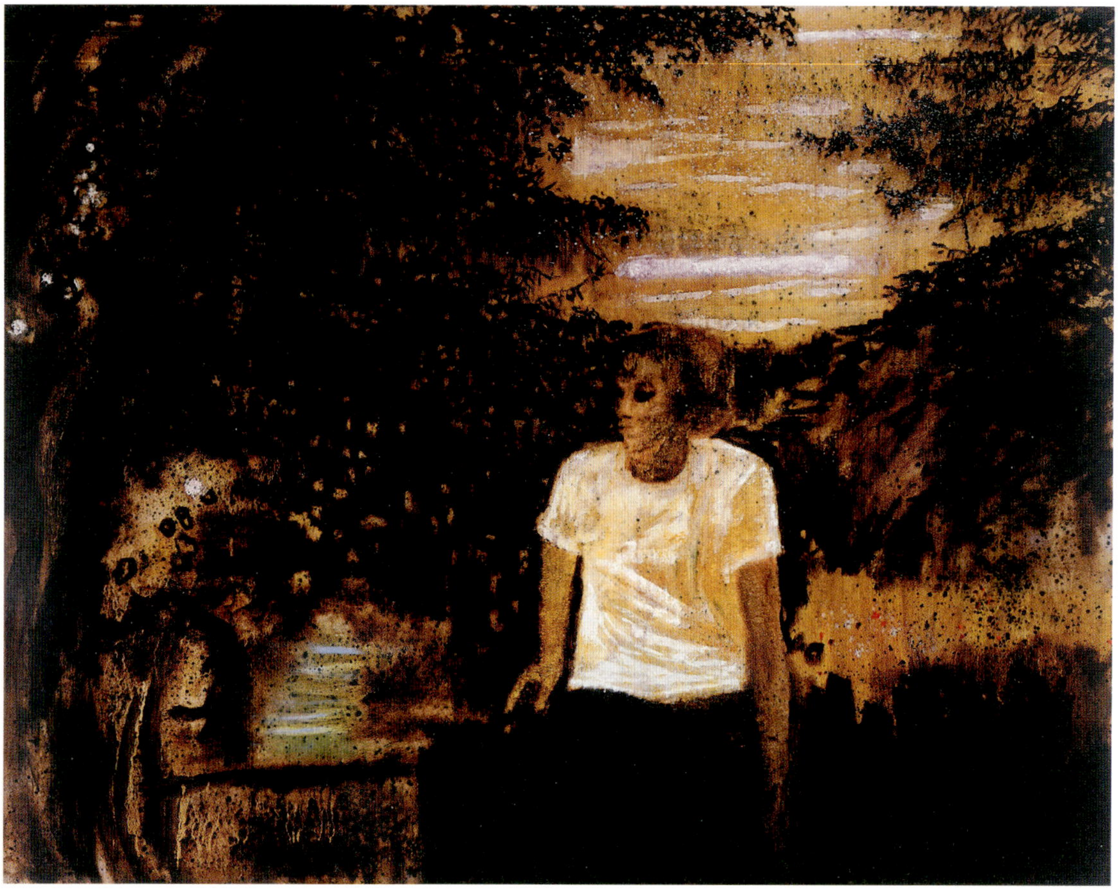

Corn Cob 1994, oil on canvas, 121.9 × 152.4

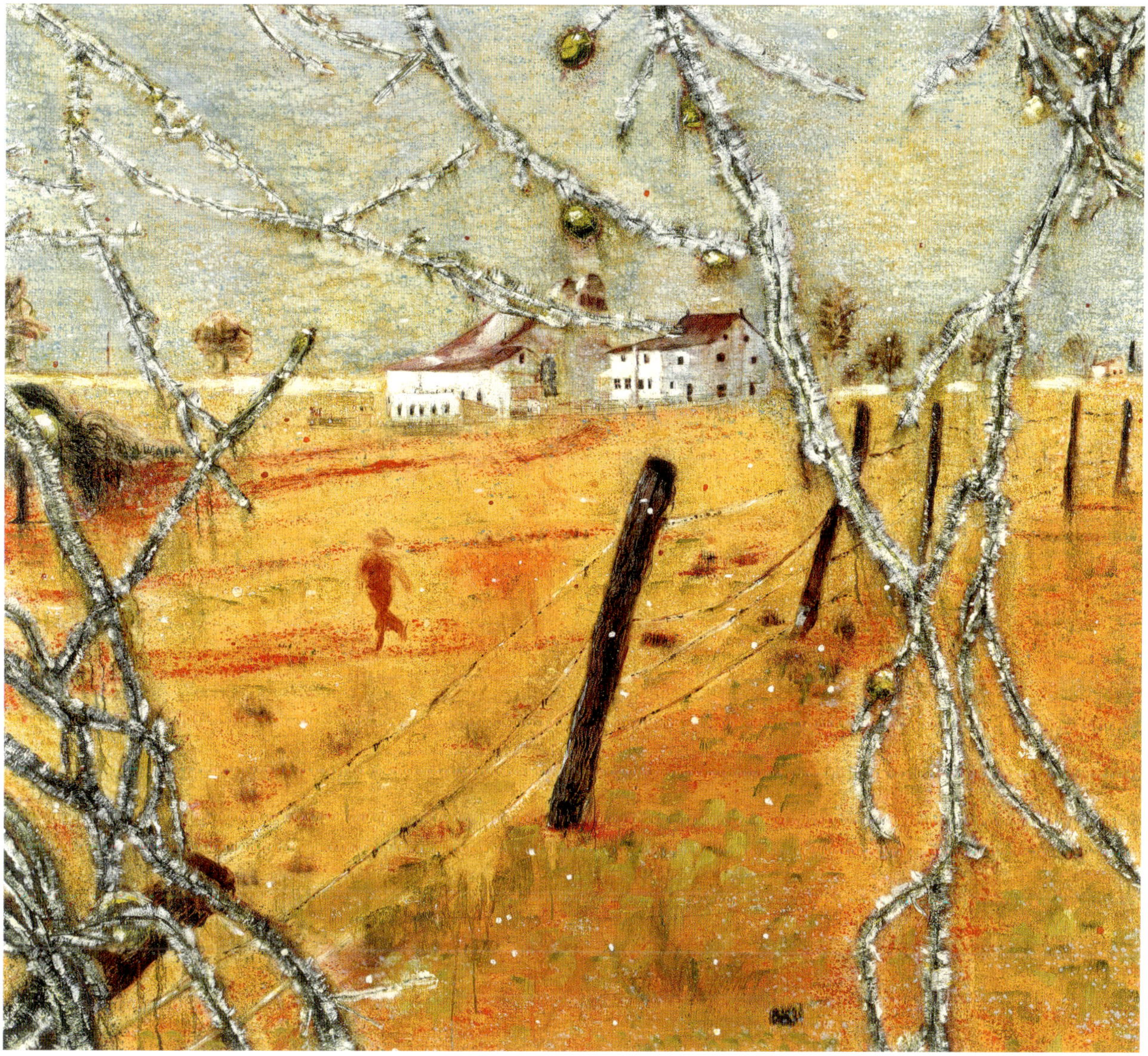

Young Bean Farmer 1991, oil on canvas, 186 × 199

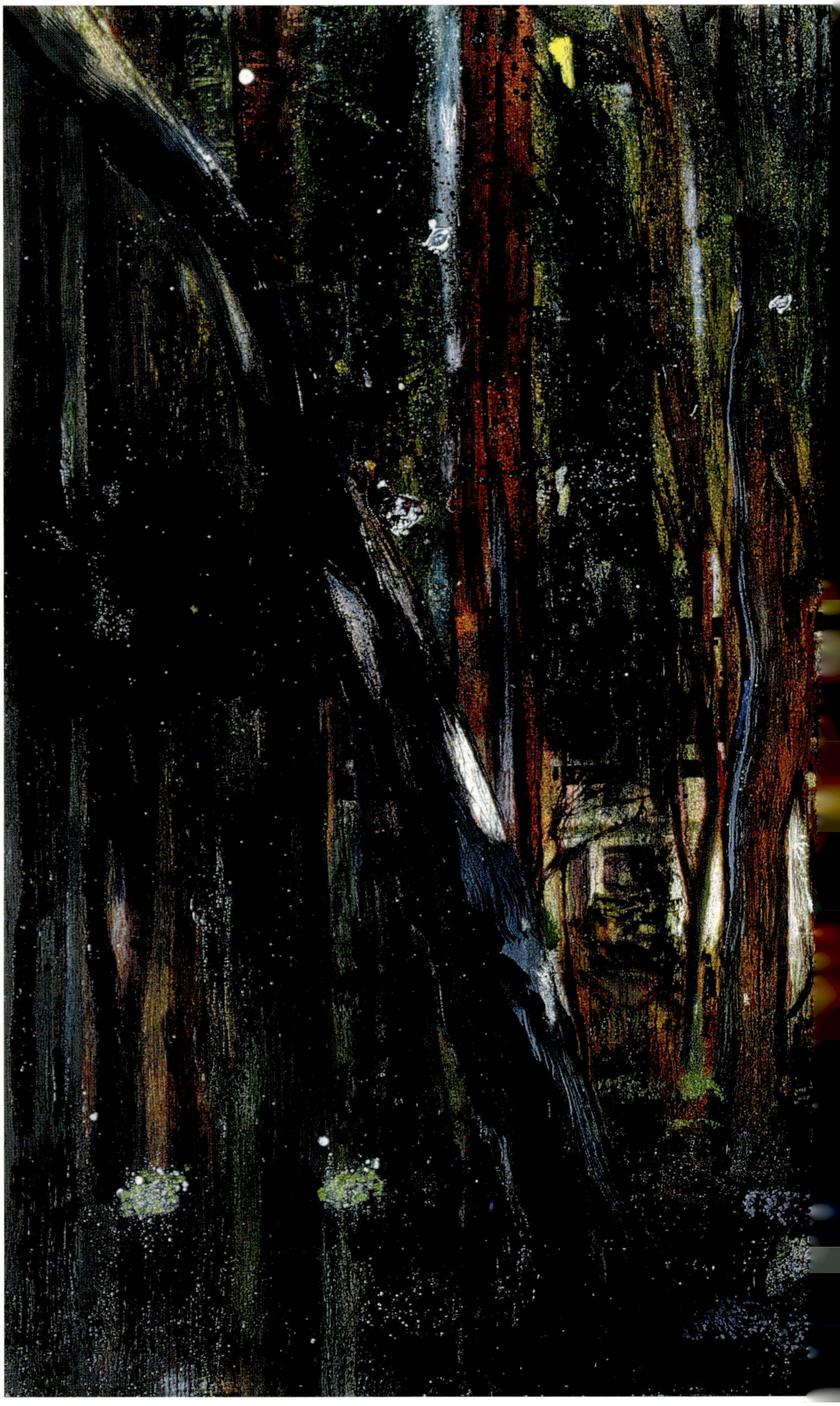

Cabin Essence 1993–4, oil on canvas, 230 × 360

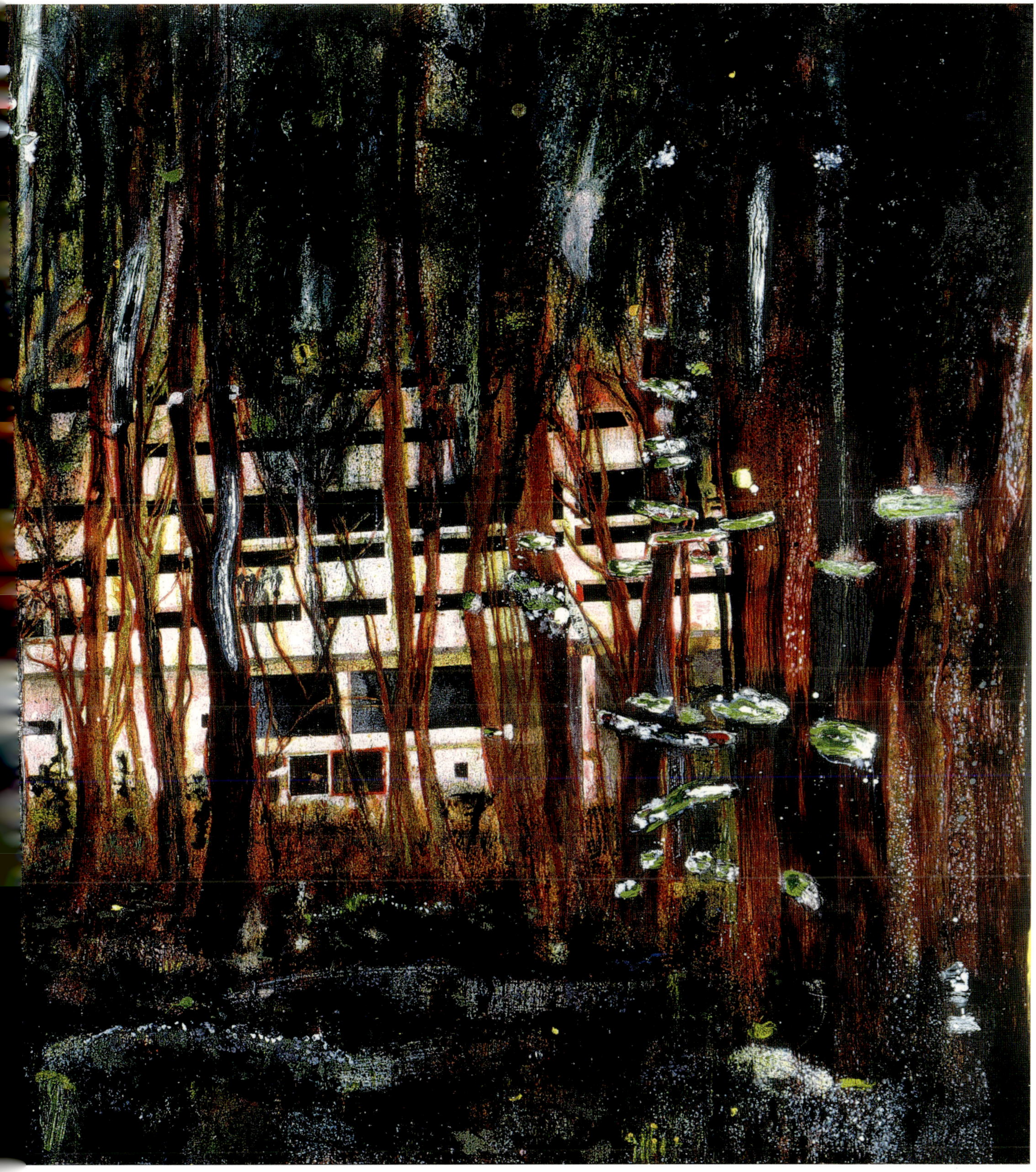

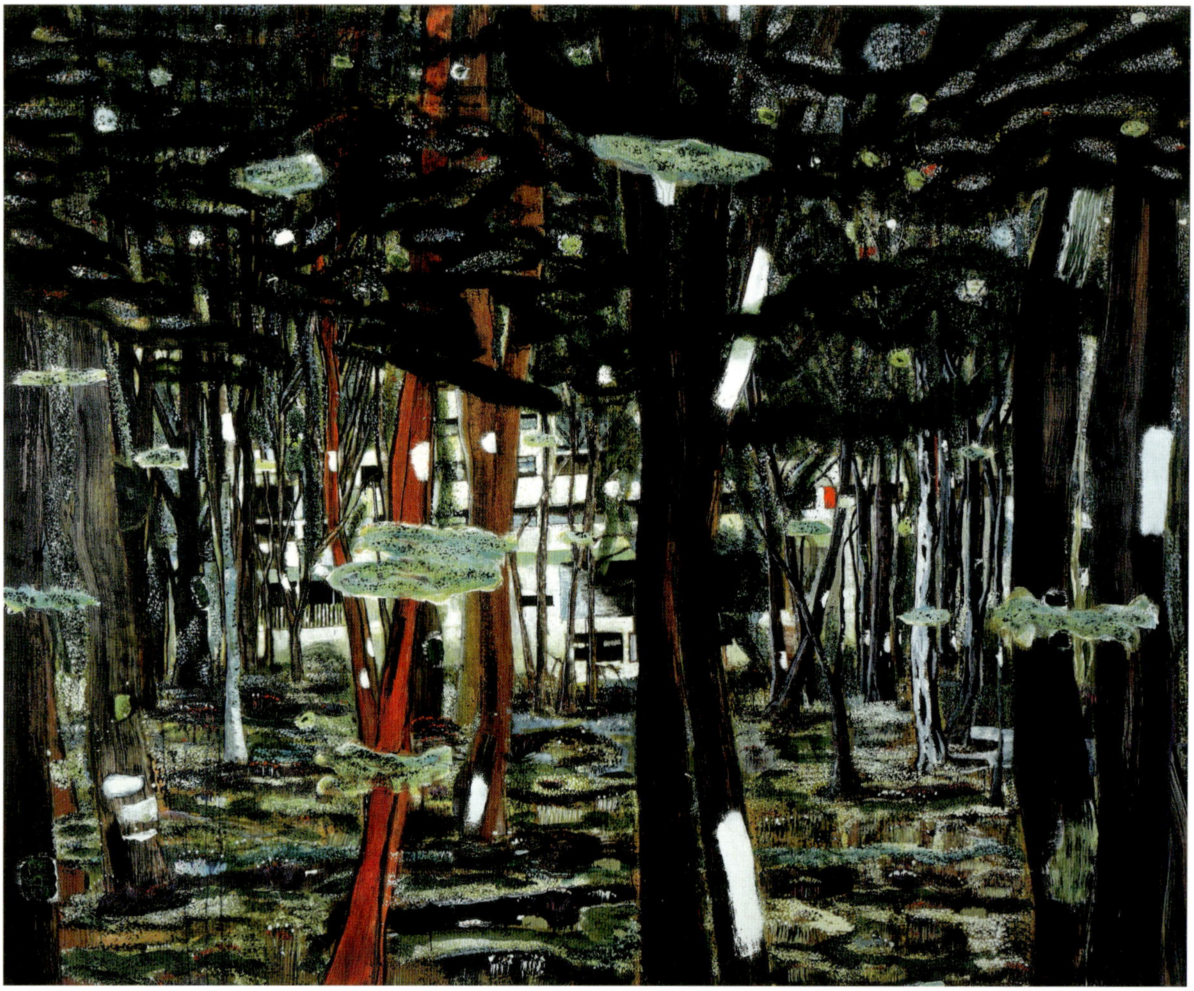

Concrete Cabin 1991–2, oil on canvas, 200 × 240

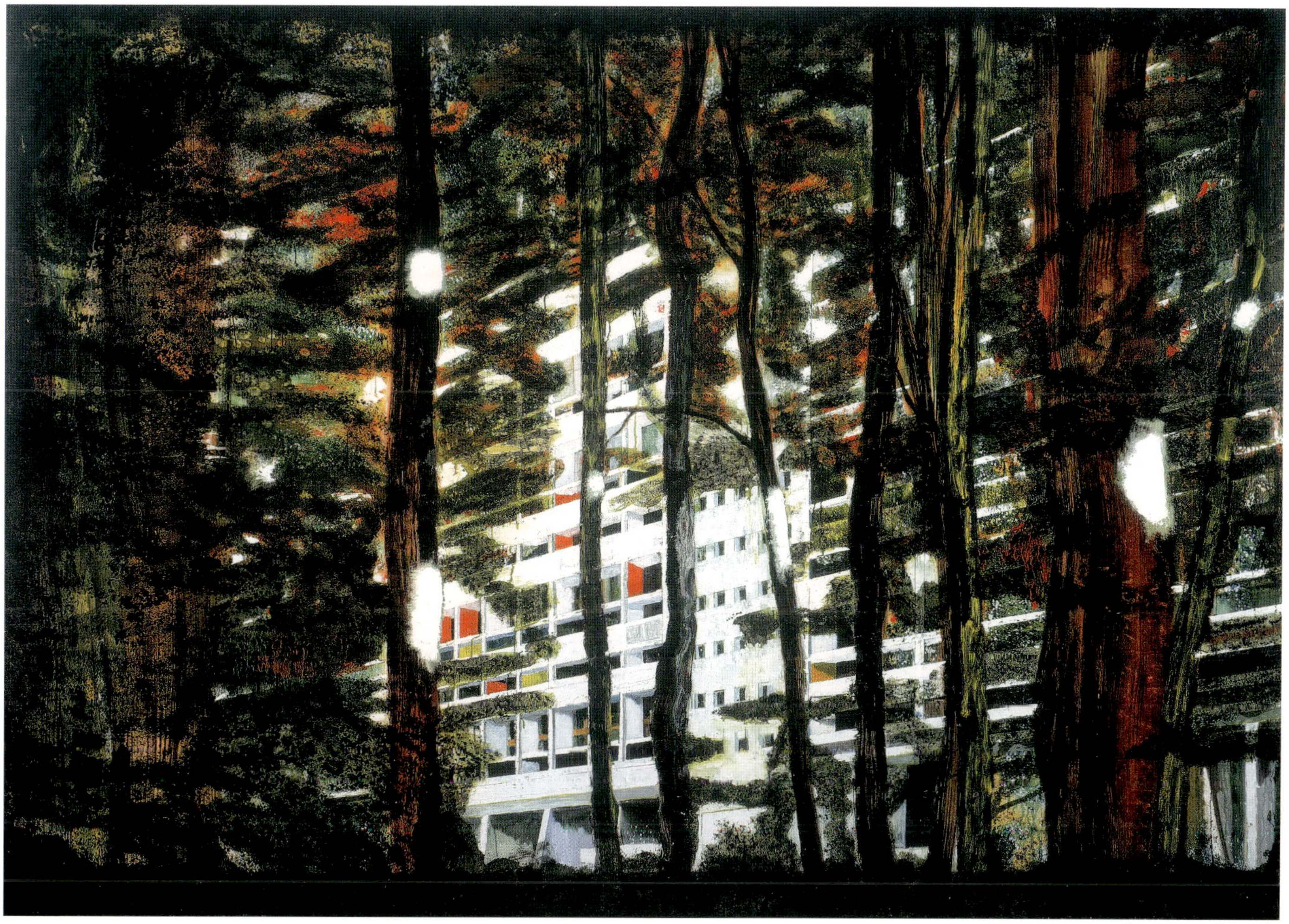

Concrete Cabin II 1992, oil on canvas, 200 × 275

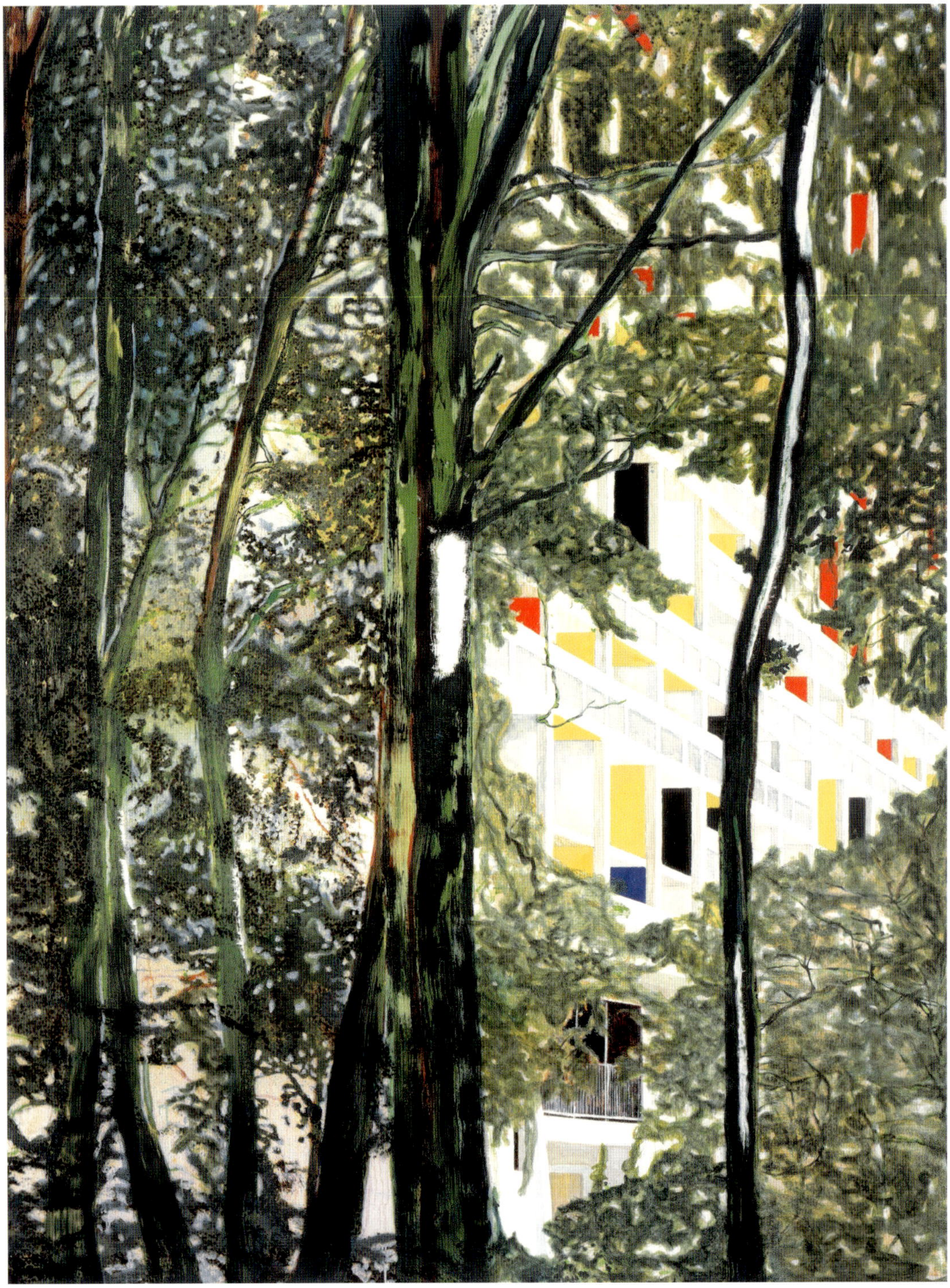

Briey (Concrete Cabin) 1994–6, oil on canvas, 275 × 200

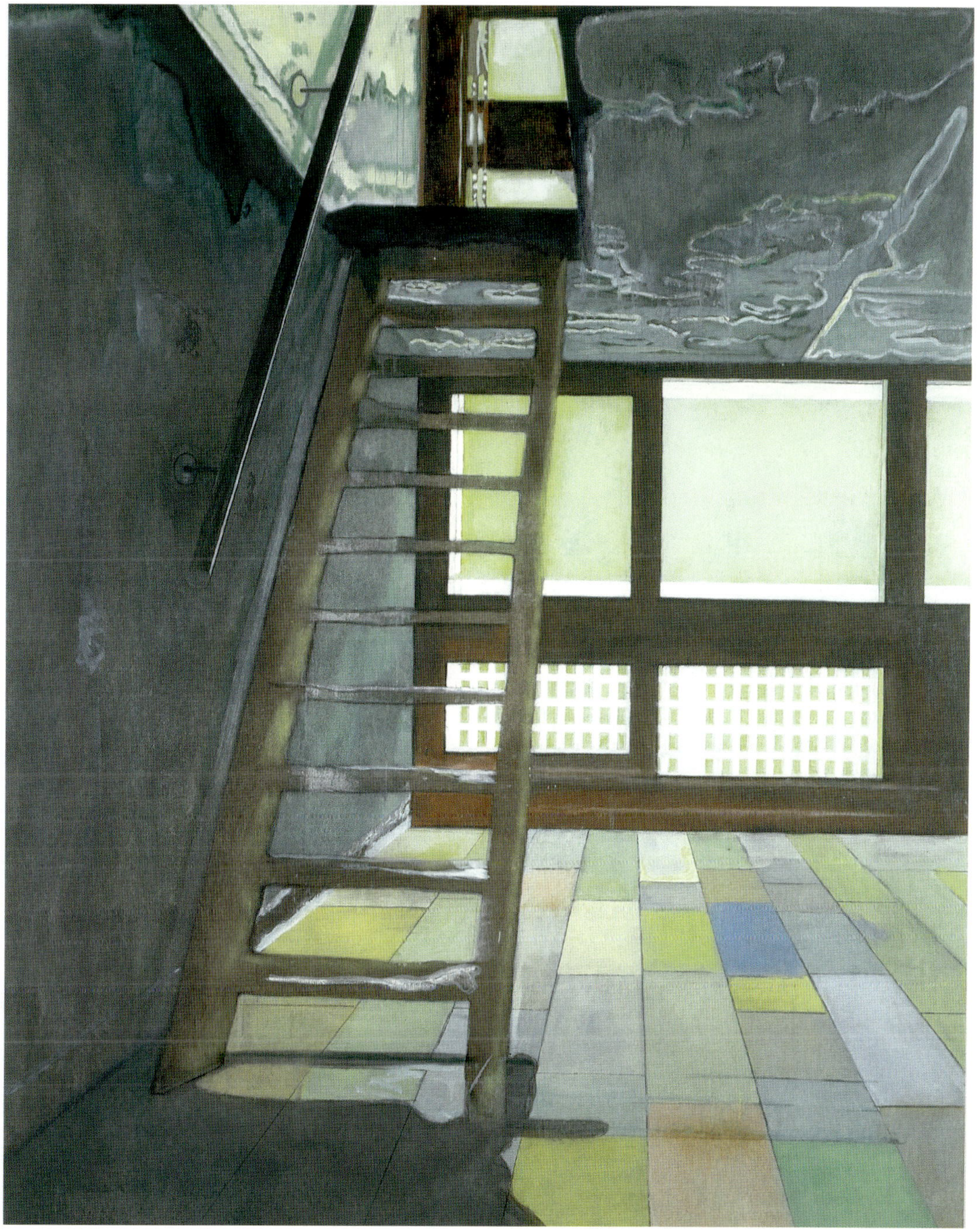

Briey (Interior) 1999, oil on canvas, 250 × 196

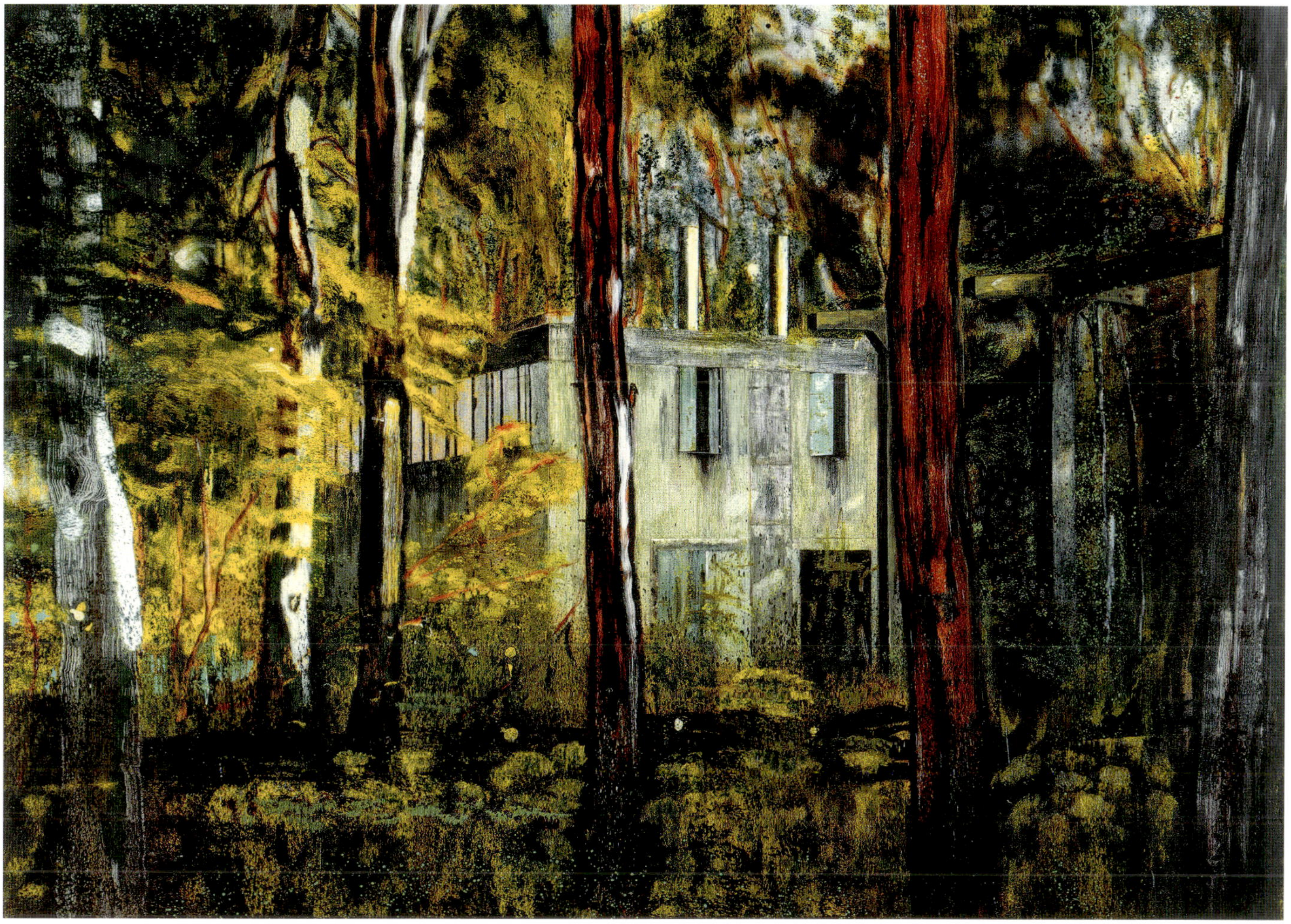

Boiler House 1994, oil on canvas, 200 × 275

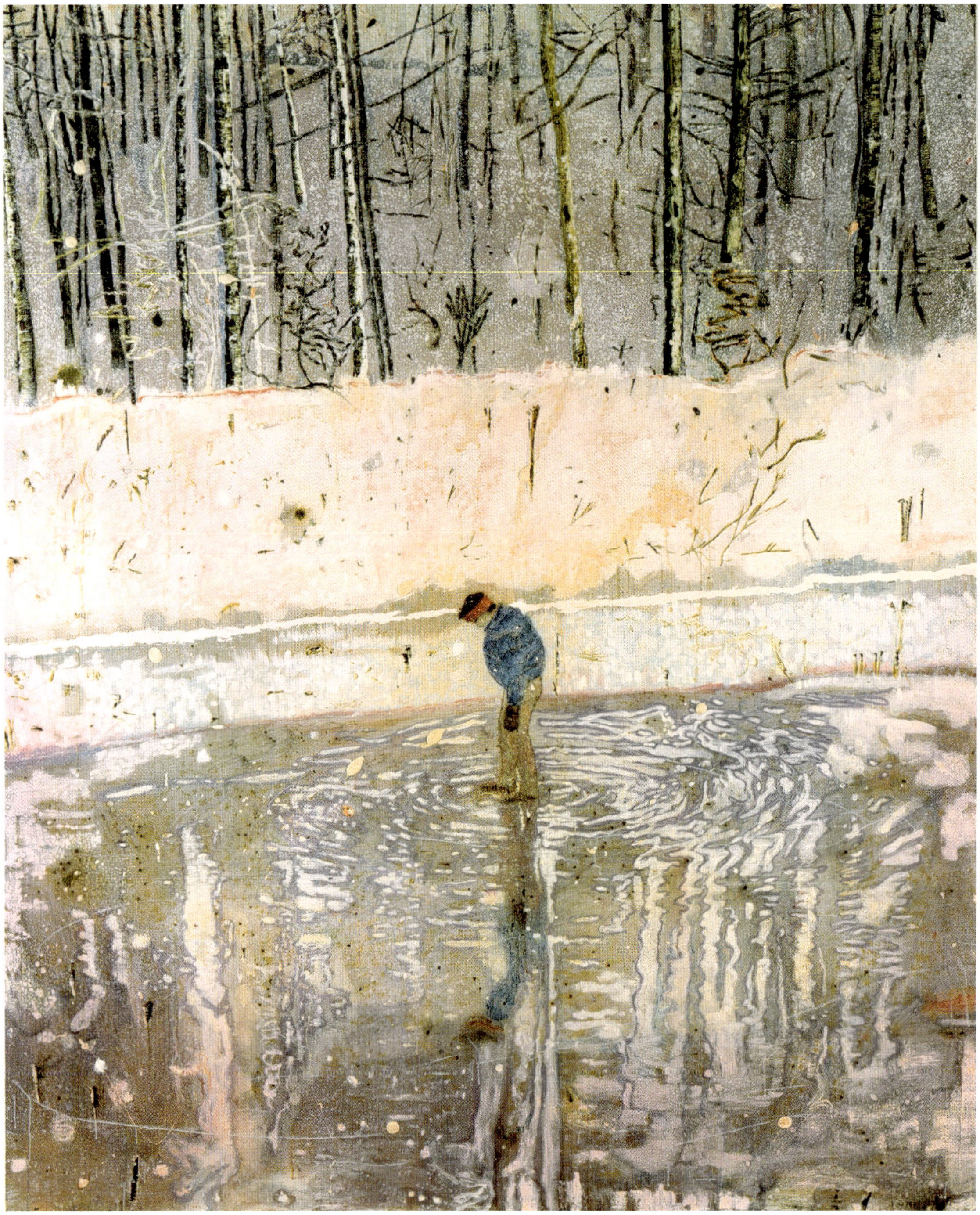

Blotter 1993, oil on canvas, 249 × 199

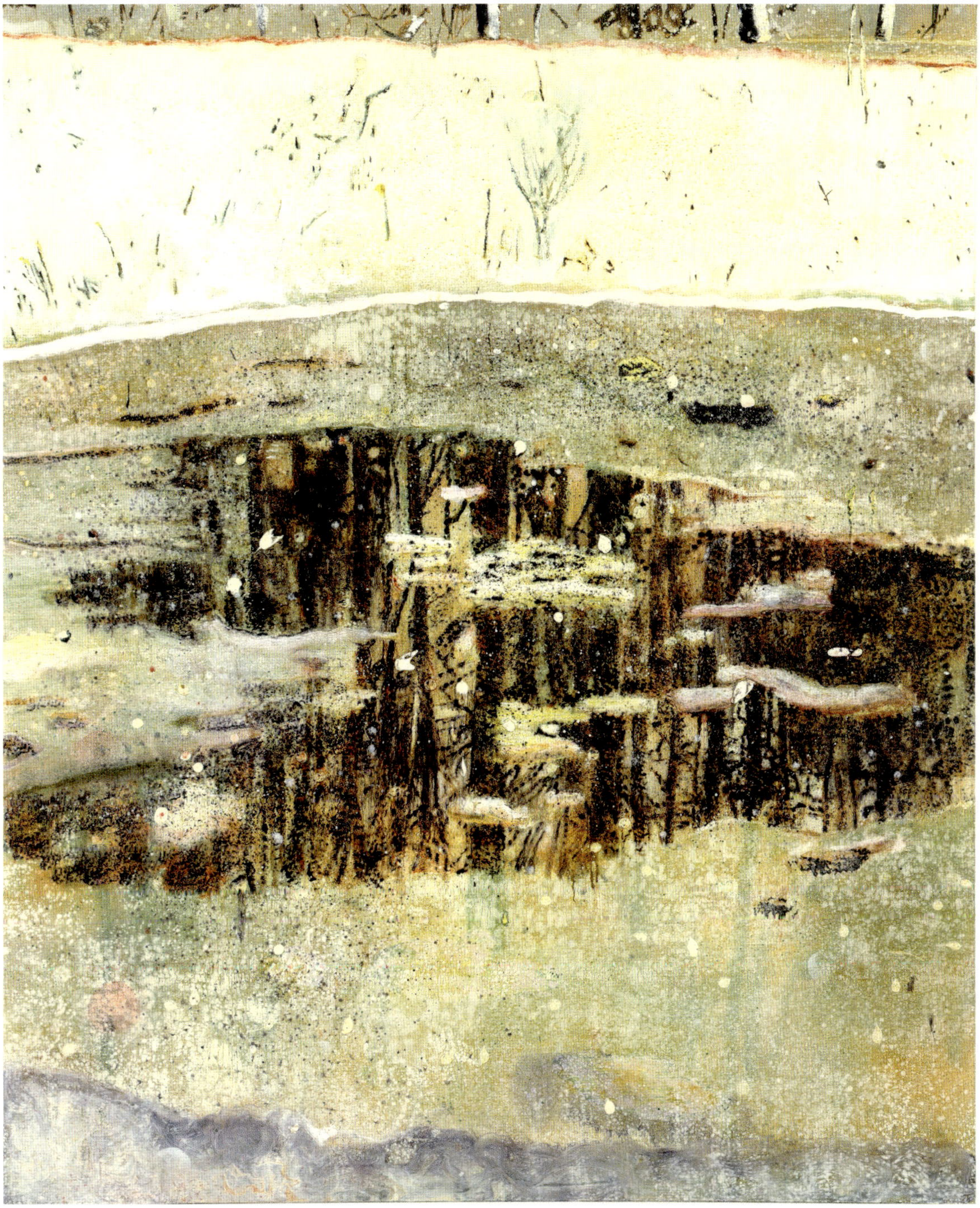

Window Pane 1993, oil on canvas, 250 × 200

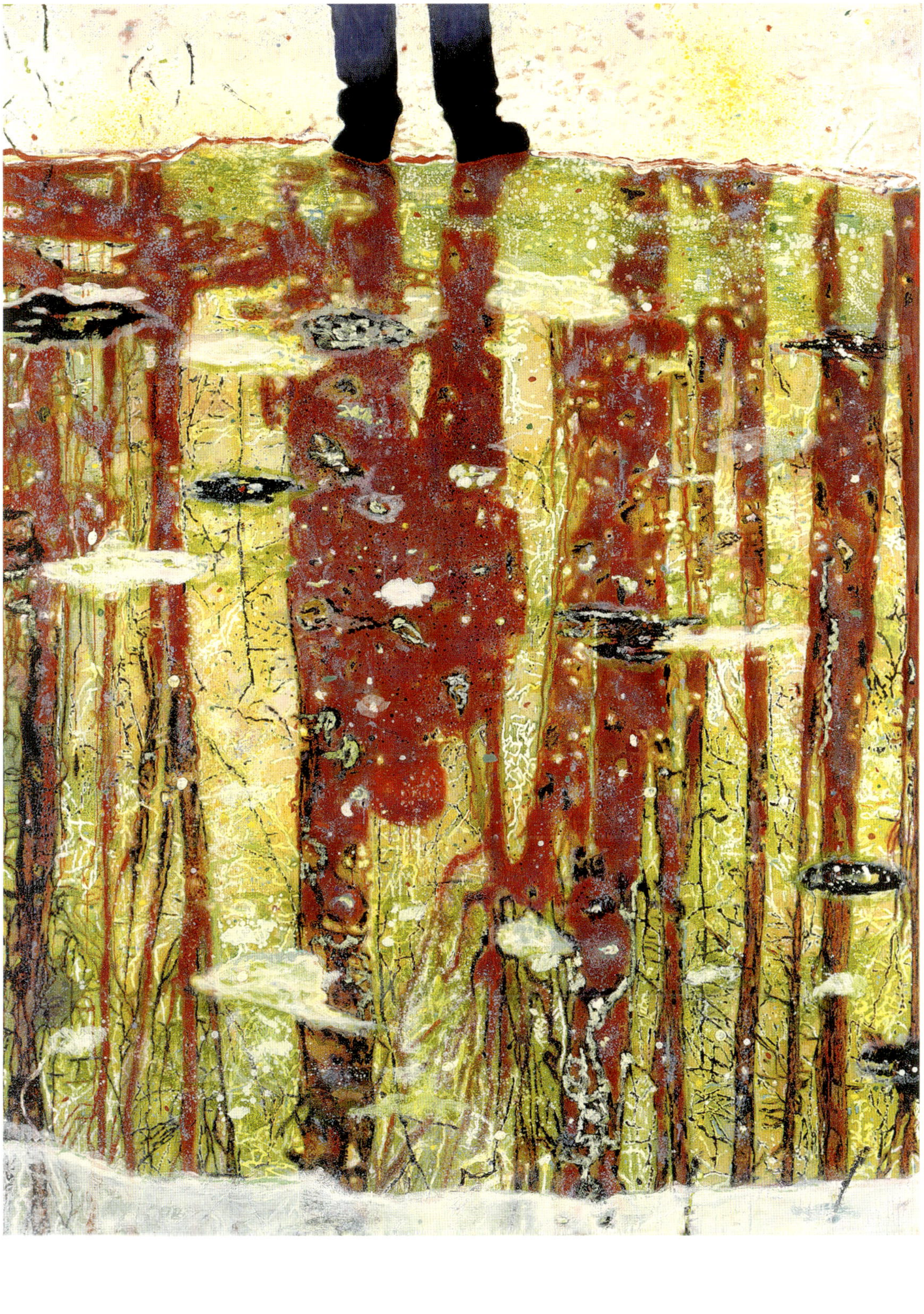

Reflection (What does your soul look like) 1996, oil on canvas, 295 × 200

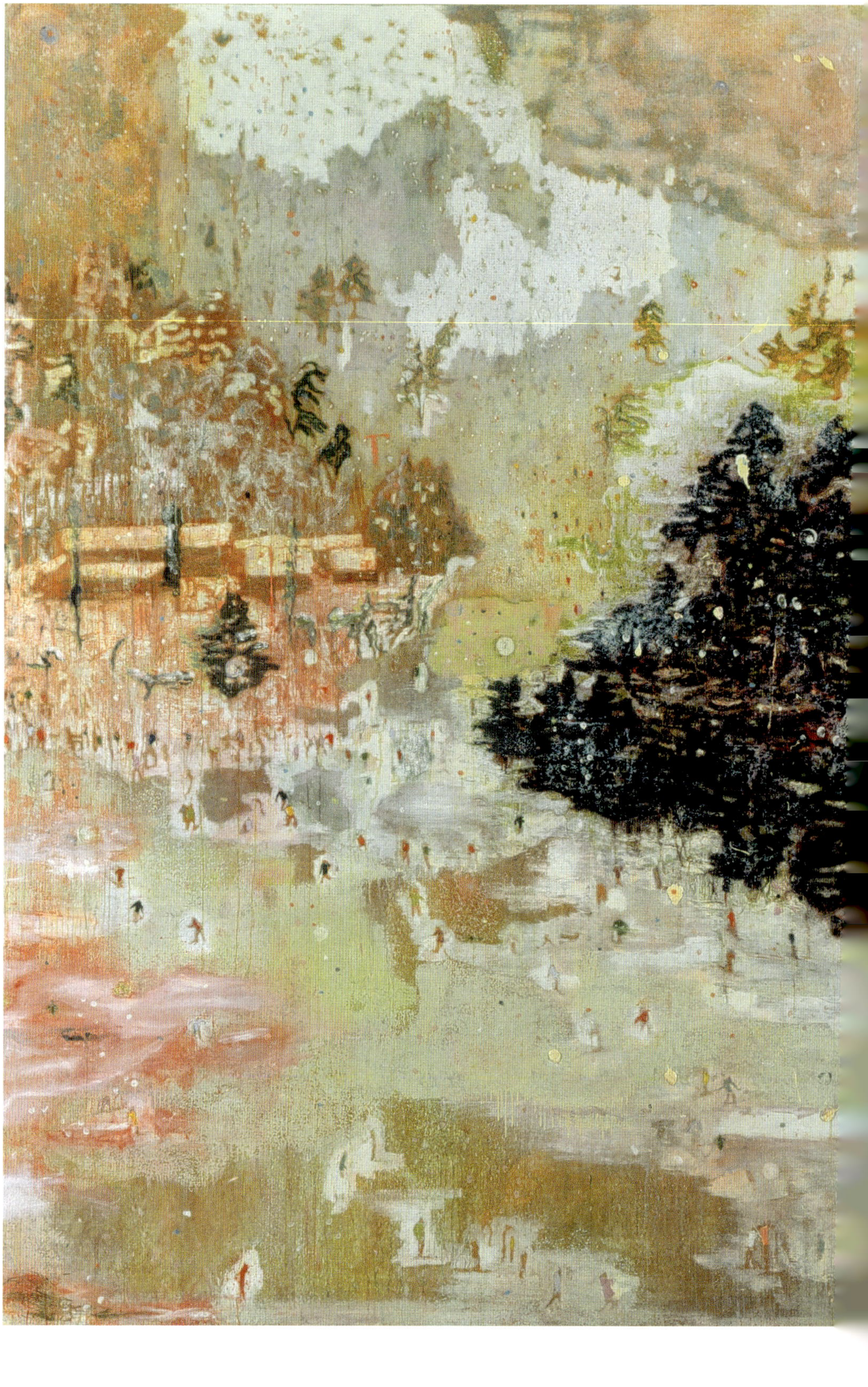

Ski Jacket 1994, oil on canvas, 295 × 190 (left) 295.3 × 160.4 (right)

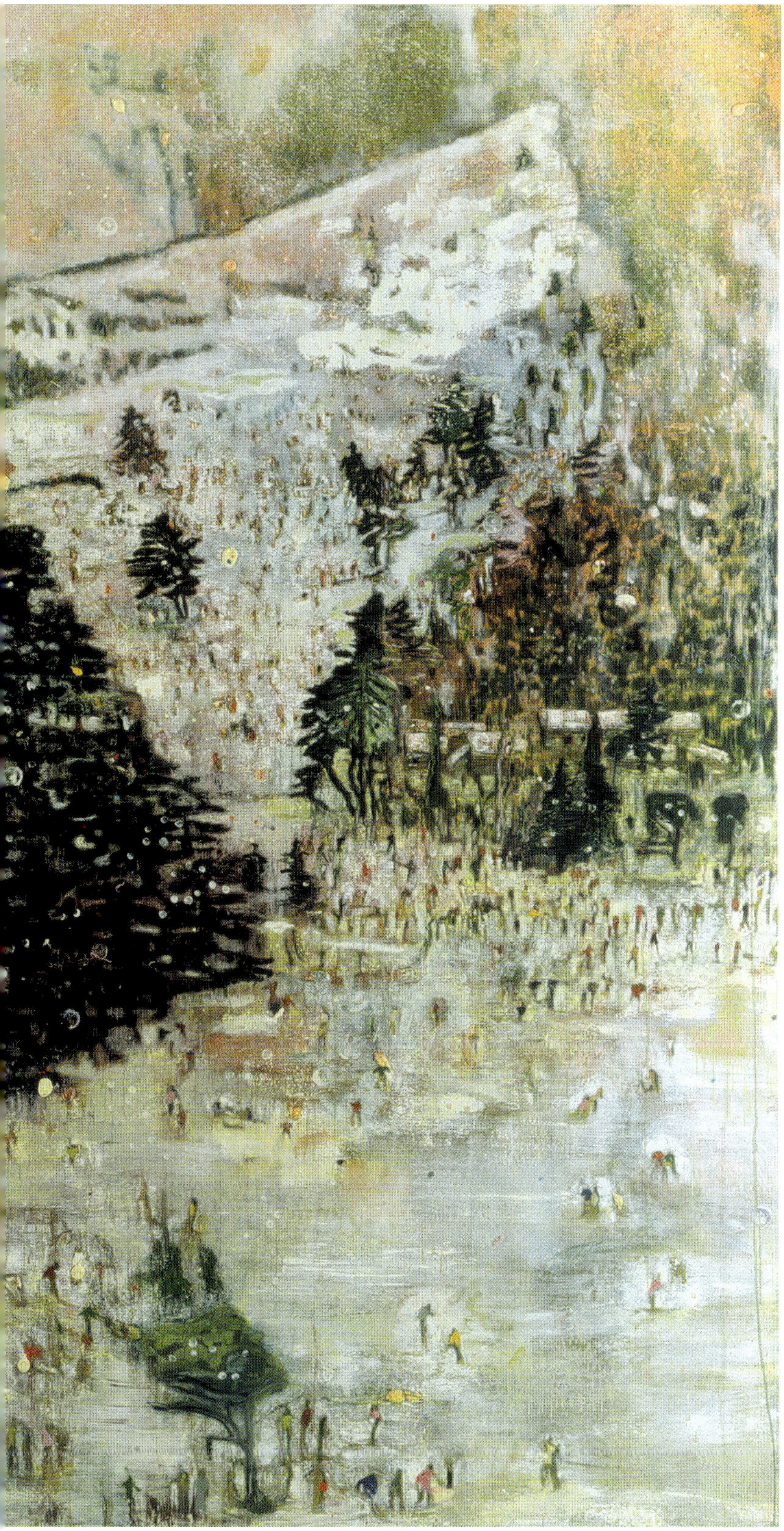

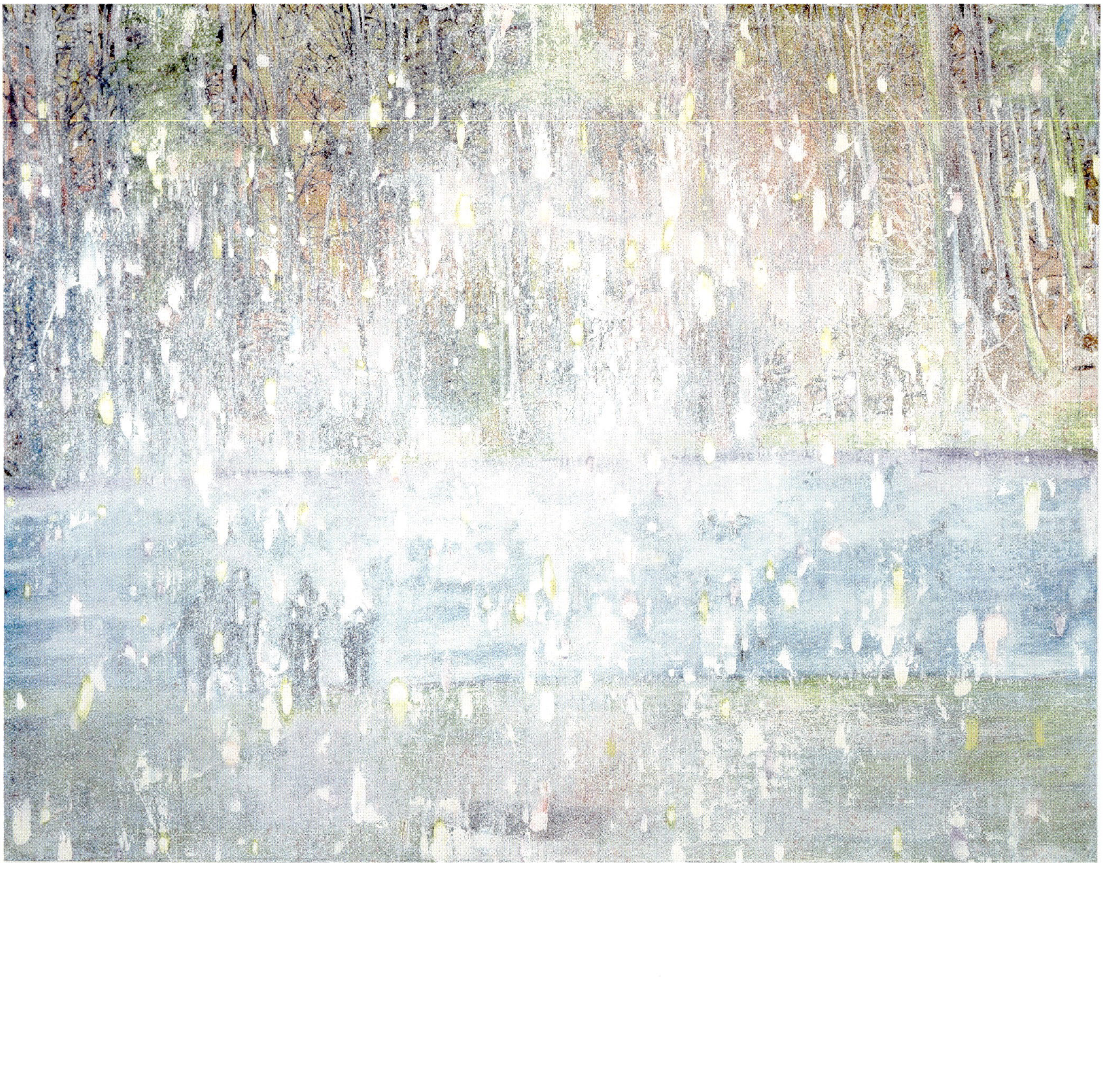

Cobourg 3+1 more 1994, oil on canvas, 200 × 250

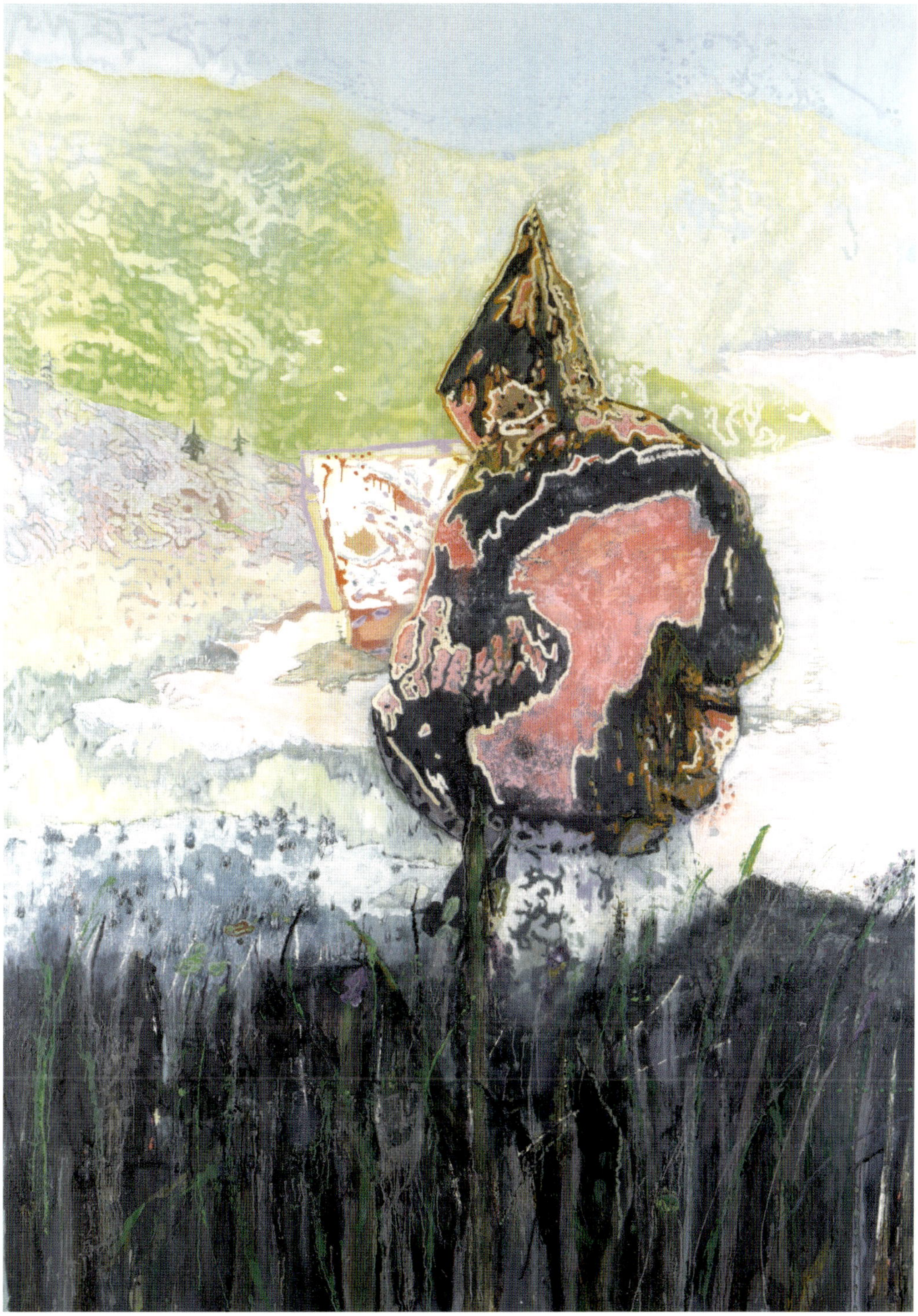

Figure in Mountain Landscape 1997–8, oil on canvas, 289 × 199.5

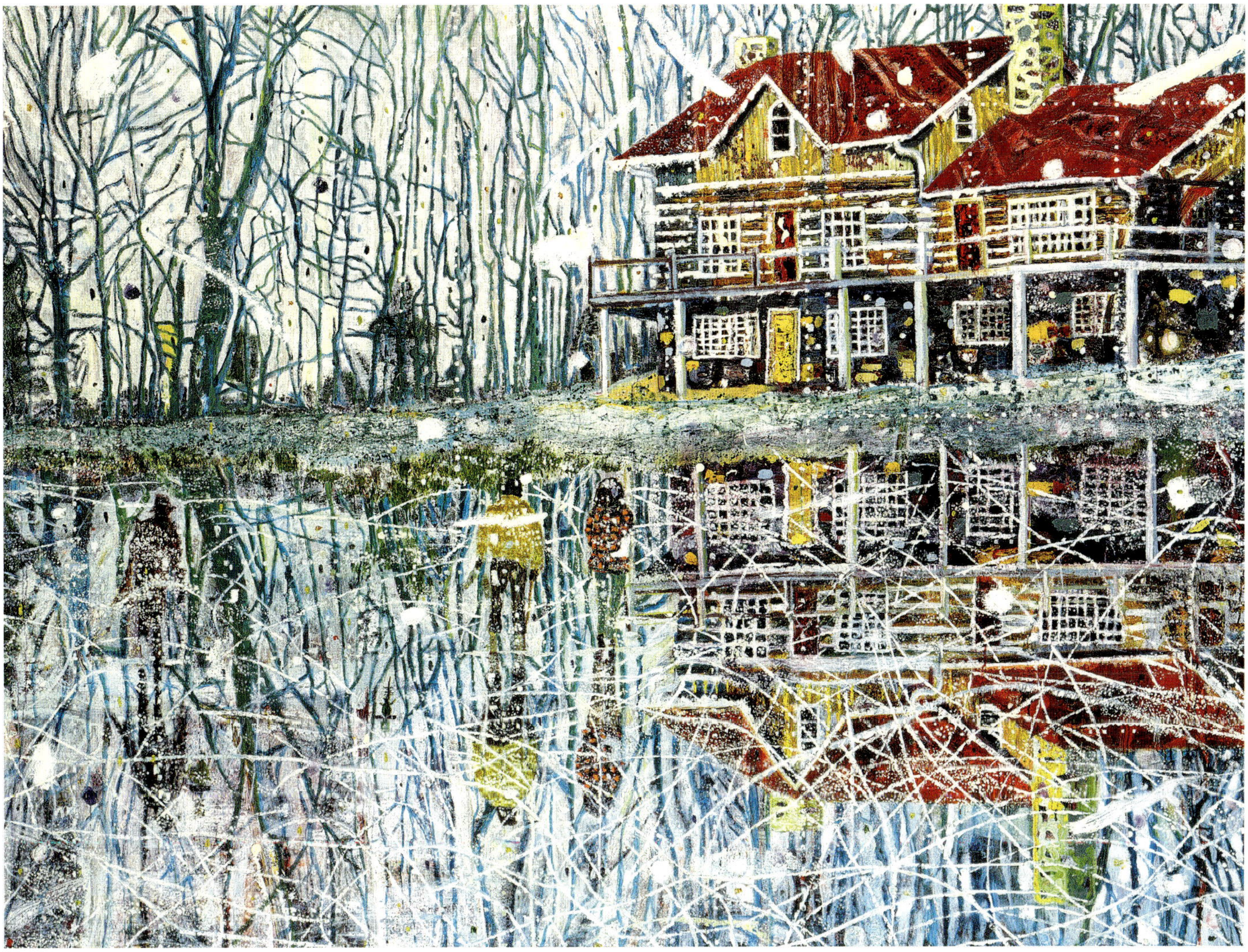

Pond Life 1993, oil on canvas, 185 × 240

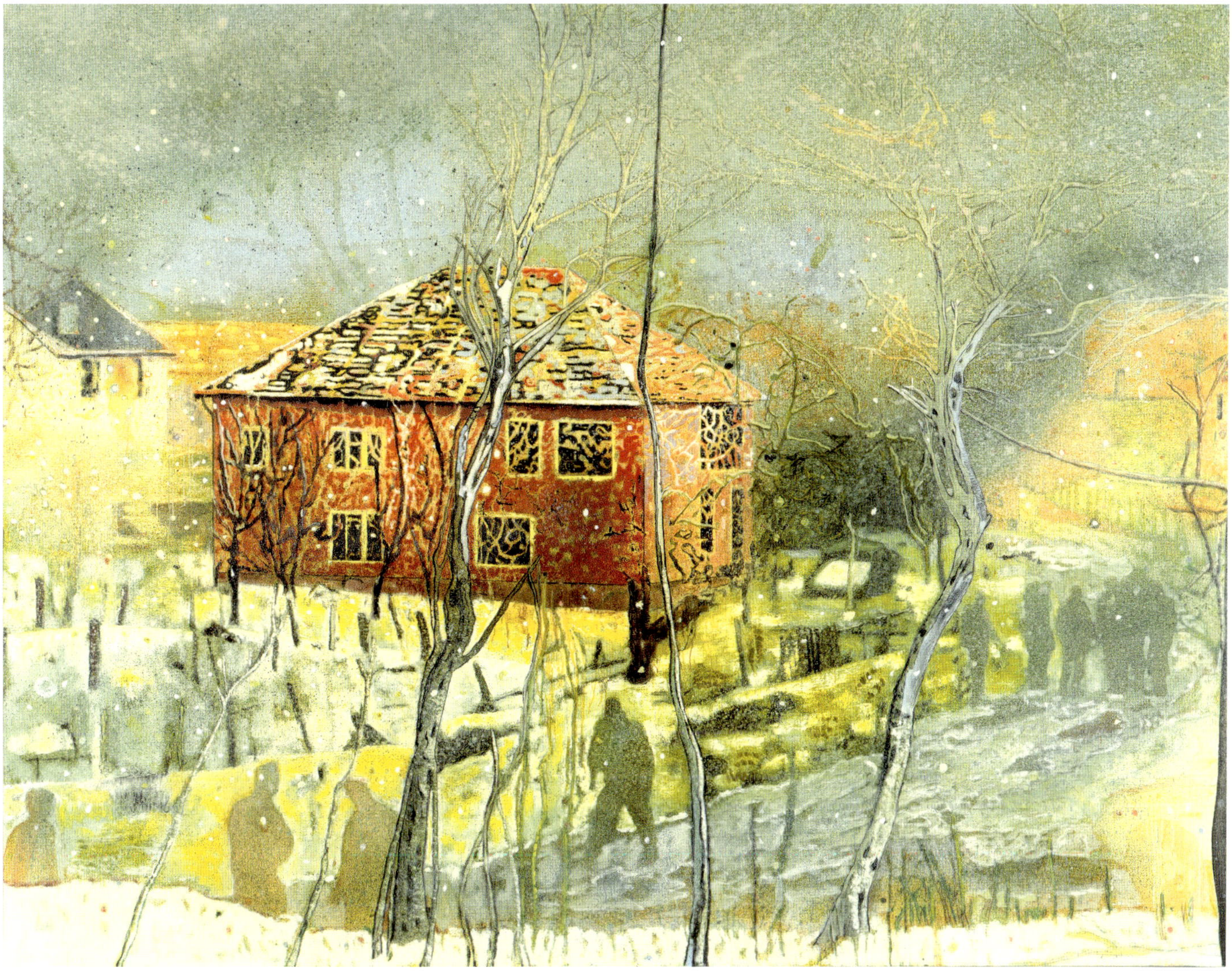

Red House 1995–6, oil on canvas, 200 × 275

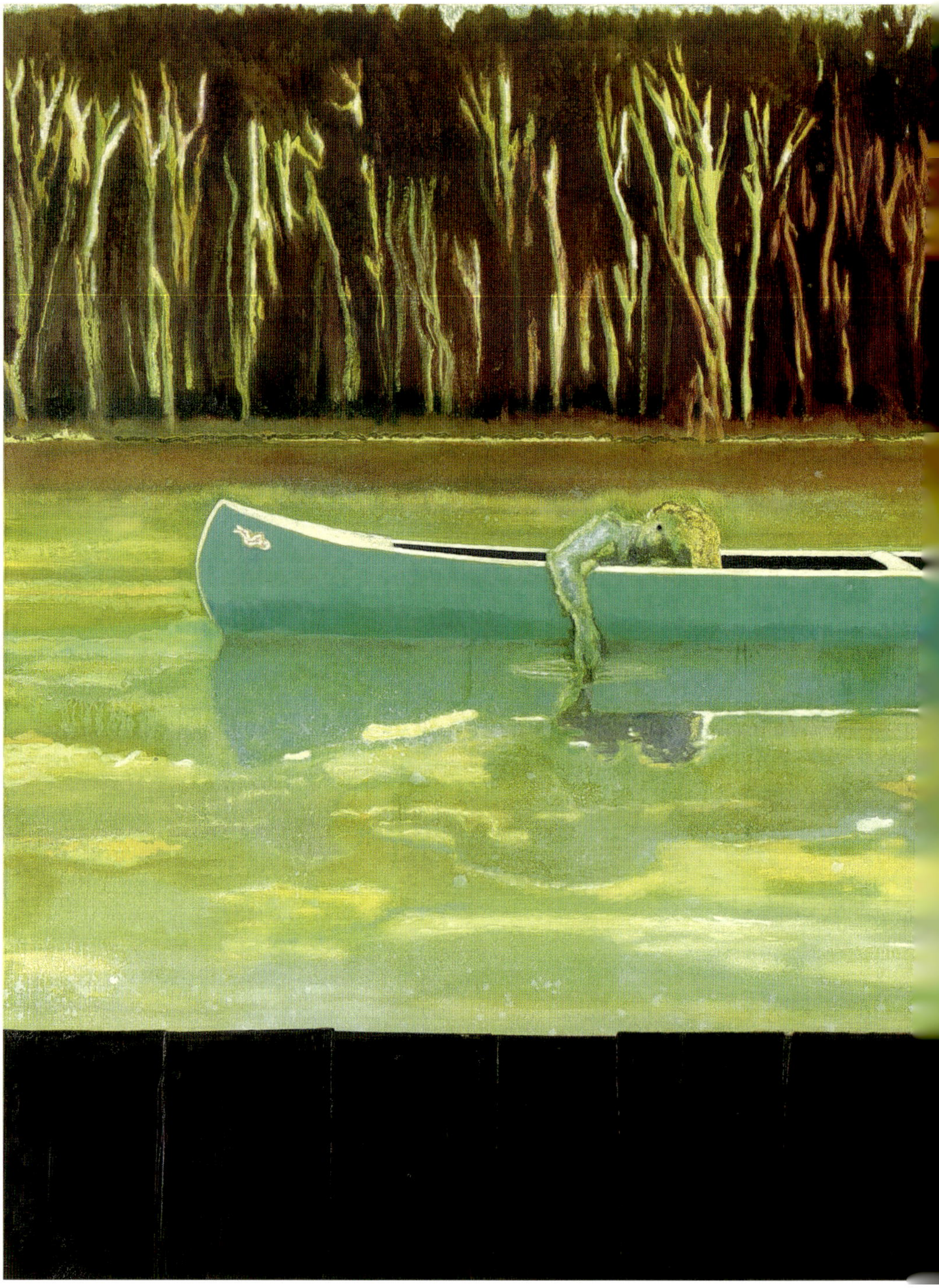

Canoe Lake 1997–8, oil on canvas, 200 × 300

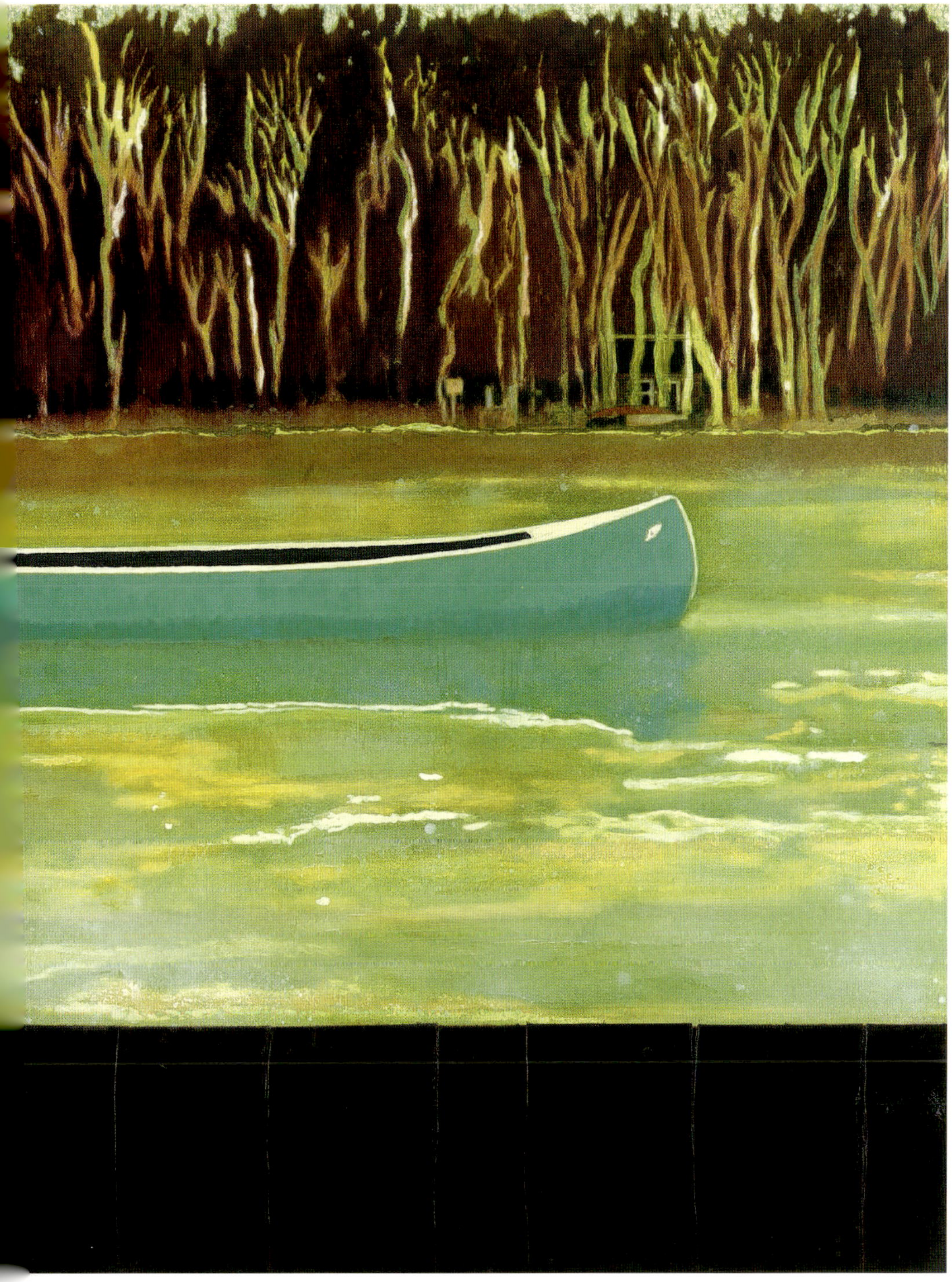

Echo Lake 1998, oil on canvas, 230.5 × 360.5

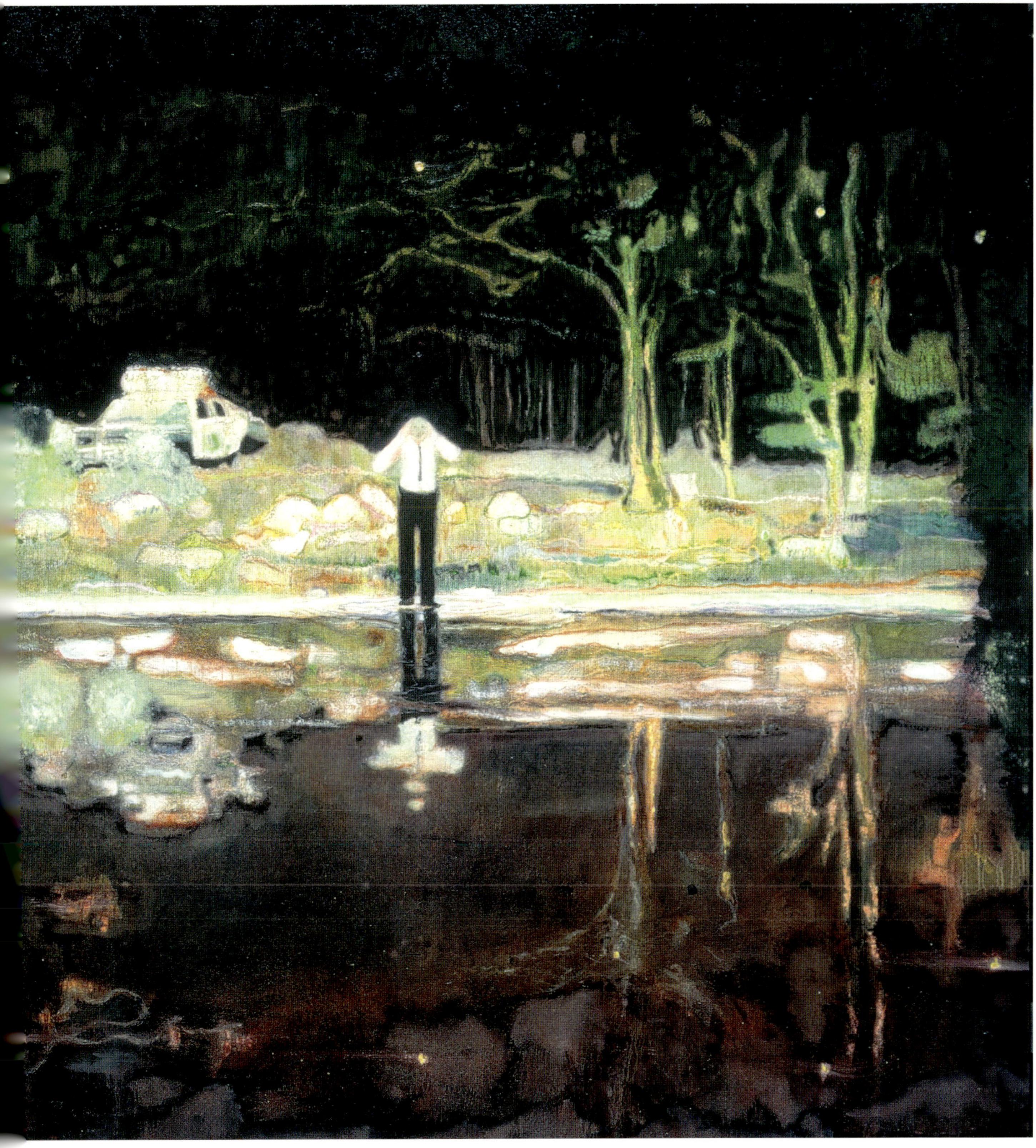

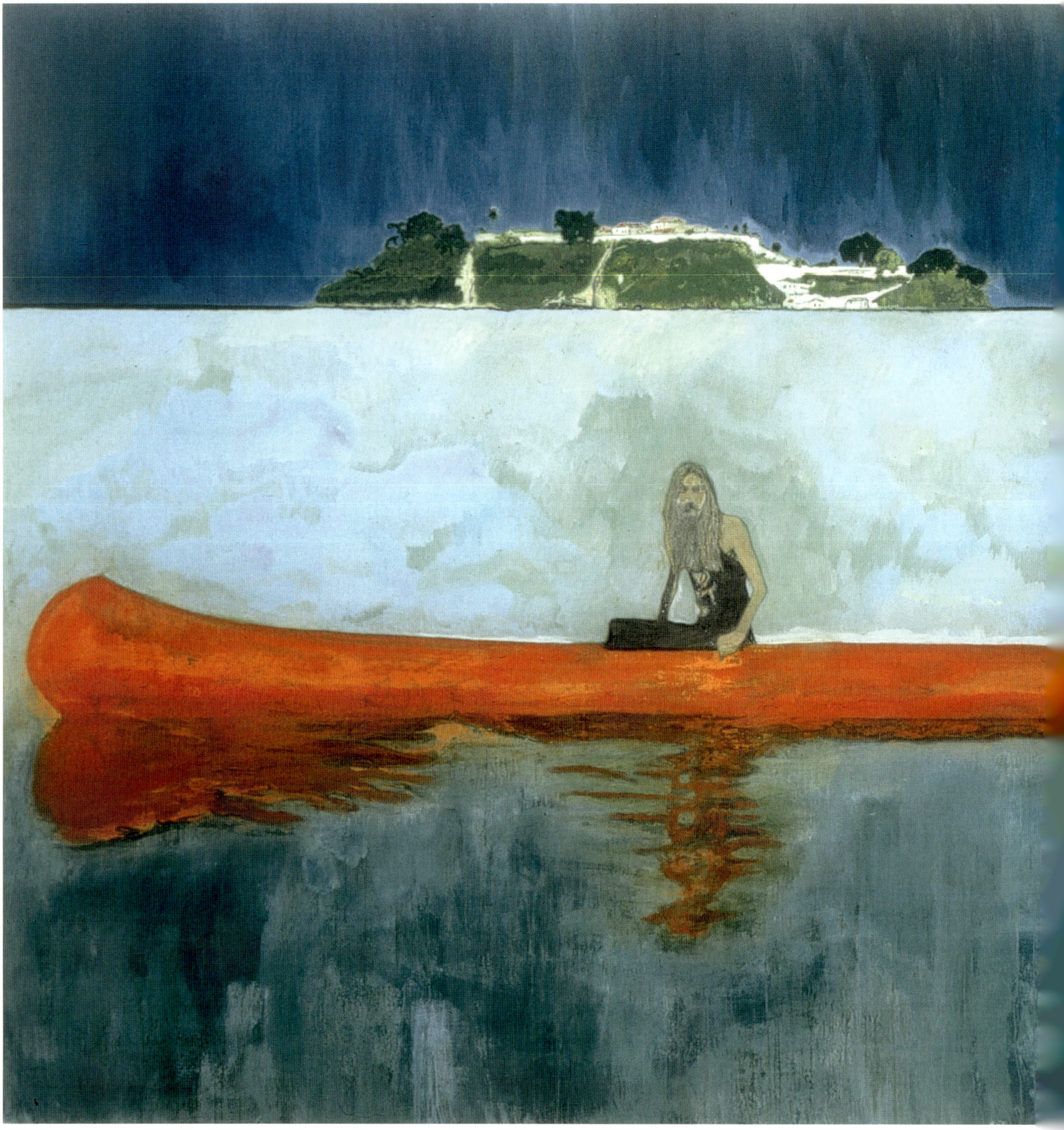

100 Years Ago (Carrera) 2001, oil on canvas, 229 × 358.5

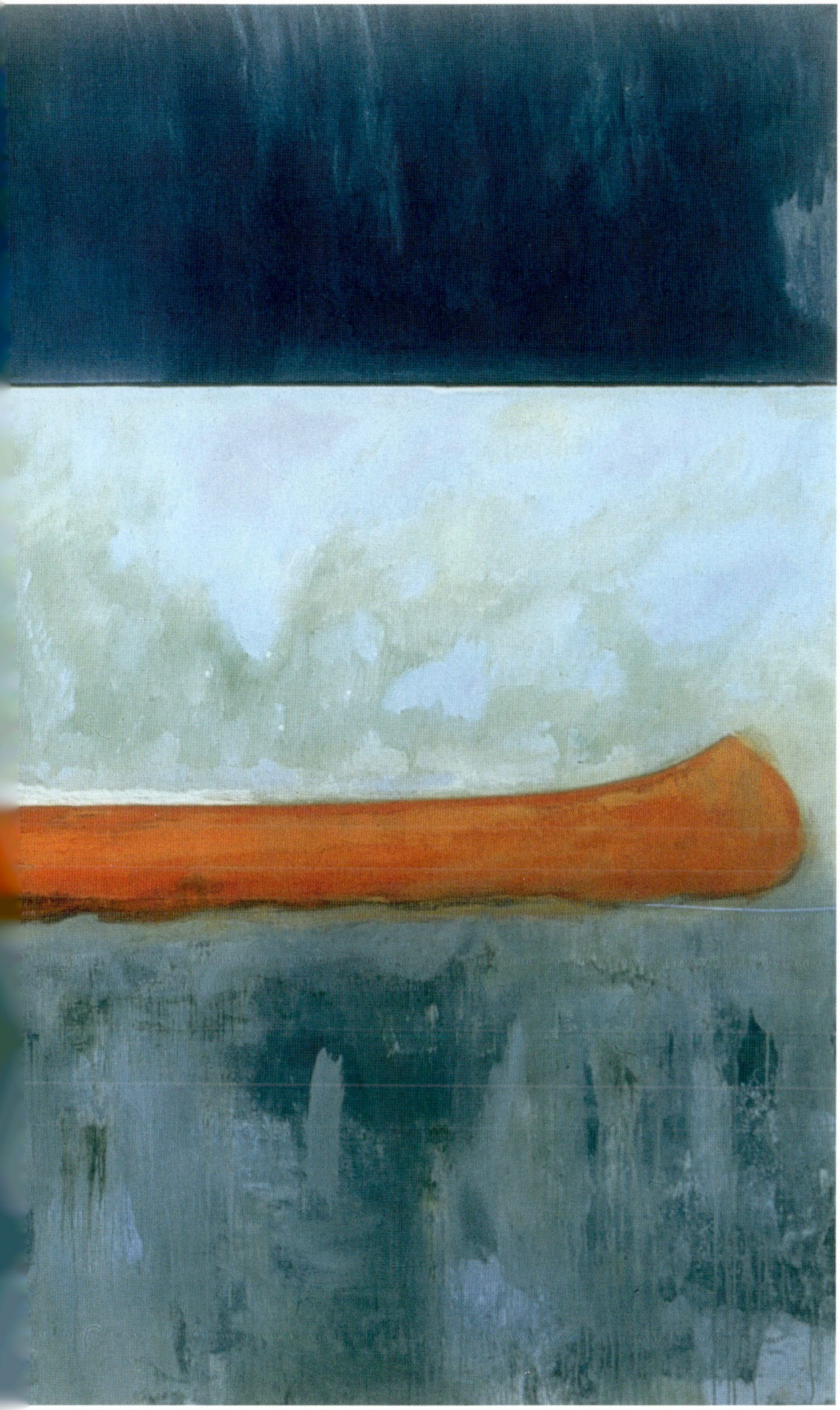

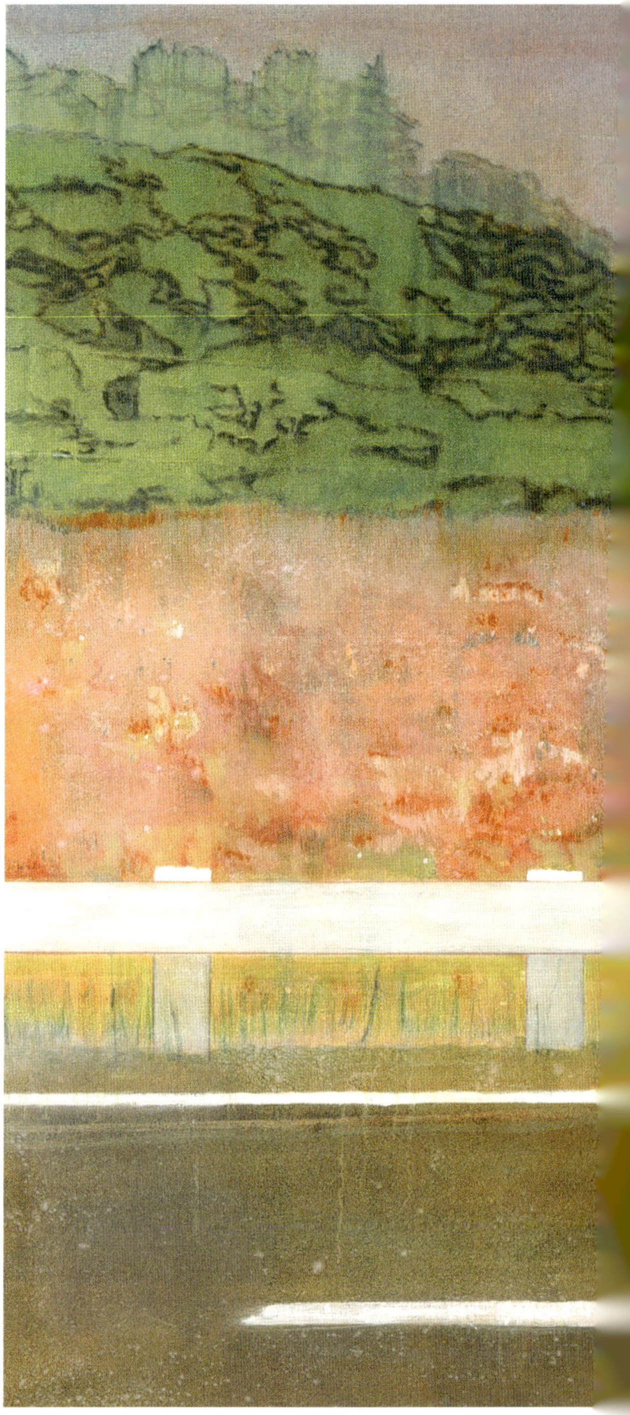

Country Rock 1998–9, oil on canvas, 202 × 300

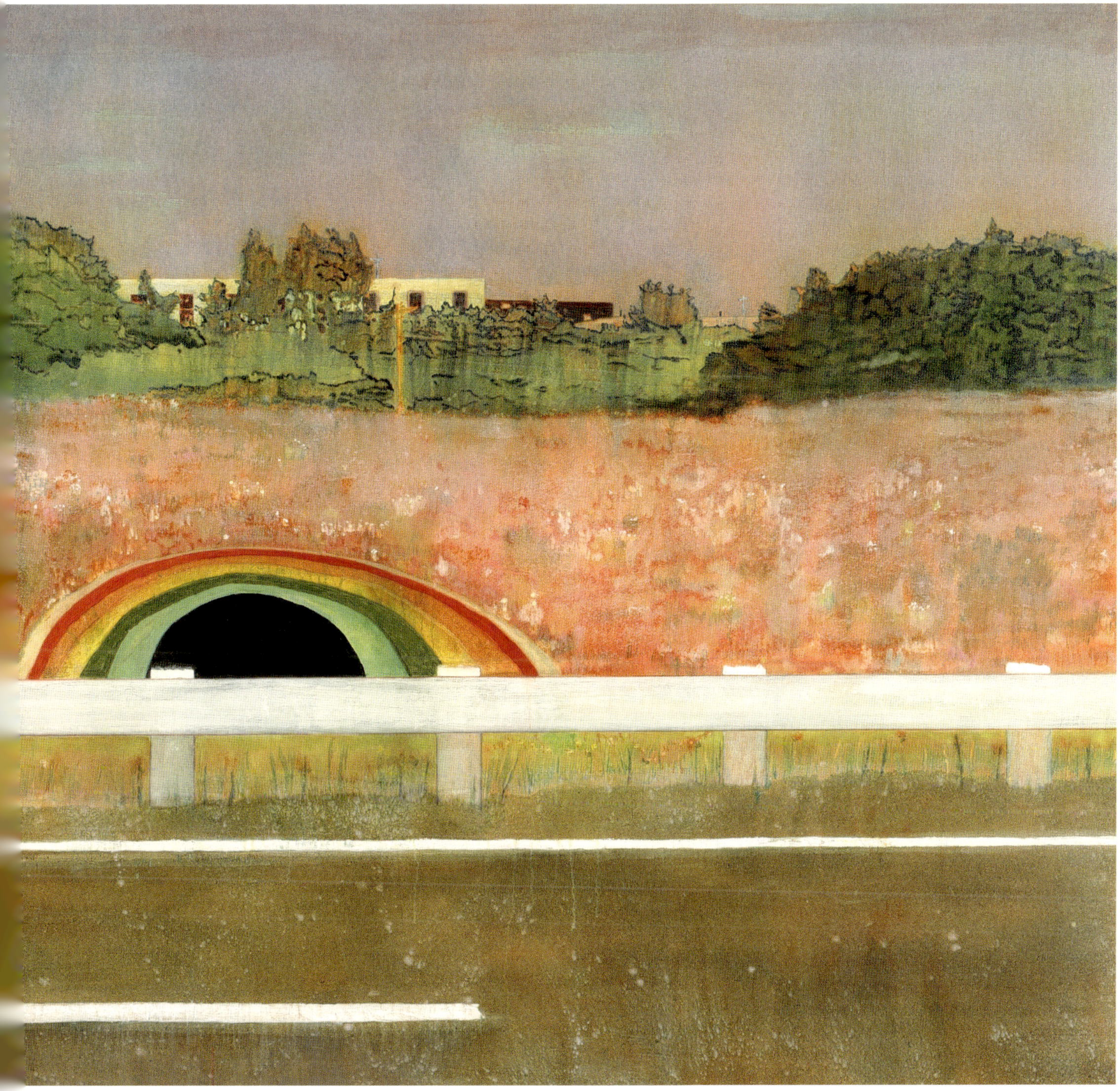

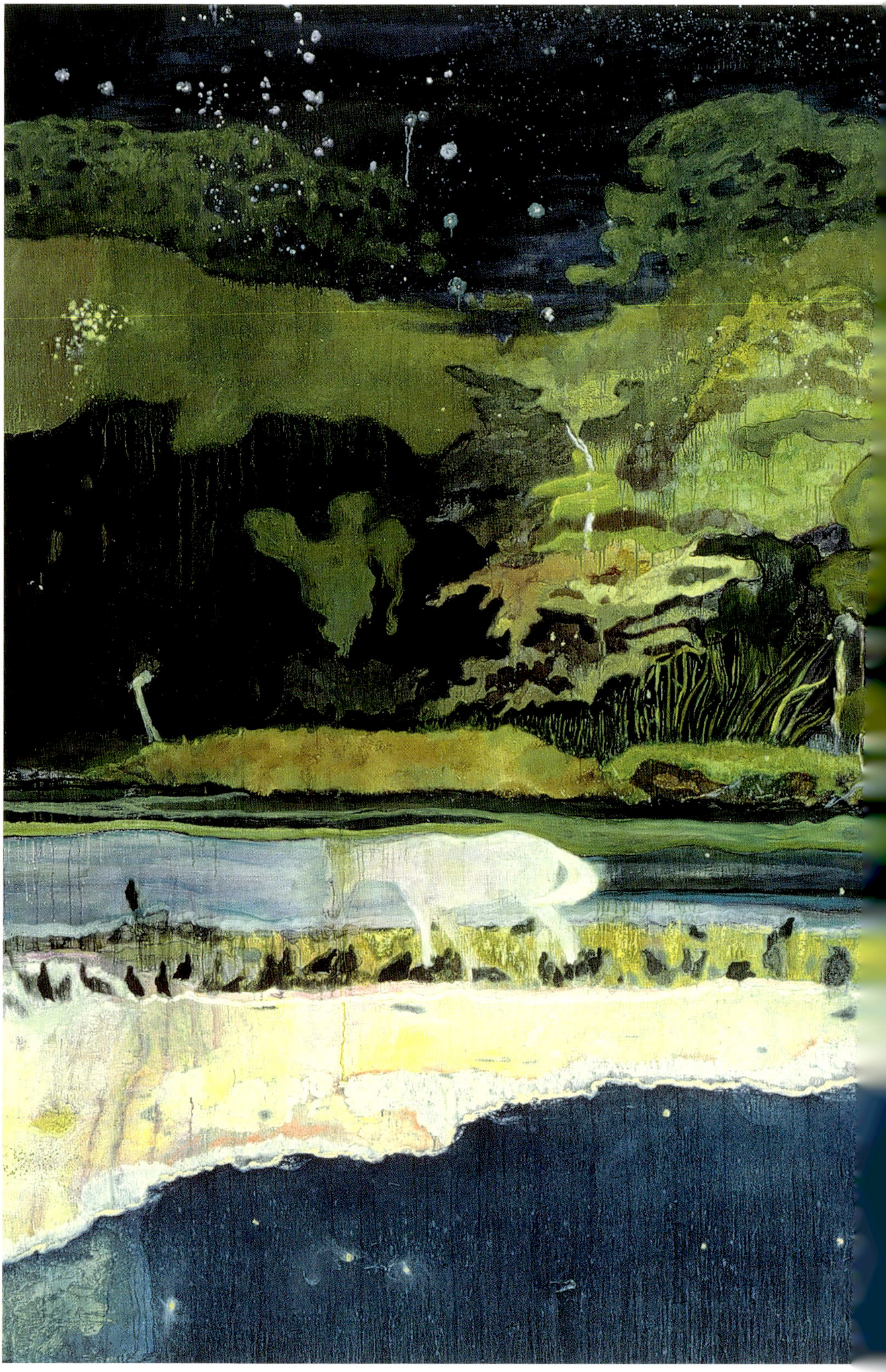

Grand Riviere 2001–2, oil on canvas, 228.8 × 358.4

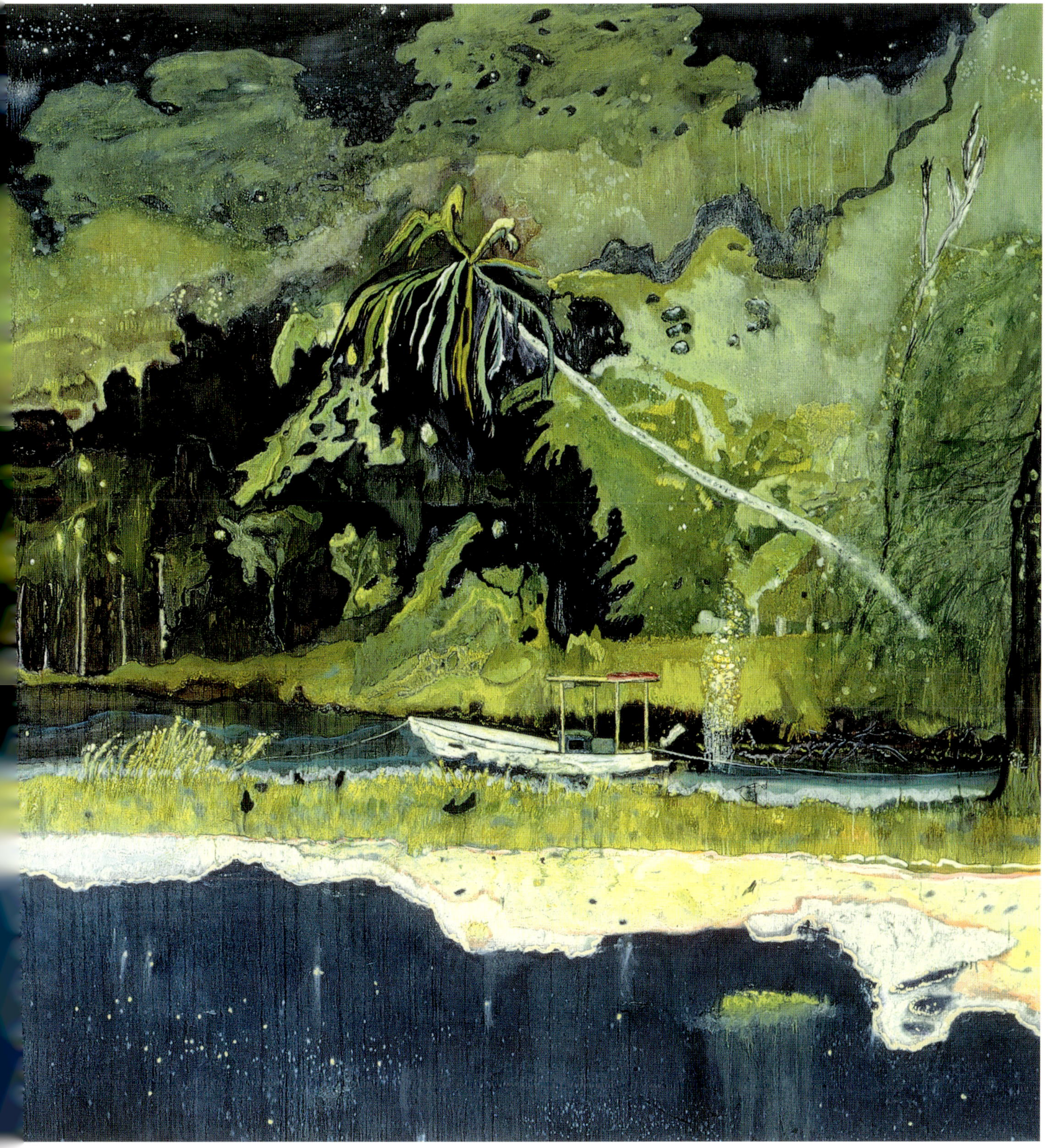

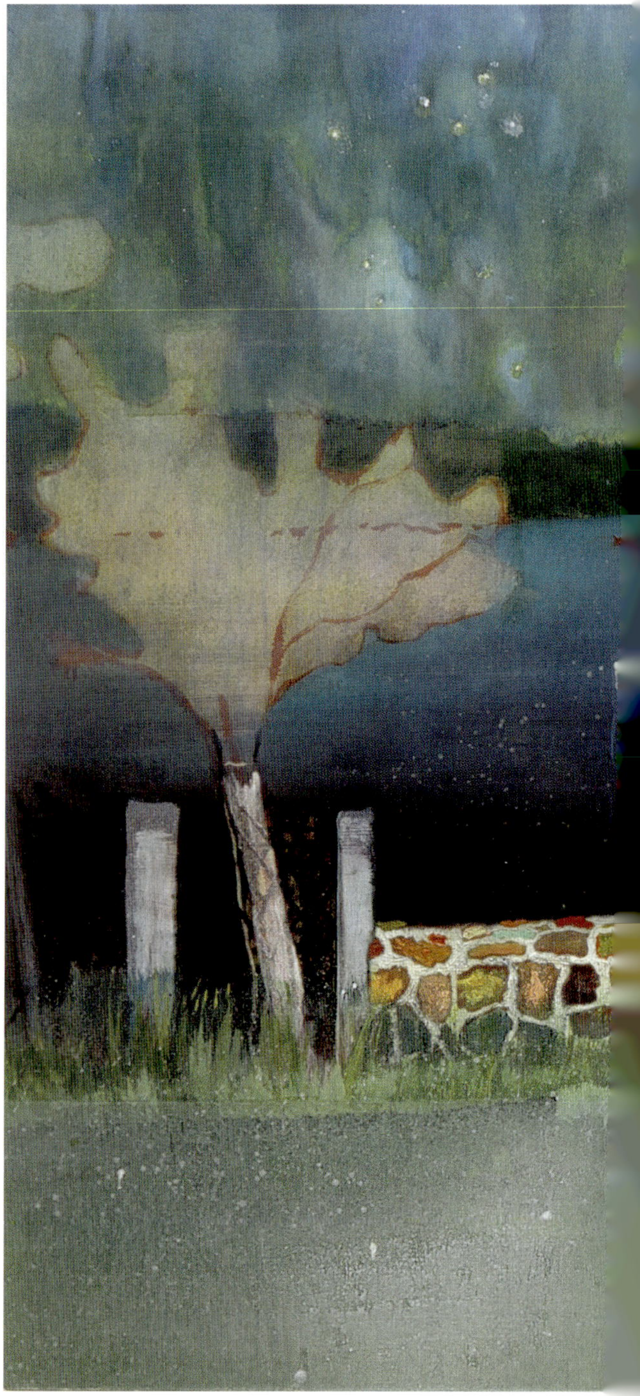

Gasthof zur Muldentalsperre 2000–2, oil on canvas, 196 × 296

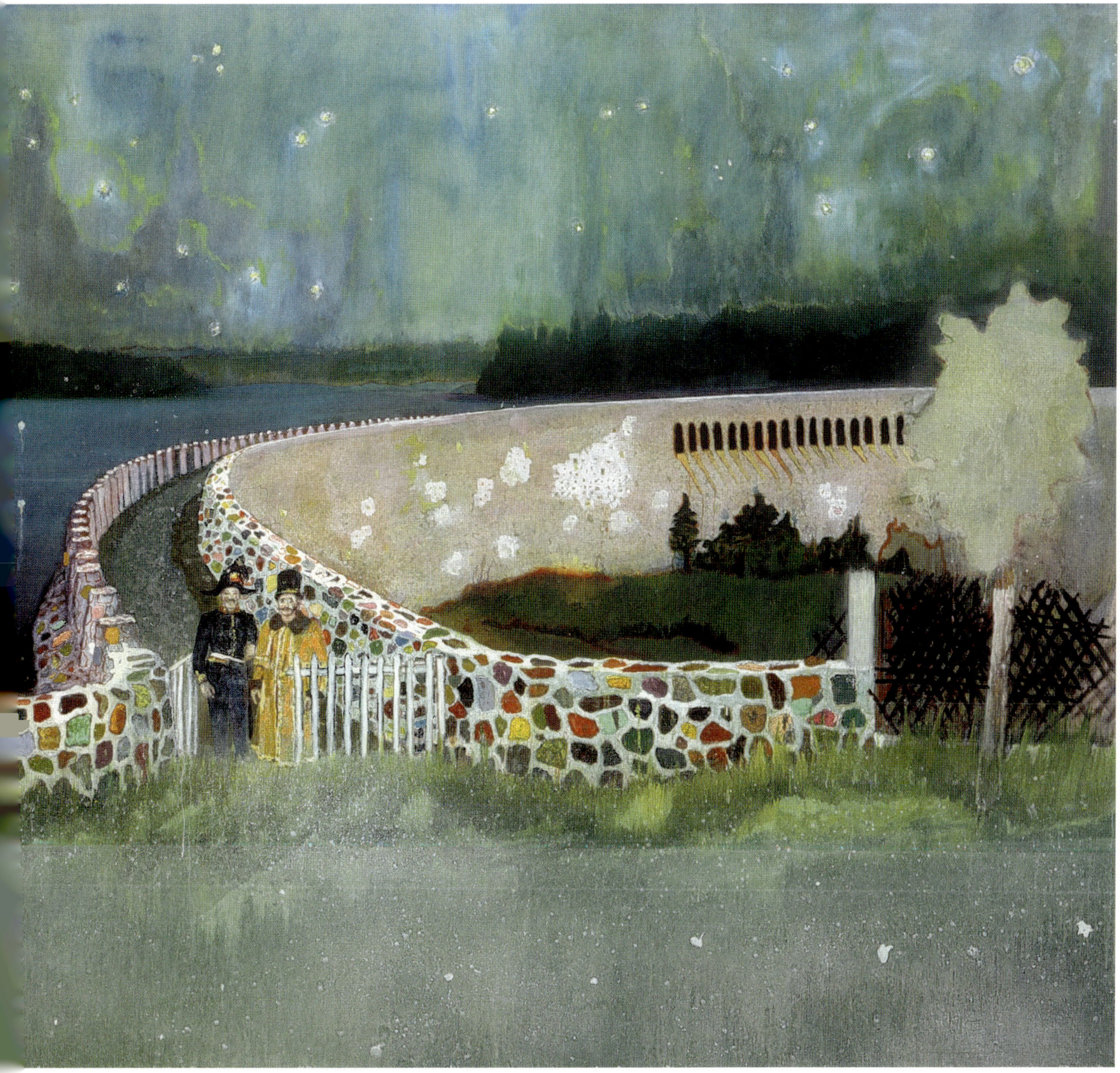

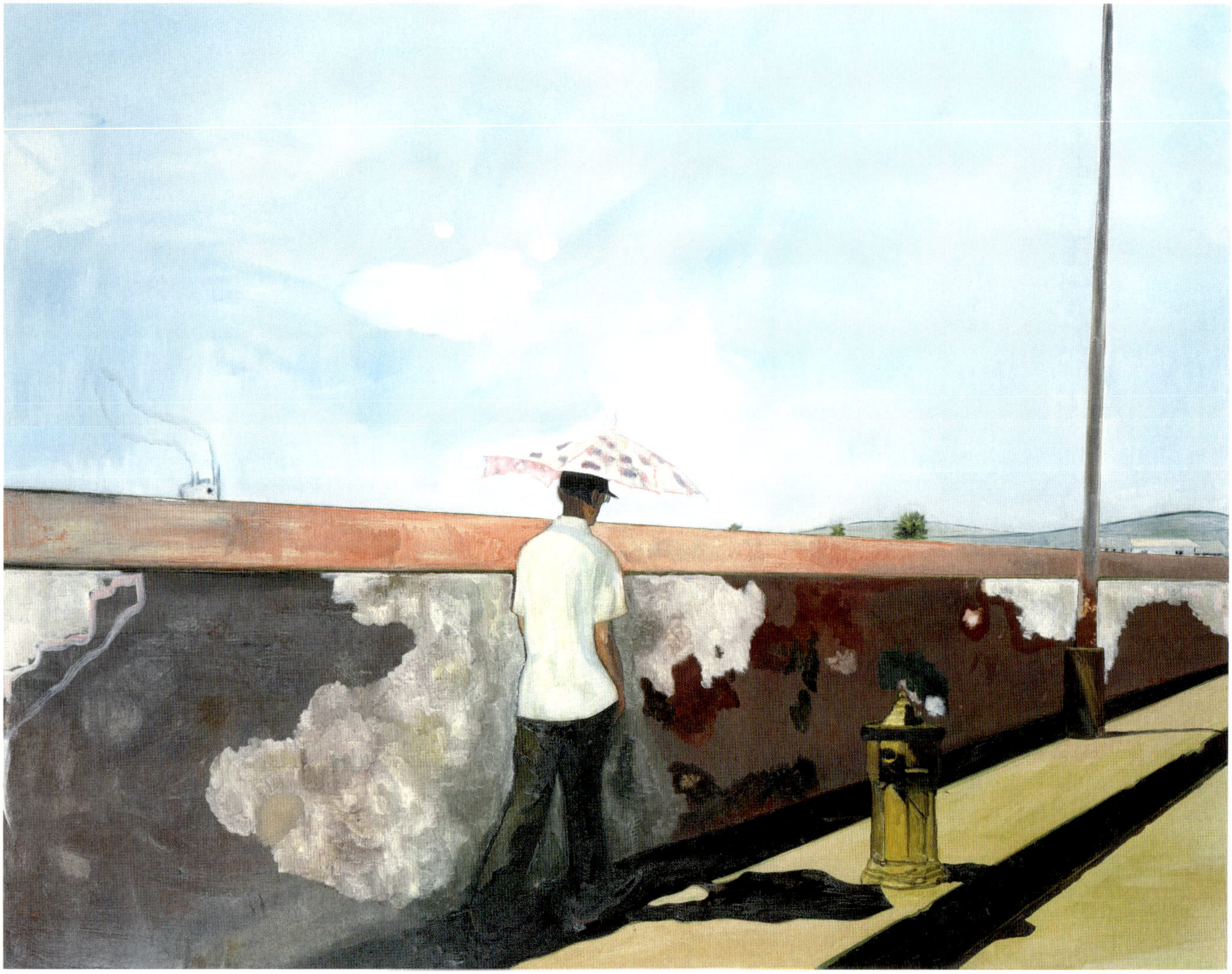

Lapeyrouse Wall 2004, oil on canvas, 200 × 250.5

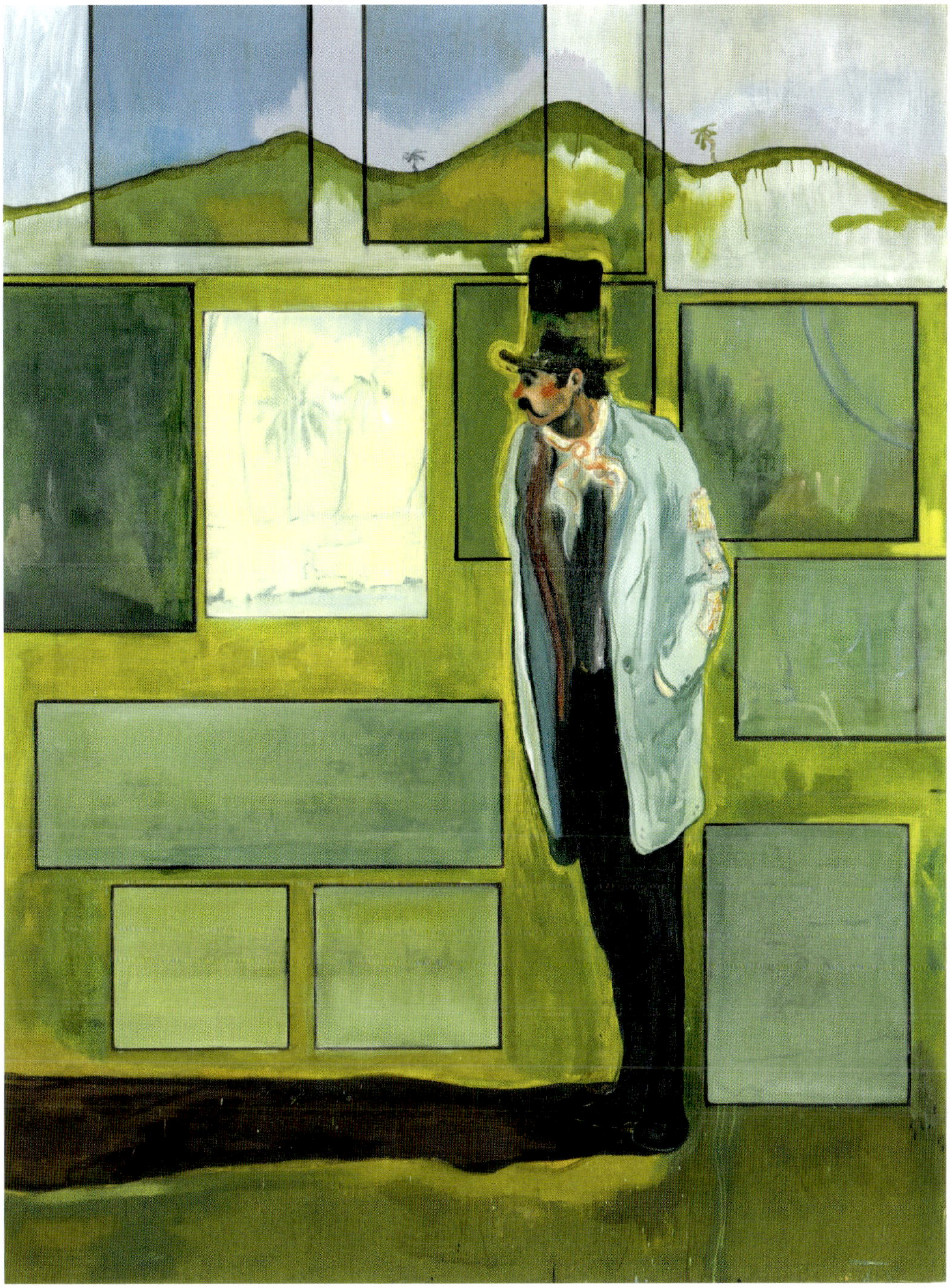

Metropolitain (House of Pictures) 2004, oil on canvas, 275.3 × 200

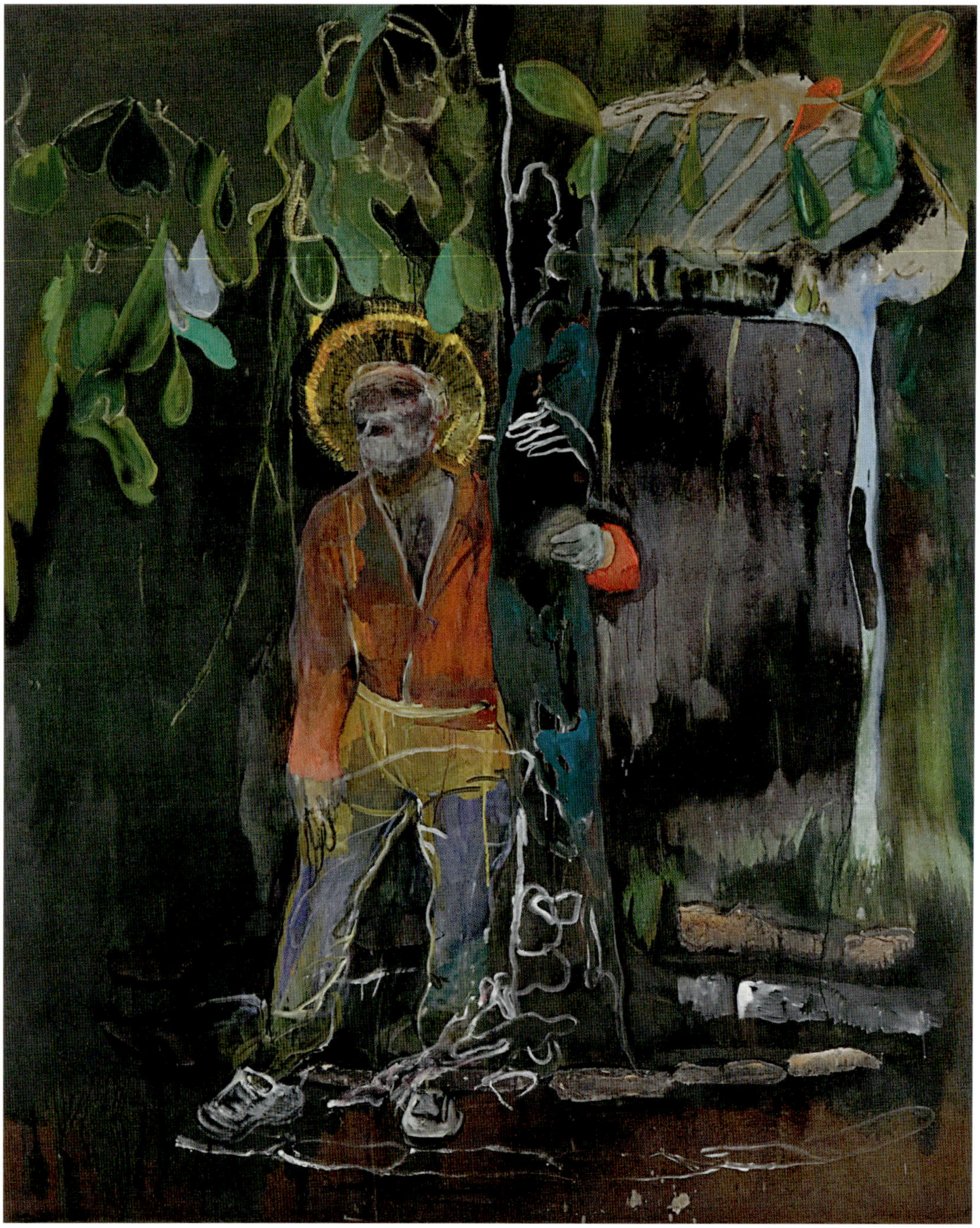

Stag 2002–5, oil on canvas, 250 × 200

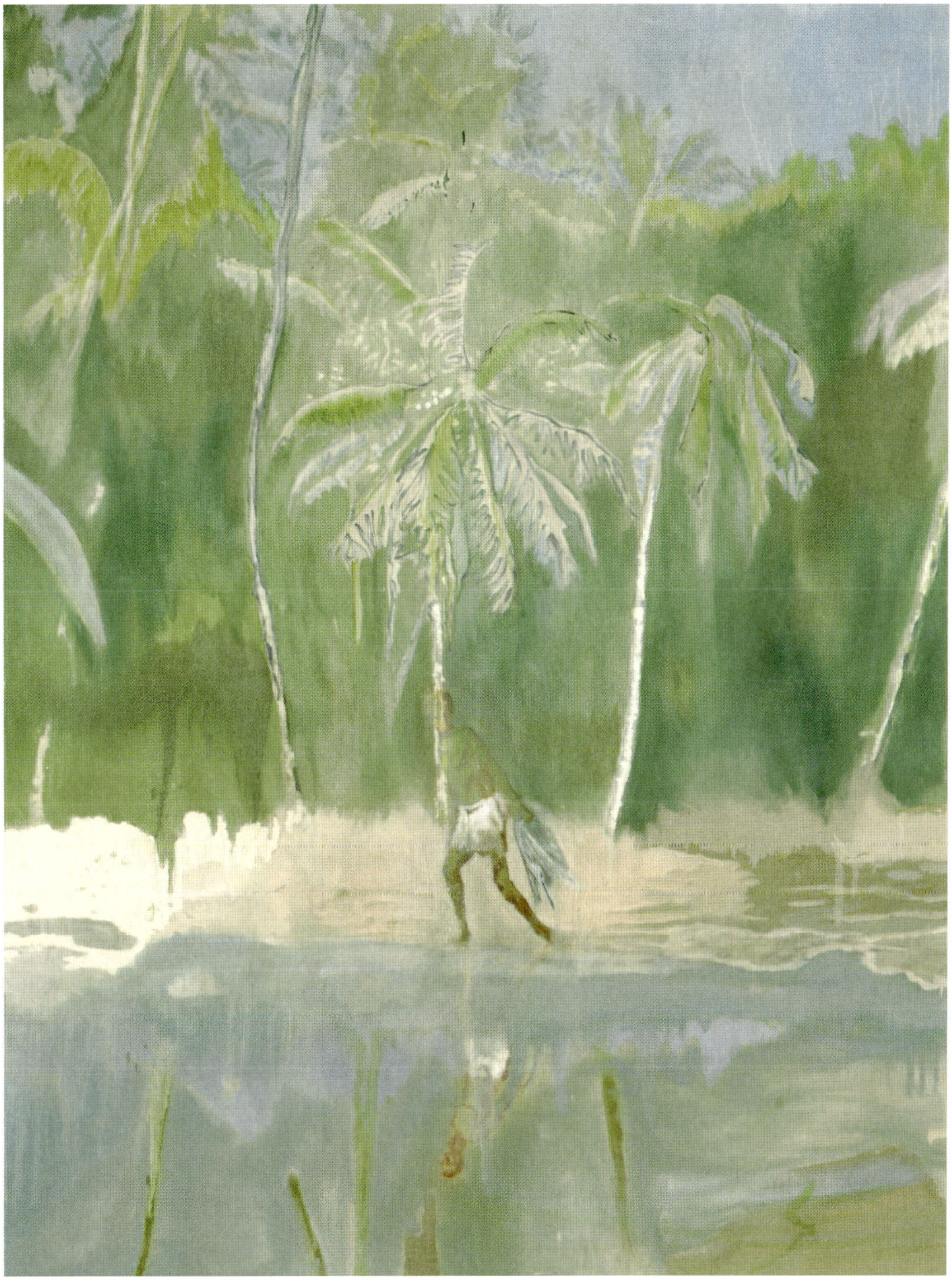

Pelican 2004, oil on canvas, 275 × 200

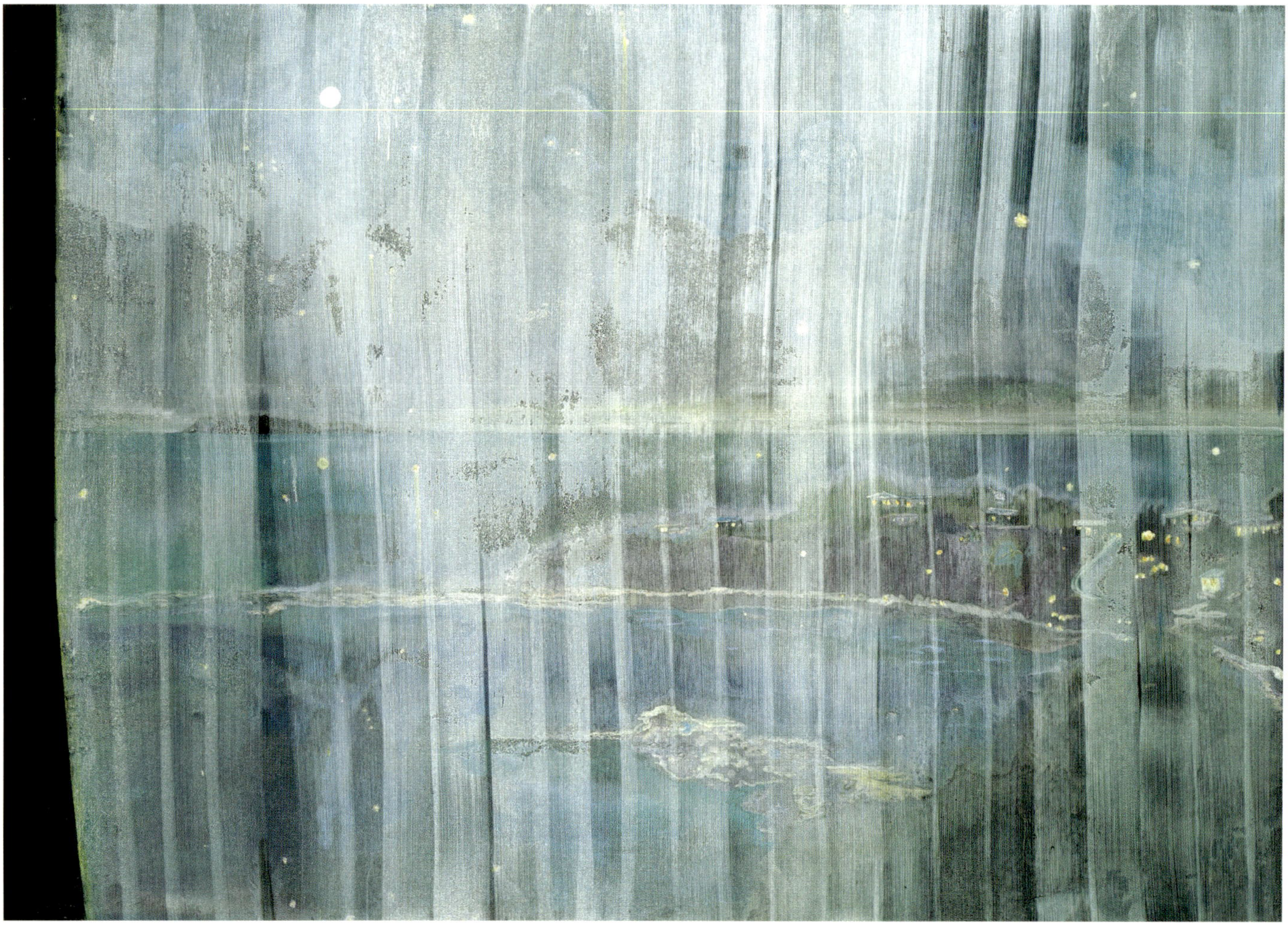

Black Curtain (Towards Monkey Island) 2004, oil on linen, 200 × 275

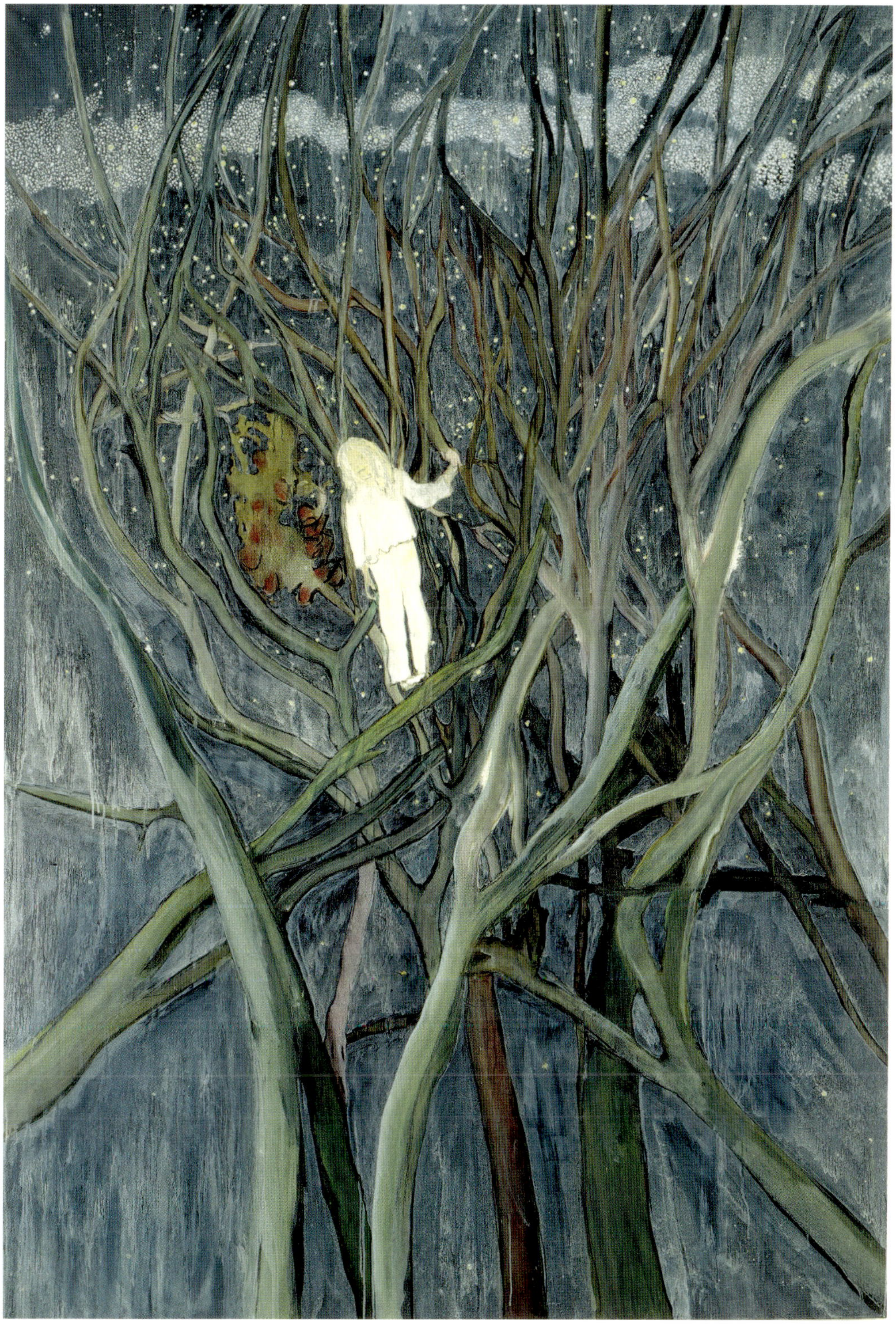

Girl in White with Trees 2001–2, oil on canvas, 300 × 200

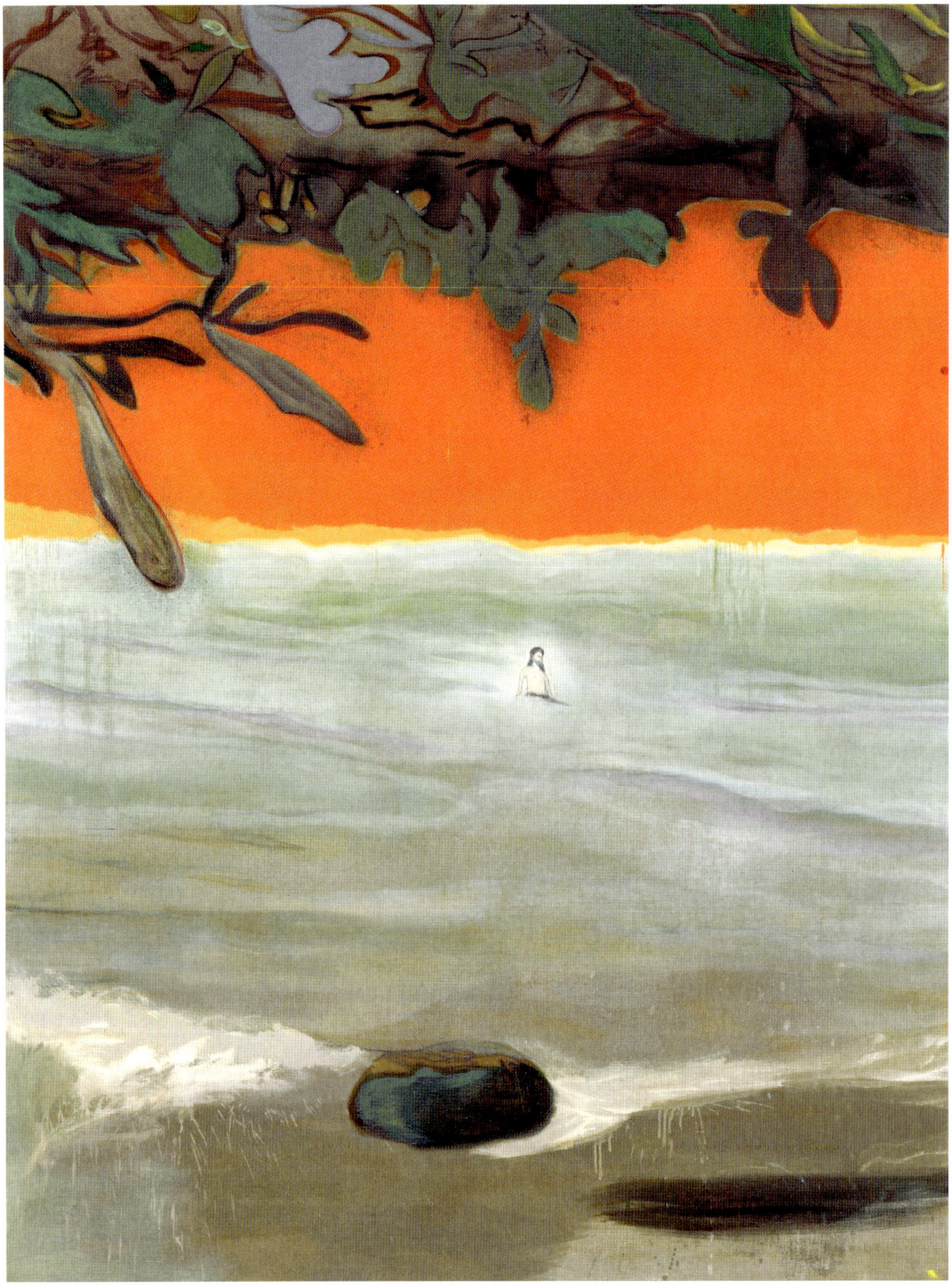

J.M. at Paragon 2004, oil on canvas, 275 × 200

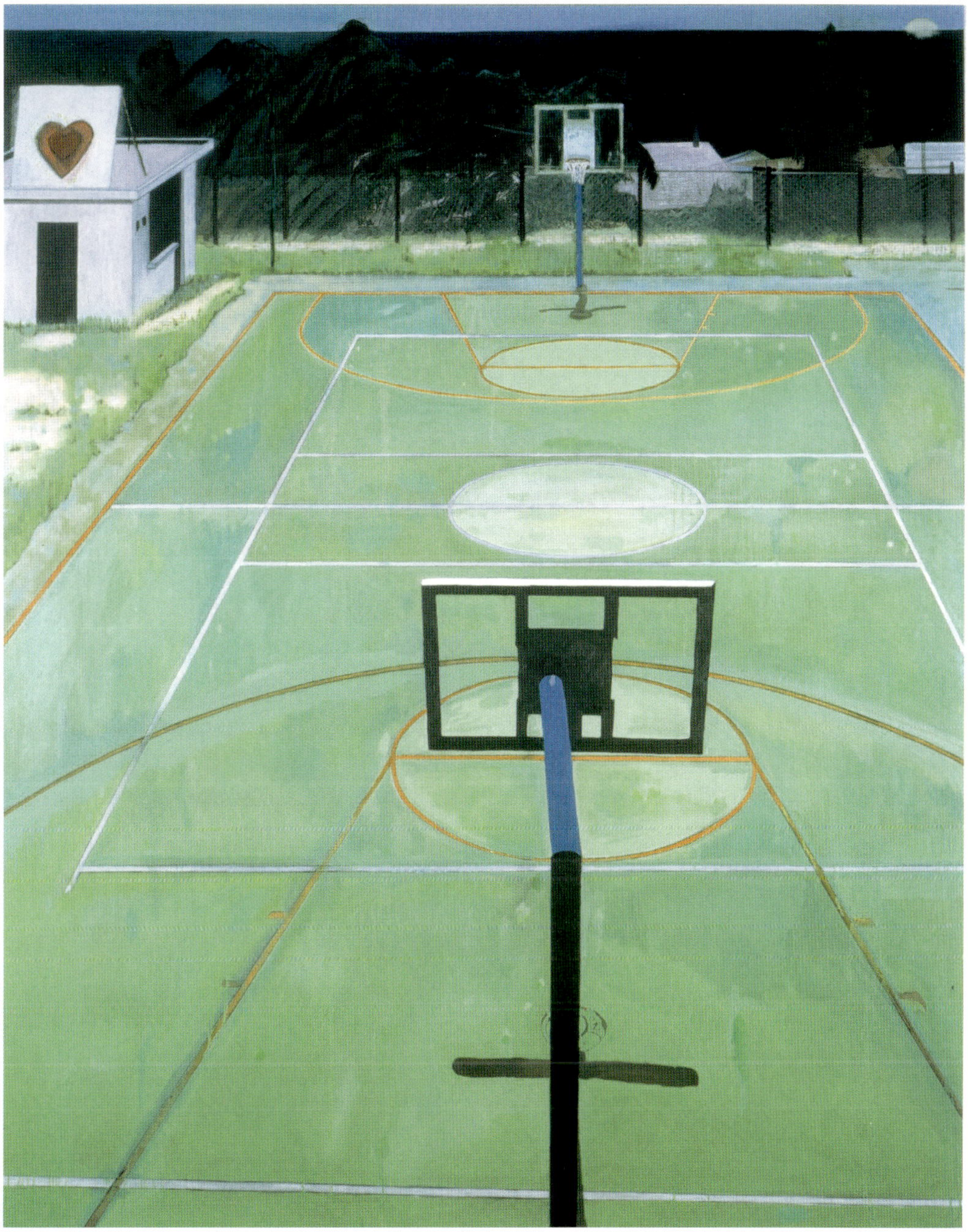

The Heart of Old San Juan 1999, oil on canvas, 250 × 195.5

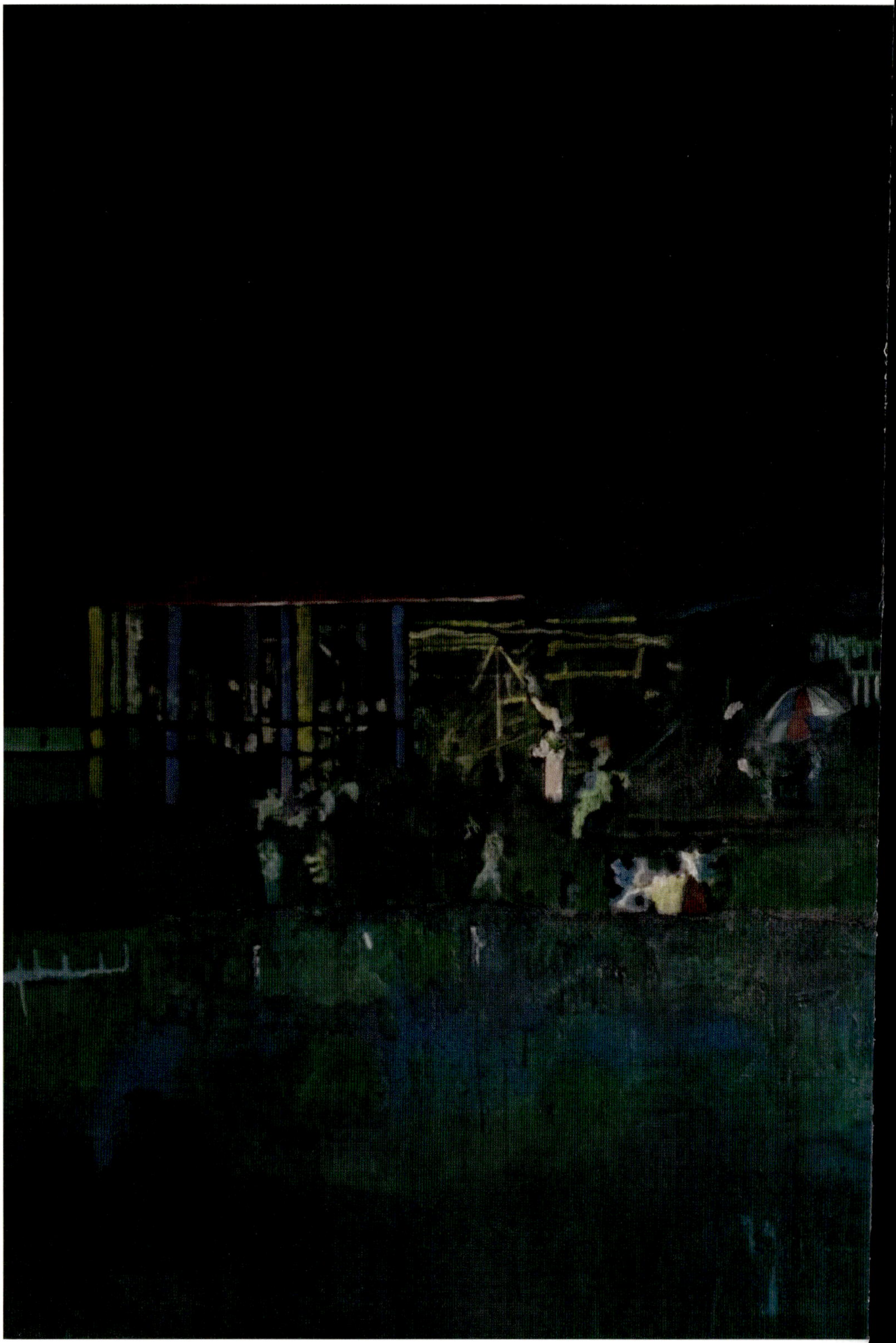

Music of the Future 2002–7, oil on linen, 200 × 330

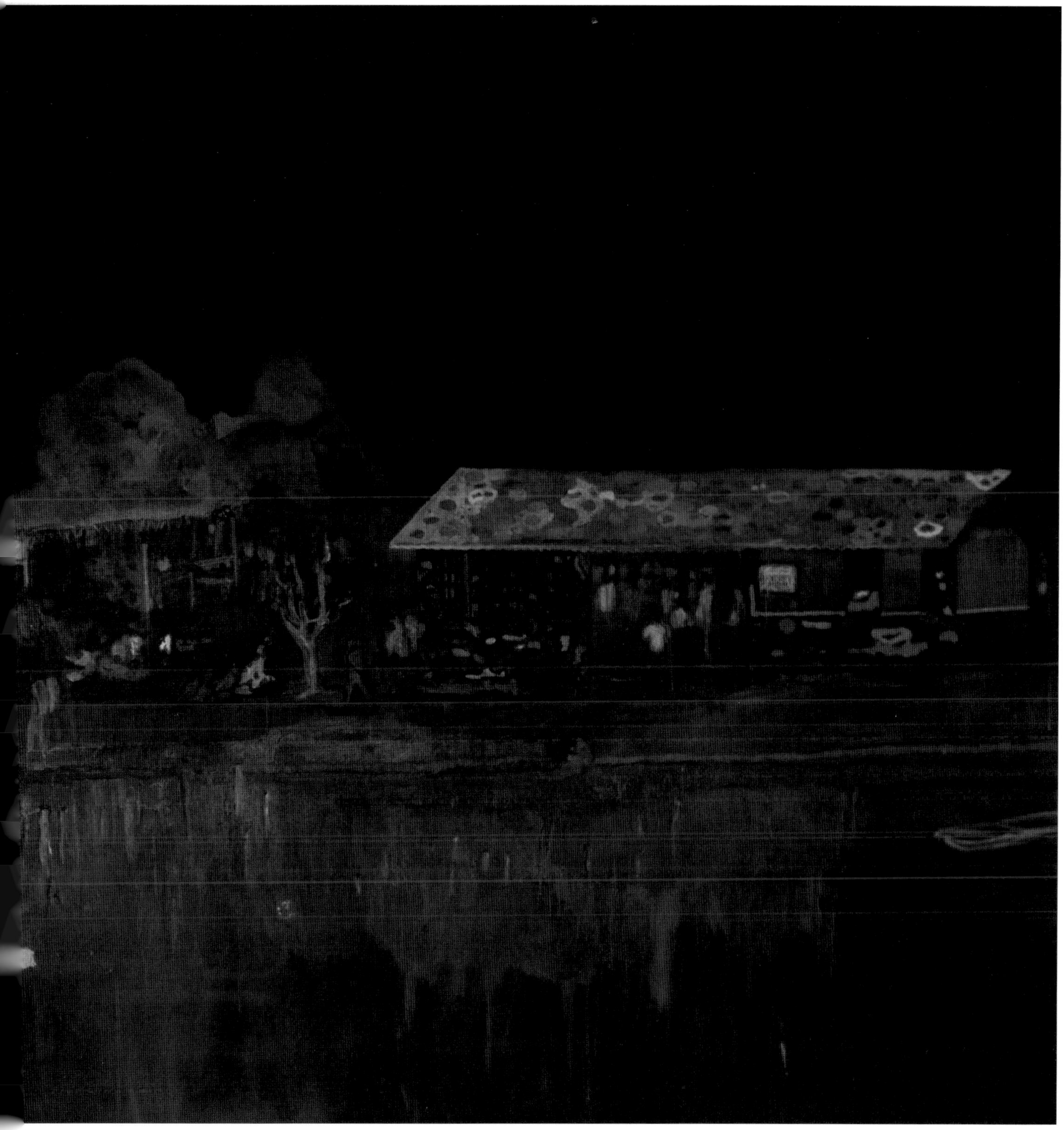

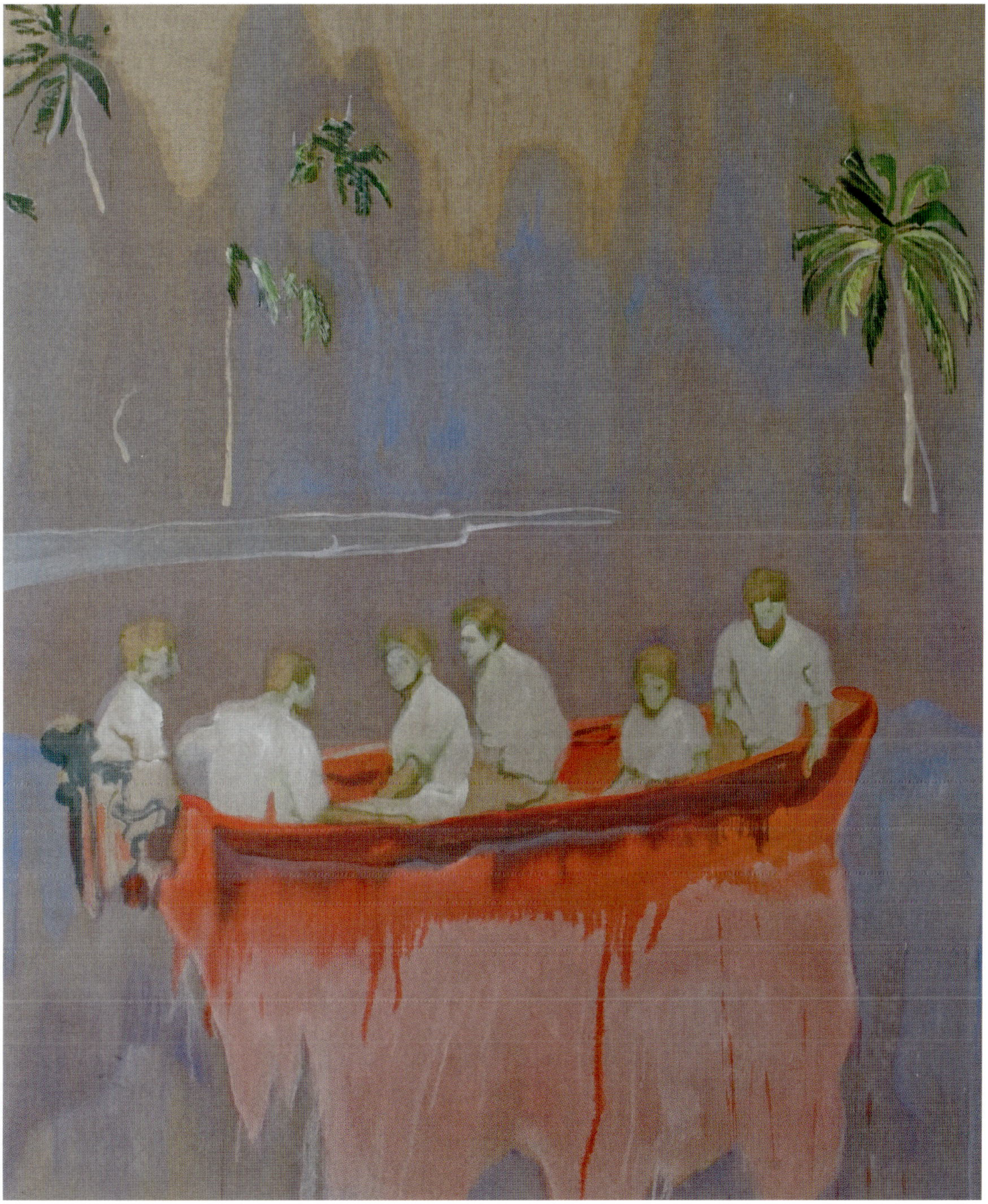

Figures in Red Boat 2005–7, oil on linen, 250 × 200

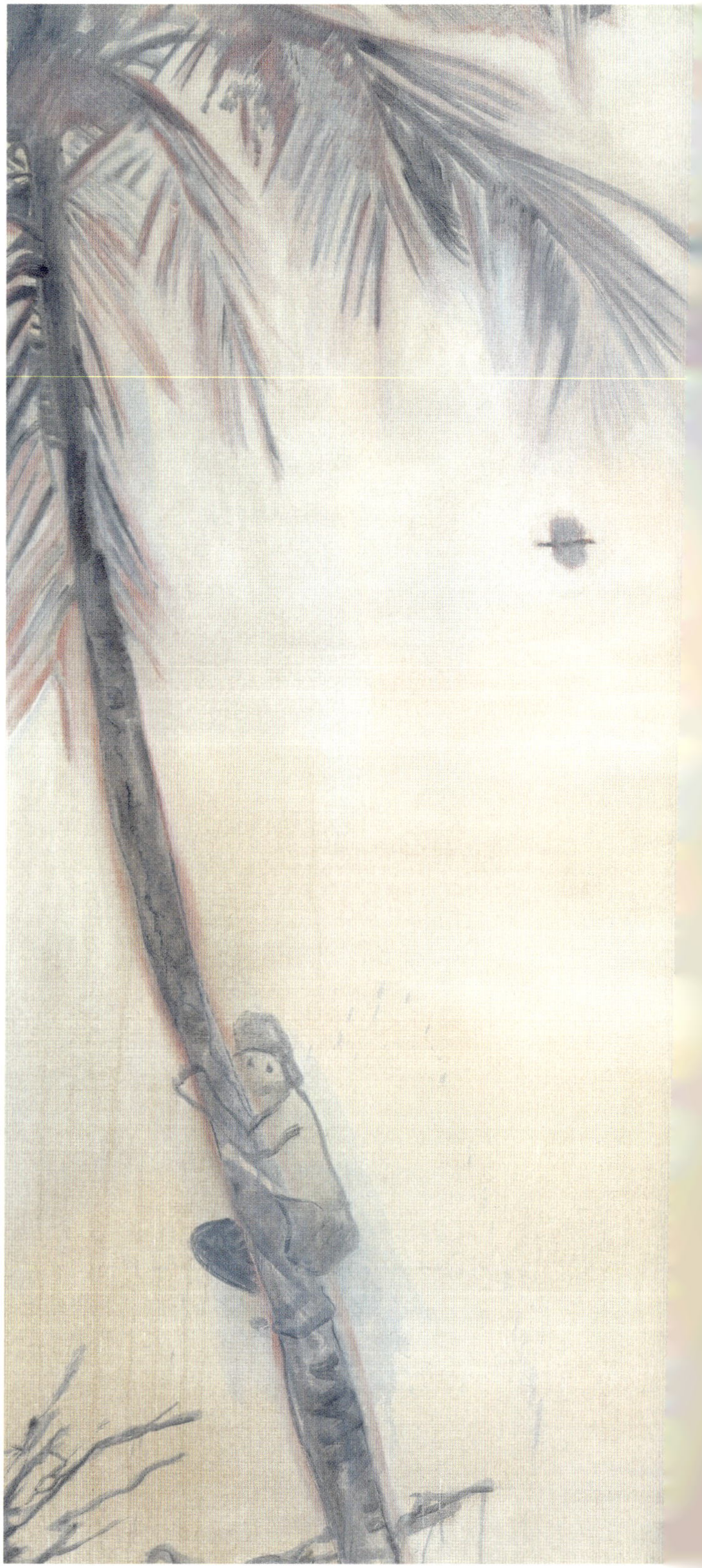

Untitled 2006, oil and pastel on linen, 300 × 350

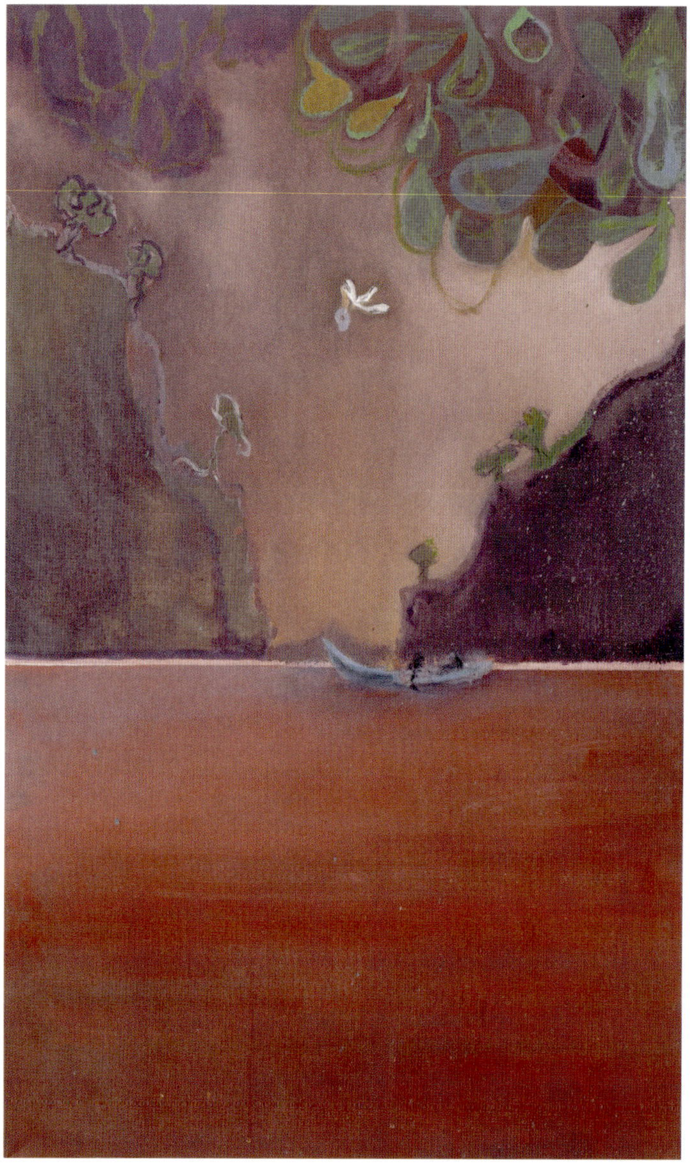

Pelican Island 2006, oil on canvas, 120 × 70

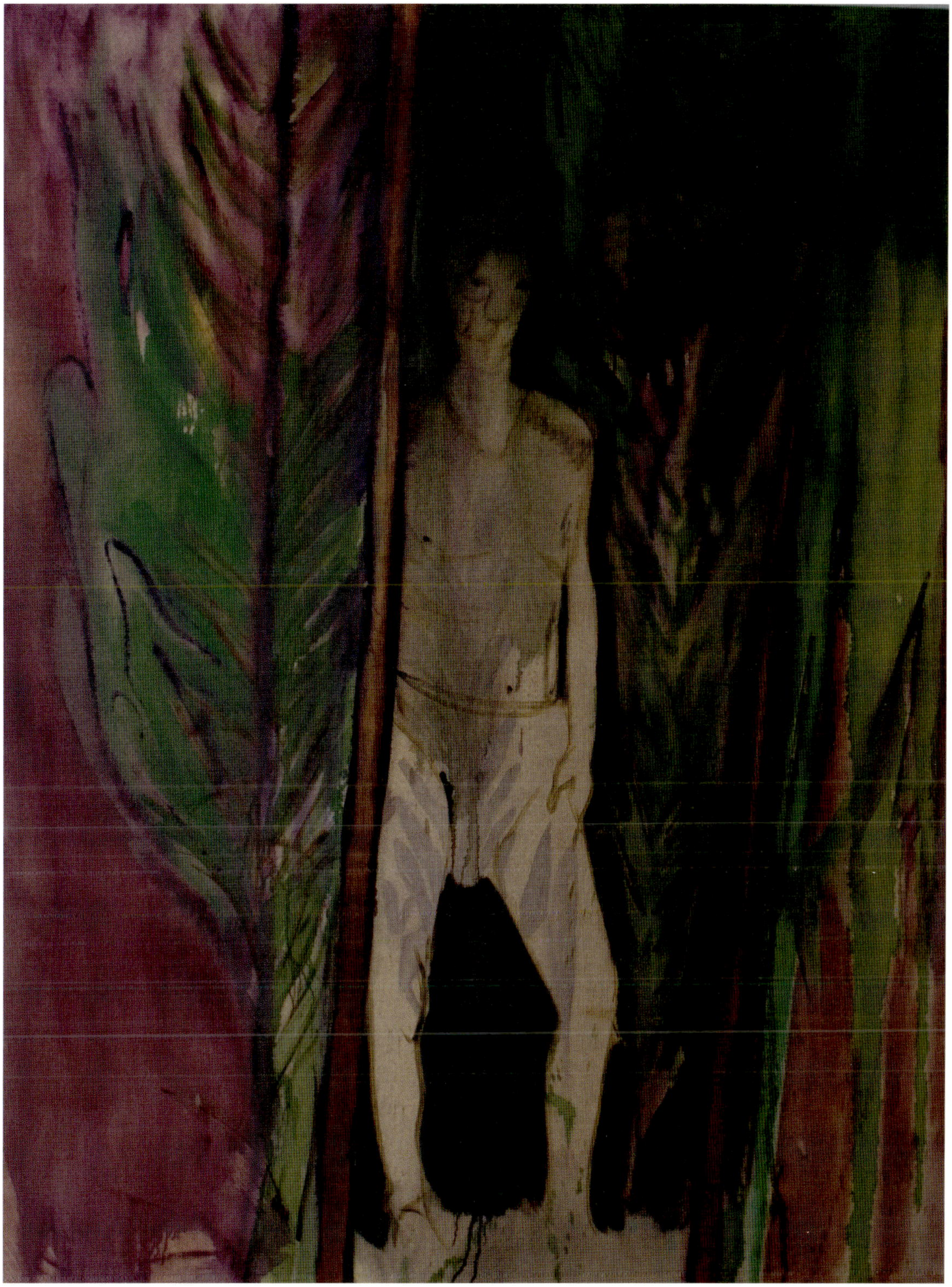

Untitled (Jungle Painting) 2007, oil on linen, 275 × 200

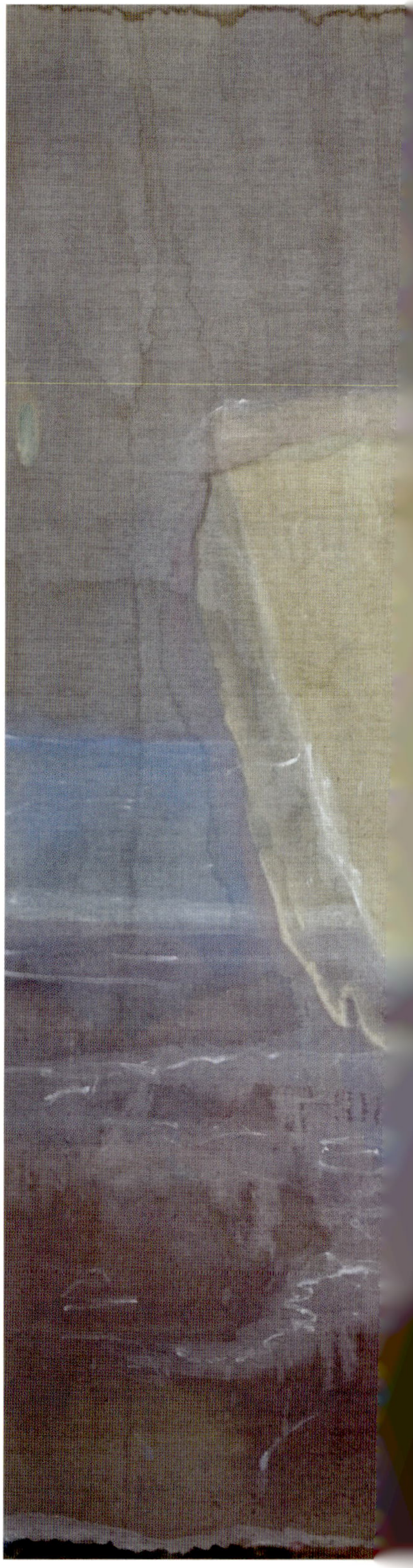

Man Dressed as Bat 2007, oil on linen, 300 × 350

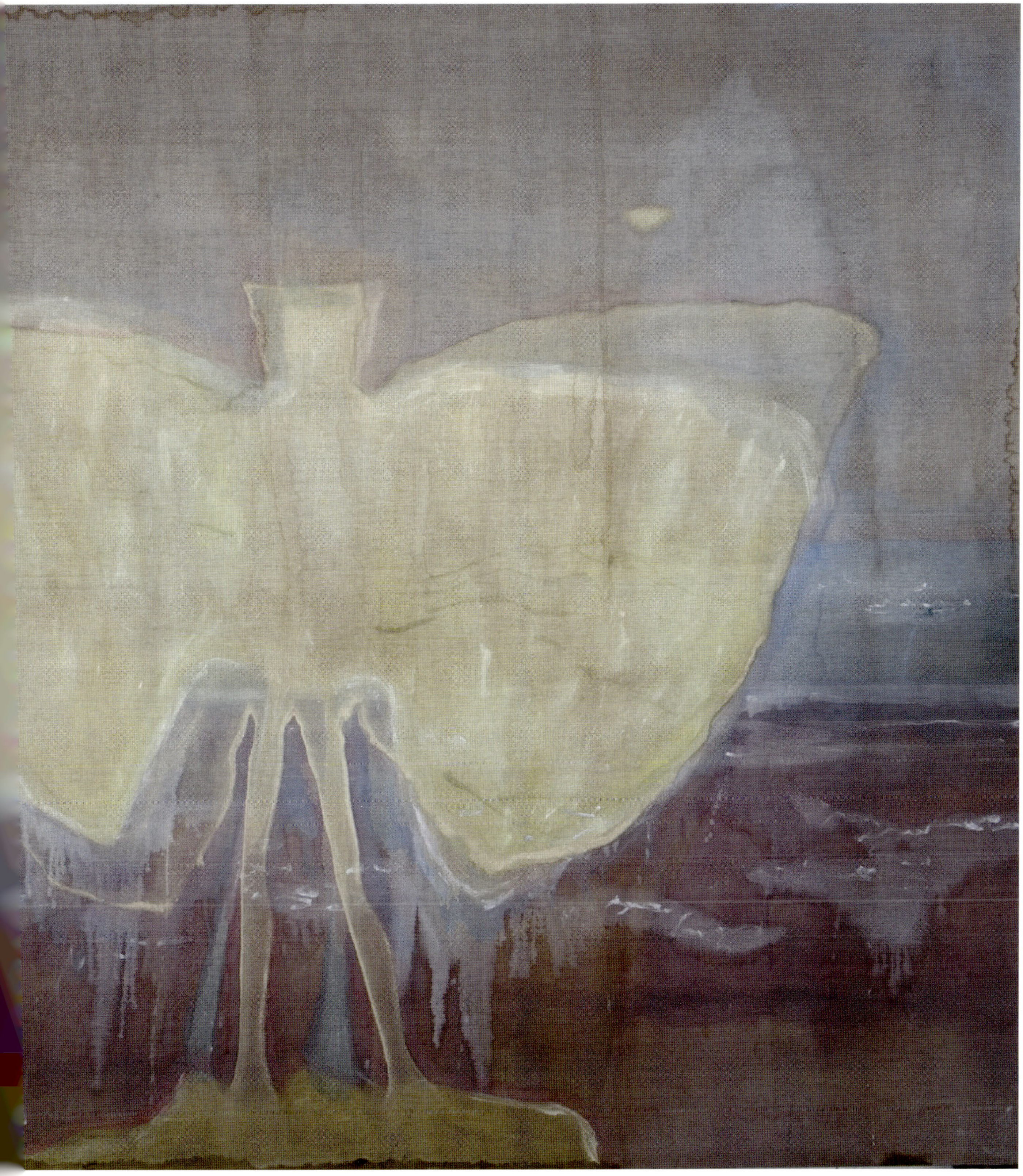

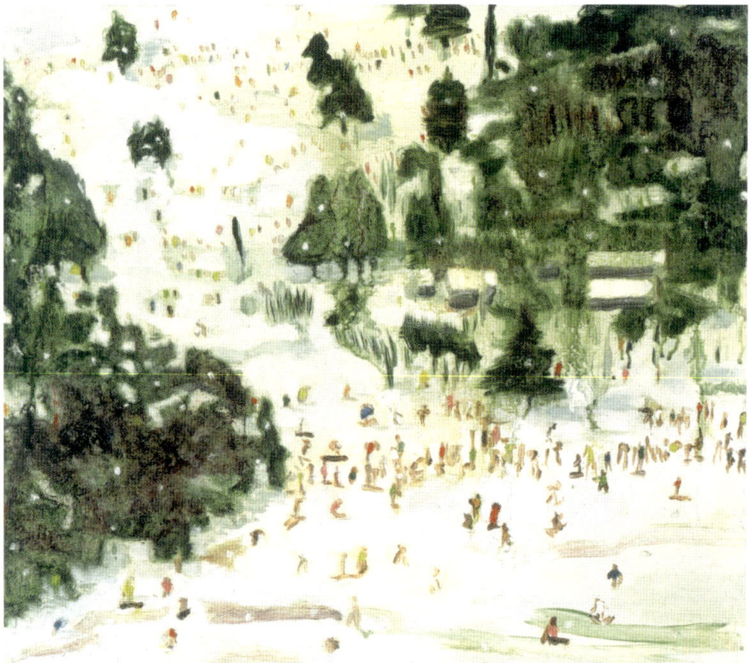

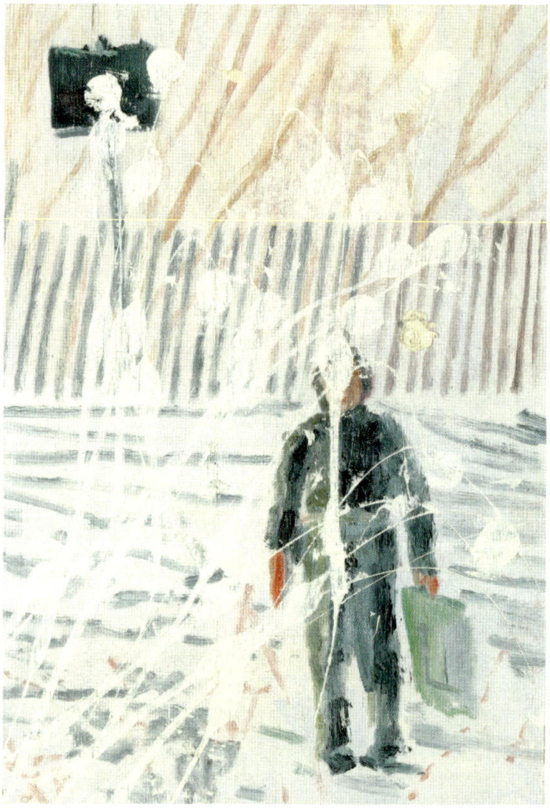

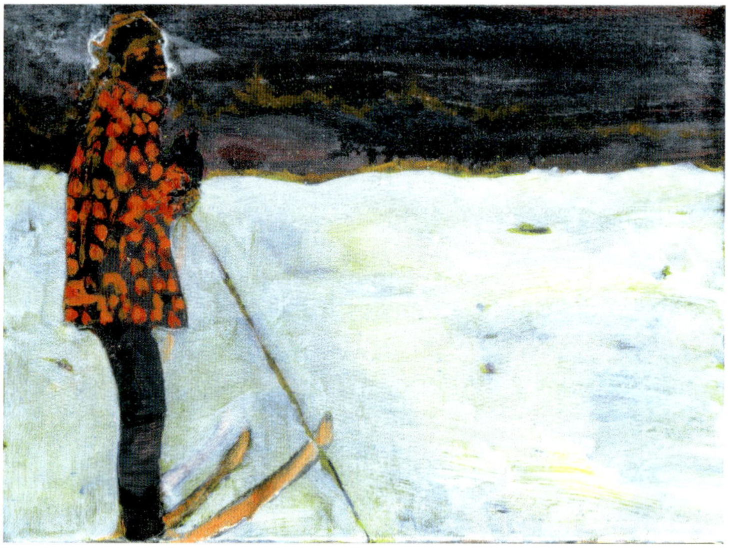

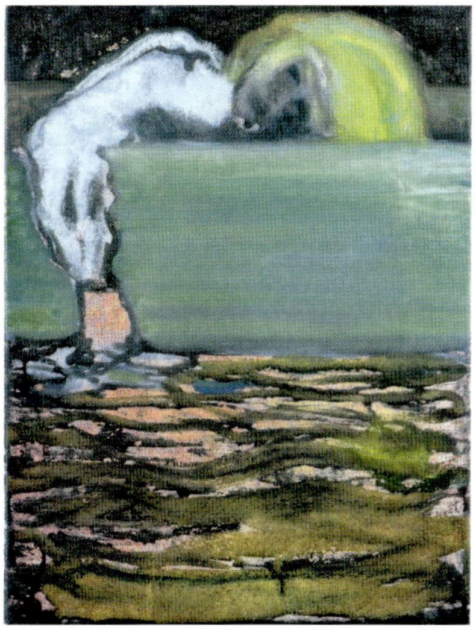

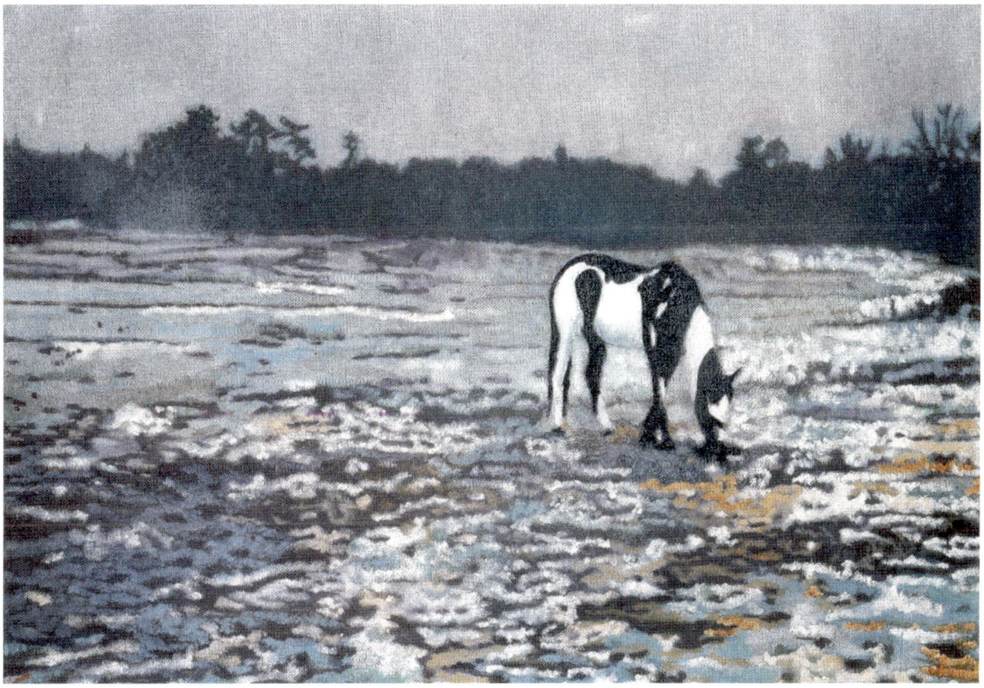

Ski Jacket 1993, oil on canvas, 51 × 46
Snowballed Boy 1995, oil on plywood, 60.5 × 40
Girl on Skis 1997, oil on canvas, 30.3 × 40.6
Friday 13th 1999, oil on linen, 35.6 × 27.9
Pinto 2000 oil on linen, 49 × 69

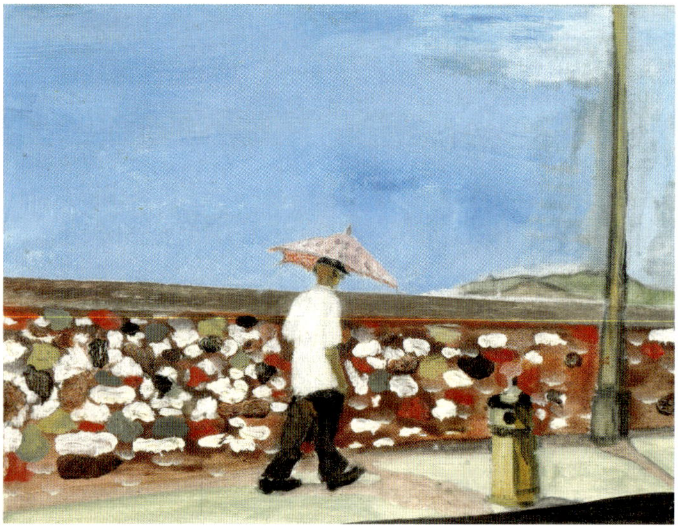

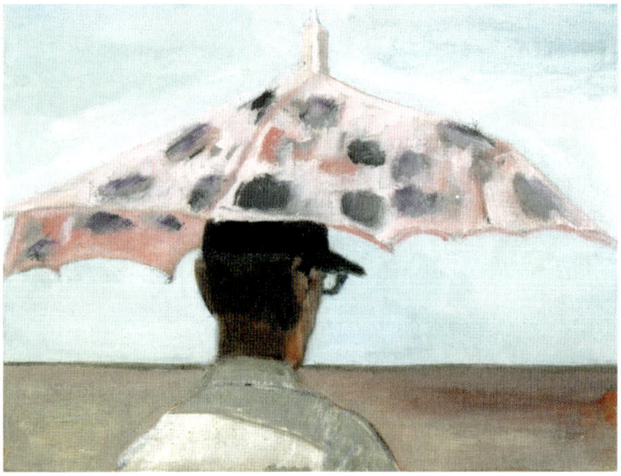

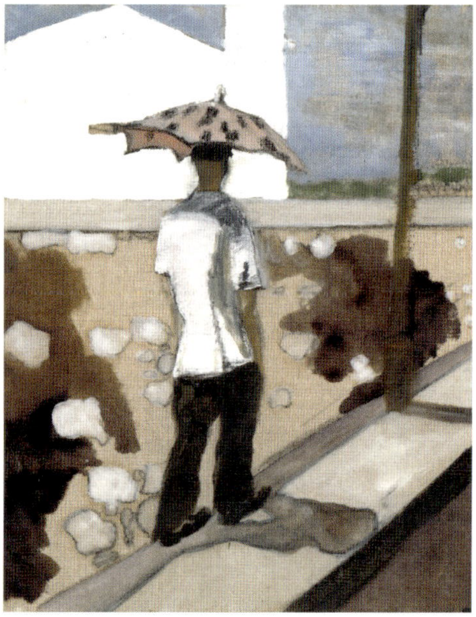

Cemetery Wall 2003, oil on canvas, 30 × 46
Lapeyrouse Umbrella 2004, oil on canvas, 31.3 × 41 cm
Lapeyrouse P.O.S. Pink Umbrella 2003, oil on canvas, 41 × 32 cm

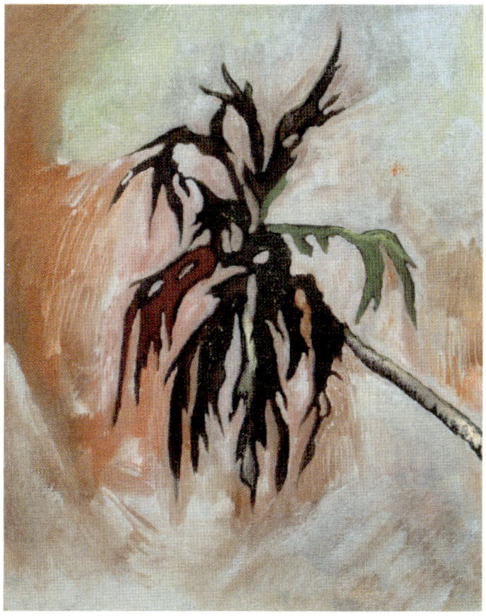

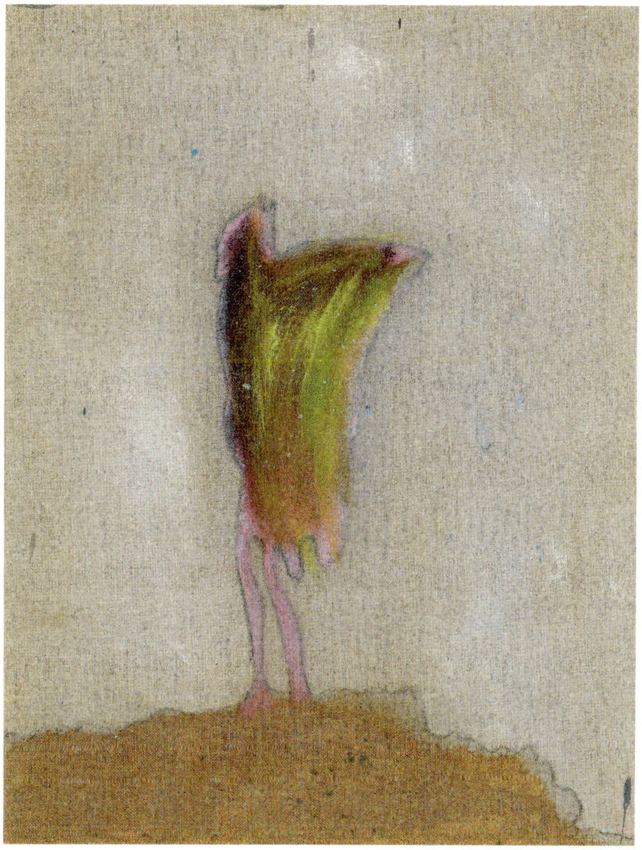

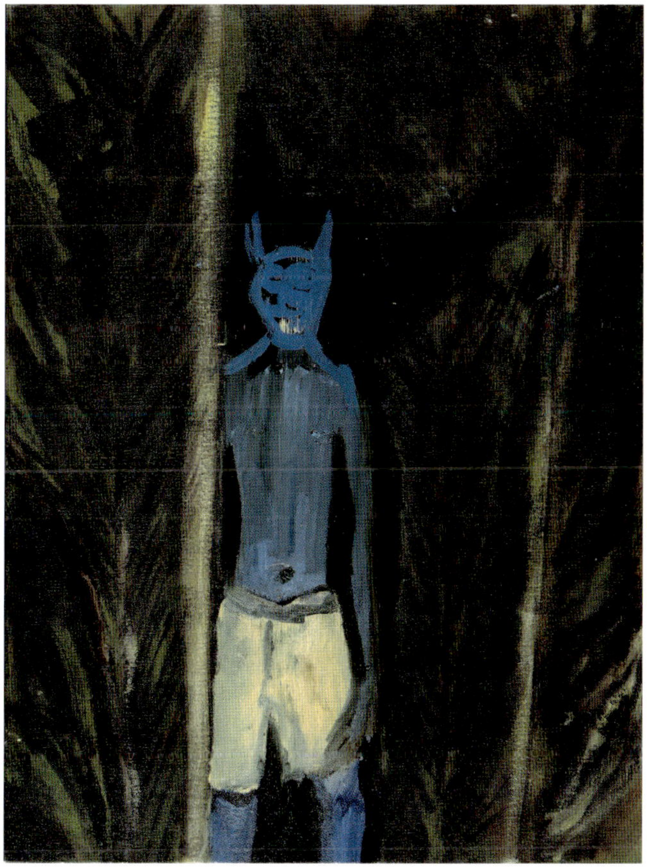

Black Palm 2004, oil on canvas, 41 × 31.3
Man Dressed as Bat (Embah), 2004, oil on canvas, 23 × 17
Untitled (Paramin) 2004, oil on linen, 58.2 × 42.9

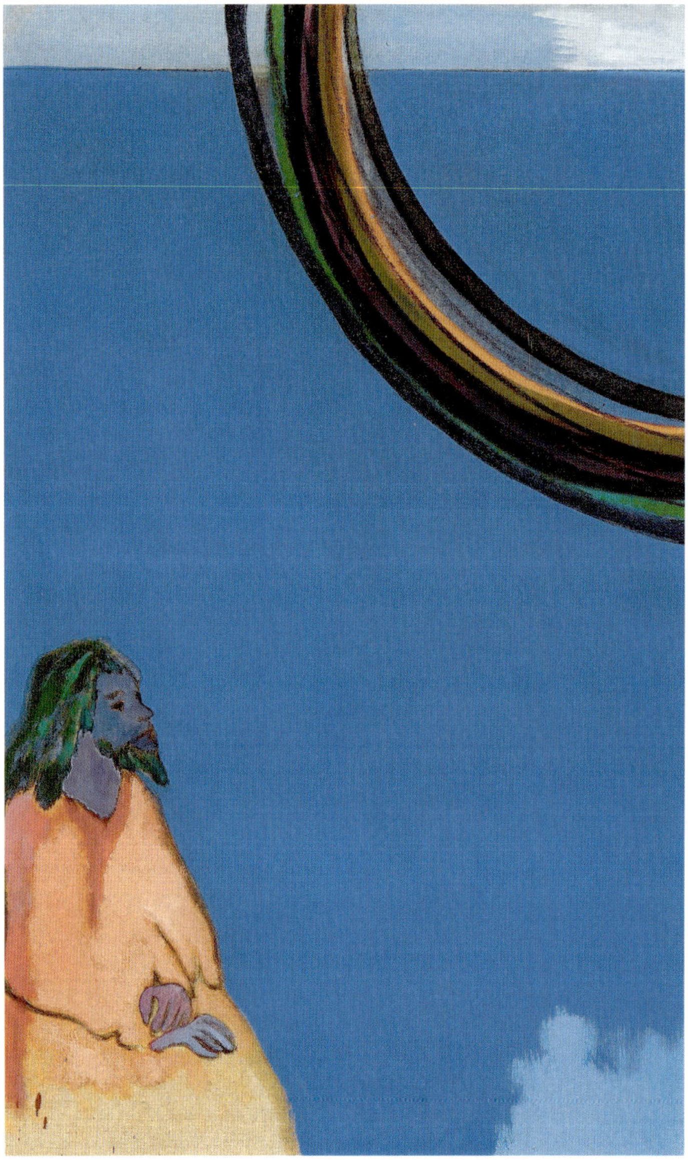

Purple Jesus (Black Rainbow) 2004, oil on canvas, 120 × 70

Peter Doig and Chris Ofili in Conversation

Edited by Rachel Tant

Chris Ofili: How do you start painting? Do you see something and say, I want to take a photo of that, so I can paint it?

Peter Doig: No. A snapshot camera is a way of recording things that may one day become part of a painting. Invariably there's a lot of editing. Do you think that as well?

CO: I might be working on a subject; it can be made up, or from other artists' work. I find a way to translate it into my own experience. Often I look at paintings I've made and I don't know if it feels like the present day. I don't know if the time that I'm living in *now* is actually the time that I'm painting.

PD: I don't think the present day is a very important thing to depict. And you don't want to make a nostalgic painting about another time that's not totally tangible. Painting becomes interesting when it becomes timeless.

CO: Do you look for that in a subject then?

PD: Yeah, the photographs we were just looking at of fishing boats taken through a telescope, there's something about that subject, when stripped away of context, of shoreline, of city. It's a blurry photograph so you can't really see what kind of clothes people are wearing. The boat is a fairly primal shape, a floating vessel that could have been from long ago or right now.

CO: The boat is a massive metaphor in this part of the world. People travel from one island to another in search of a better way of life, the discovery of new lands. But when do men in the boat stop being that? What's the transition? Is it in one's head, or the picture?

PD: The photograph is really just an extension of memory.

CO: With a photo you can record something, but at the same time, actually being there provides so much more information.

PD: It's 360 degrees, plus sound and atmosphere.

CO: Do you think you can capture any of that in the photo?

PD: I don't think you can. A photograph is a way of remembering shapes. It's not so much about the people in the boat, it's about what a strange phenomenon form is. Sometimes it's useful just to be reminded of that because you're seeing so many things all of the time.

CO: You freeze a moment.

PD: I suppose it depends what type of artist you are. You seem to be an artist who has been quite rigorous in some ways, but in other ways, there's room to actually drop something else in.

CO: An exit.

PD: An entry point.

CO: Yeah, I think an exit point. Sometimes in your career everything starts to get a bit claustrophobic. I suppose just like life, you find ways for things to be exciting, and not so predictable. Sometimes you just have to kick in the door and move the work, paint differently.

I had to make that decision not so long ago, to actually stop painting in a particular way, in order to move forward. Essentially the problem wasn't with the work, the problem was more with me, and I felt frustrated. Some people will say, but everything was going so well.

PD: That's not really the point.

CO: Some people think that *is* the point, that the paintings look good. The process of making is about making them look good, rather than exploring life.

PD: The process of actually making good-looking paintings is not as important for me as the process of actually feeling like you're making good paintings for yourself.

CO: But how do you measure that?

PD: It's a personal thing. I sometimes think I could make paintings along the lines of other paintings I've made, but I would just get bored quickly. I don't like repetition in process. I want to avoid that way of working.

CO: Why is that?

PD: I think because of a short attention span [laughter]. But it is really important to have a lot of time to come to terms with a painting. It's not so much the hours making it, but allowing it to be ready.

CO: That's one of the most challenging things. When you're actually looking at the work and figuring out whether or not it can remain like that, or if it should be changed. And this can be down to a type of brushstroke, or just something that's there.

PD: When you start out, you make a painting by adding, you feel you have got to build it from start to finish, and it's finished when it's built. As time goes on you realise it's what you leave out that's important. You can only arrive at that point through your own terms. It's the classic comment the teacher makes to the student: 'Stop right there! You've done enough! That's it!' Unless a person can actually decide that for themselves, and see and feel it, it doesn't mean a thing.

CO: Sometimes you allow external things to finish the paintings for you. The date of a show will stop the process for you, and you decide, they've got to go because they've got to go.

PD: Sometimes it is to do with deadline, but also with that entry point into the world, saying, this is now complete. Having said that, I did exhibit a painting that I decided was unfinished.

CO: Do you have to exhibit them?

PD: Well it's something I discuss with my students. I tell them, you don't have to sell a painting. You don't have to exhibit. These are things you're conditioned to do. When you and I were students, it was very difficult to sell a painting.

CO: Well, exhibiting and selling weren't really part of the curriculum. If you had an exhibition it was to challenge yourself. People could pounce on you, and say: 'Right, what is this? Why does it look like that?'

PD: You're in public debate.

CO: In the studio I guess that all goes on privately.

PD: Maybe artists nowadays show too much. Perhaps we don't need to see work every eighteen months? Why not wait five, ten years? It's a kind of trap that the system has imposed, and it takes a strong will, or a fanatic, to react against it, especially if their work is desired.

CO: I like exhibiting just as much as I like not exhibiting. The anticipation of doing a show is exciting.

PD: At a time when I wasn't making very much work you said to me: 'You have to remember, it's not a job.'

CO: But you don't approach it like a job. You have a lot of distractions. You juggle a lot of options in your day. When I look at your work I see all the stuff you do when you're not painting; things you've seen and experienced. It's like looking at a metaphysical diary. The anecdotes drive your work.

I wondered if the formal changes you've made in the work had something to do with the subjects that you were depicting, or if it was a way to liberate yourself from a way of working?

PD: Looking back, there's often one painting in a group of paintings, or one painting in an exhibition, that's an odd one out, that was made for a reason; maybe to obliterate other ways of working, or to find another way forward; to find another subject. The ski jump painting, *Olin MK IV*, was the first painting I had made that was very open; there was no 'screening' as in paintings like *Pond Life*. I felt I was making paintings with devices, or there was a methodology to the way I worked. And I wanted to make an open painting, not as open as, say, Alex Katz's paintings but to be up front like that. Just to see if it could work ... I made maybe two or three others like that, which are actually considered to be part of a series over time. *Concrete Cabin*, the first painting I made of that Corbusier building in Briey-en-Forêt, France, was a bit like that, even though it looks very different on the surface. It was an odd painting, an odd one out when I made it. I made the next ones over the next four years. They were never made back to back.

CO: I find sometimes that having used paint in a particular way, for the next painting, all I want to do is change the consistency, or use a bigger brush, or have fuller shapes, or use a ruler; anything to change direction.

PD: Is this true for the works you've been making since you left London?

CO: What's been exciting is living somewhere where you want to take photographs every day. That's something people normally do when they're on holiday. Your visual awareness is heightened by a change of location and being somewhere where everything has different values. Leaving England was a relief; it's been like leaving behind what I was, starting the engine again. It felt like going back in time, to values I had when I was at art school, where making art was much more ruthless, and there was a hunger to make decisions.

PD: At art school you have this incredible momentum that's created by all the other artists who are working there. There's an incredible energy, which is the first thing you miss when you leave. I can't really imagine you photographing or taking your camera around London with you; there's nothing really to catch your eye on the streets. Maybe there will be in ten year's time when you go back. However, it's strange, when I went to London as an eighteen year old, I did take a lot of photos, because London was as exotic as Trinidad is to me now. That's because I hadn't lived there, and I was totally excited by it.

CO: After a while the visual vocabulary becomes so familiar. It's like listening to the same record over and over again. At some point you have to switch to see ... if there's something else.

PD: I started painting this idea of landscape in London, via my experiences in Canada, but that didn't come for a long time, not until I'd been in London for almost ten years. And it was filtered through found images that I chose. It was an escape to make these paintings in the studio, because what was outside the door was so different. The work became a different world. Perhaps that's always the case but it was exciting trying to find this other place

Untitled 2007, oil on card, 56 × 36

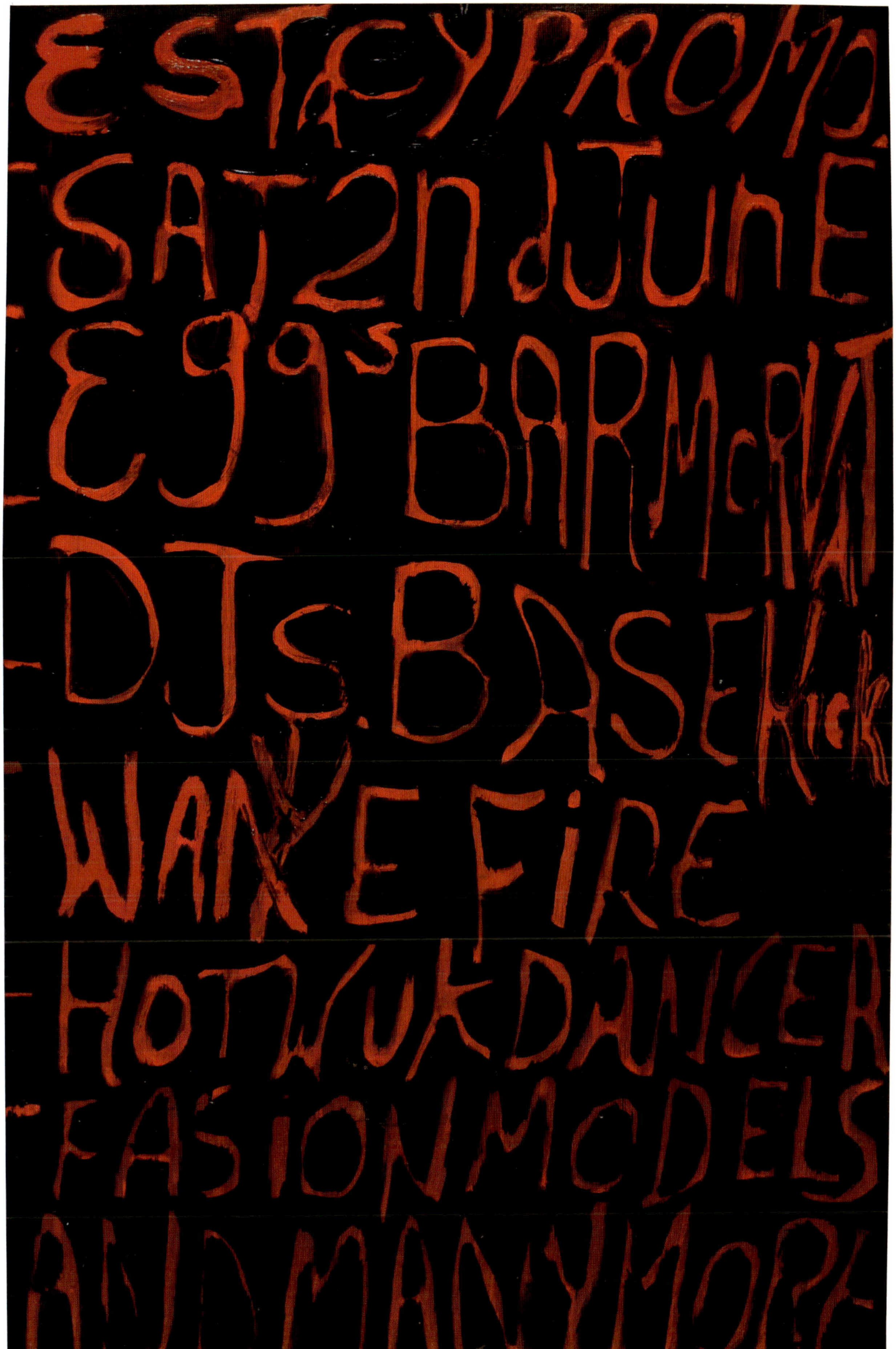
ESTACYPROMO
SAT 2nd JUNE
DJS BASEKick
HOTWUKDANCER
FASIONMODELS
ANDMANYMORE

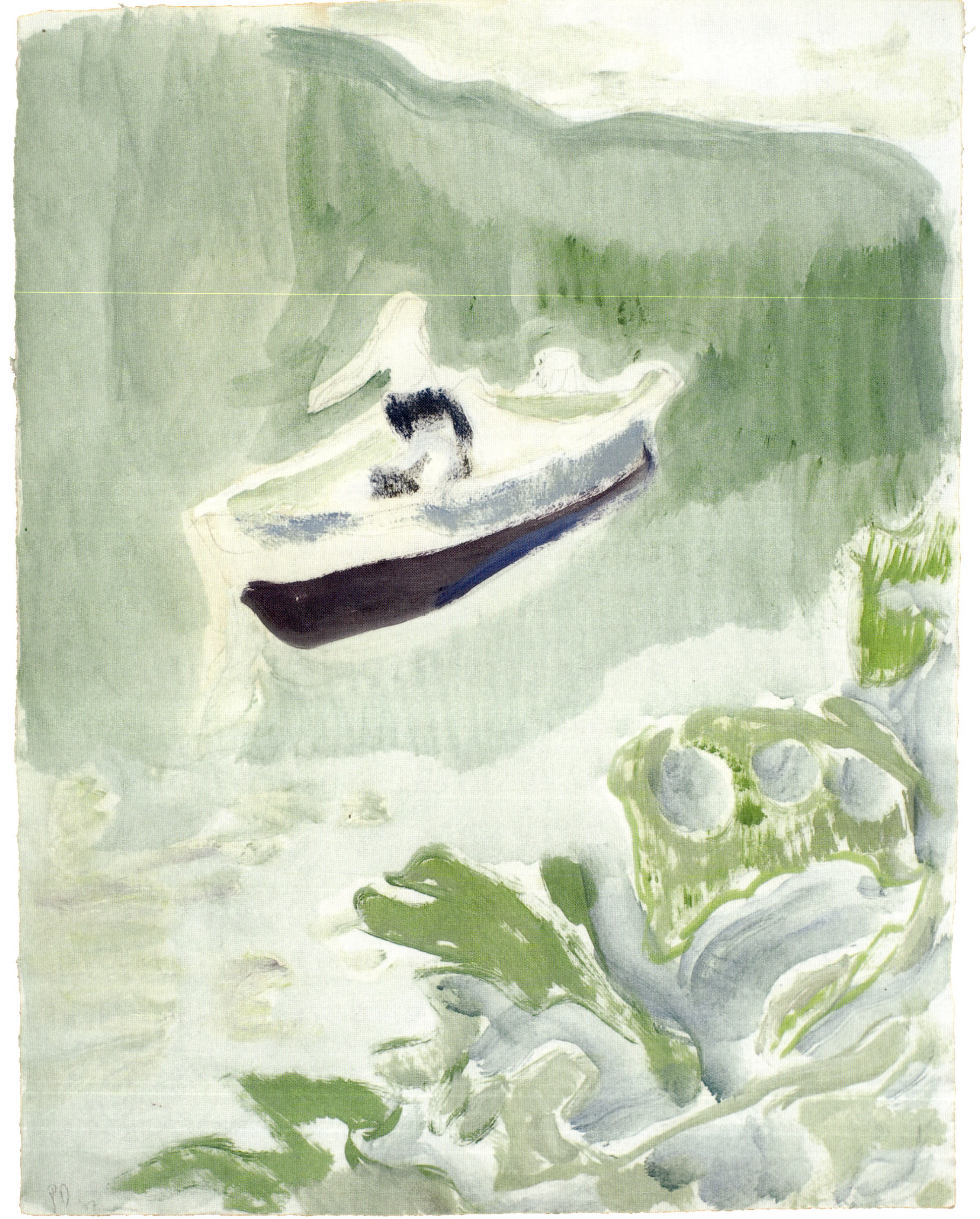

in my urban studio and in my head; the canoe paintings, the ski paintings, things like that.

CO: Why would you paint those works when you're not in the place?

PD: Because it's about thinking about the place.

CO: Through distance.

PD: In Trinidad the landscape is so present and powerful. But for me having grown up in Canada, it hit me again. The challenge is trying to make art in this environment where you're quite close to the things that you're being inspired by.

I question, all the time, what is a legitimate subject. What can I use that I feel comfortable with?

CO: Are some subjects here not ones that you could use?

PD: Possibly. Sometimes I think that if I was a Trinidadian artist there would be a lot more that I could deal with in my work. But there are subjects that haven't even been addressed internationally by local Trinidadian artists and it feels like territory that's not mine to take.

CO: There's an image of the Caribbean that historically has been projected through paintings.

PD: Happy people working the land; happy people at their leisure; but it's a view from outside. Whatever you do is going to be adding to that.

CO: As a white foreigner, painting images of Trinidad … what's the fear?

PD: I suppose that it's a naïve view; a naïve romantic view.

CO: Because you do see those things as you drive through the countryside.

PD: You see it depicted in paintings; the halcyon days of plantation life. They're not painted like heroic paintings glorifying Soviet workers or socialist projects. It's an 'above-the-mantelpiece' type of art; a naïve type of pastoral, harkening back to the type of paintings made in the nineteenth century by Millet, for example.

CO: It seems awkwardly appropriate then to talk about cultural difference. How culture functions in Trinidad.

PD: White culture here is quite marginalised. Local white people make up 0.67% of the population. Culturally they seem to have no power whatsoever or no voice. There are very few writers, a few rock musicians and very few artists. Naipaul wrote about the phenomenon in Trinidad where the white and French Creole classes have no locally developed culture.

CO: People are quite curious as to why anyone would come here and settle from a place that's considered better, like the US or the UK.

PD: Trinidad and Jamaica are traditionally places that people want to leave.

CO: To have a better life. There is a certain suspicion by Trinidadians as to why you're here.

PD: It's not an easy question to answer.

CO: I'm actually quite comfortable with not knowing.

PD: So you said sex, sea and sand. [laughter]

CO: No, that was you! [laughter]

PD: Going back to what's legitimate and responsibility towards local subjects – in the west, in the big cities, anything is game as far as subject's concerned, because you have access to so many images; you're bombarded with things. There's such a culture of borrowing and collaging images, making comparisons, jokes and ironies.

CO: The way people here talk about their history and who they are is in relation to who their parents and grandparents were. It's personalized and home grown. So to branch out and take from other areas and subjects is not really done. People stay quite local in their attitudes. So to paint an image of anything here, locals expect there to be a deeper meaning and one must go through a complex narrative explanation. I suppose that made me quite hesitant in combining or juxtaposing two things that were apparently not related – people playing instruments and a dead hanging figure – in my painting, *Iscariot Blues*. I think people think it was a comment on Trinidad's society.

PD: People look for what they can recognise of their place in the work we're making here. My painting, *Music of the Future,* which was in the same exhibition, was misinterpreted too. Some people thought it was a painting of down the island. A place where people have holiday homes.

CO: Particularly rich white people?

PD: It was not that at all, it was summarised completely.

It's a river scene at that dusky time of day when there's no illumination other than from the sky or what is reflected off the water. There are only shadows, figures and traces of colour. The source of the image is a postcard I found in London. It's actually a riverscene in southern India that very much reminded me of here: the colour, the landscape, even the shapes within the photograph.

CO: It's a distant scene; the image is taken from the viewpoint of

Untitled 2007, oil on paper 51 × 40

someone who's not there.

PD: A boat on a lake, looking back to the shore, or the other side of the river. It's hard to tell what it is. What separates you from the action is this body of water; the figures are a microscopic view of a Seurat-type scene, but far less …

CO: The view you've used shows the whole scene. You're dealing with perspective to achieve this distance from the subject, to get that feeling of foreground, mid-ground. These three horizontal planes are used a lot in your work.

PD: I started the painting quite a few years ago. I'm not happy with it yet as it is too much like a picture. I want it to become more abstract, like *Ski Jacket*, which dealt with a similar distant view of people going about some kind of activity.

CO: *Ski Jacket* is based on a photograph from a newspaper; it functions as a painting about colour on a flat plane.

PD: A flat, white plane. *Music of the Future* is almost a negative version of *Ski Jacket.* It's a difficult painting for me to resolve.

CO: Context is everything. If that painting is to be shown elsewhere completely different values will inform how it's read. The painting stays the same, but the way people read it can change.

PD: My paintings of lakes, canoes and cabins were interpreted differently in a Canadian context. Canadians related to them in a way that other people didn't. Canadians listen to Neil Young in a very different way than Americans listen to Neil Young.

CO: Is he Canadian?

PD: He is. [laughter]

CO: Everyone's Canadian to you.

How much of what you say about your work influences how it is seen … forever? For instance your canoe paintings; I know the imagery came from one of the last scenes in *Friday the 13th*.

PD: But if I hadn't told anyone that…

CO: If you hadn't told that lie the first time around, that lie wouldn't be perpetuated.

PD: People always talk about me making paintings based on film stills as if that's all I've ever made. But that's the only painting I ever made from a film still [laughter]. Just that one. Well, maybe three related paintings. Things tend to get repeated and quoted like Chinese Whispers.

CO: There's nothing like walking into someone's studio and seeing an image for the first time. You get that rush of information coming at you, unmediated. The less you know, the purer the read.

PD: The way people look at paintings in public spaces or even in studios, is very different to how they look at just about anything else. It's a strange, lost scrutiny. Maybe you're focusing a painting; it's not fixed, like a photograph is?

CO: But it is still, isn't it? Everything that's there, be it an image of a face or a landscape, is completely still. But there's something about how a painting works optically.

PD: It's all illusion.

CO: It's still substance on a flat surface.

PD: It's form and illusion in space.

CO: I think you're talking about a certain type of painting, a certain type of image making.

PD: No, I'm talking about abstract painting as well; painting in general. The same type of illusion applies. There's only so much depth in a painting.

CO: I never really studied painting when I was young. We didn't go to museums when I was a child. So I always went into making paintings based on what I knew and was interested in, not in relation to art history. I feel that some of the healthiest areas to cull from are your own experience.

PD: Do you think you're still doing that now?

CO: Yeah, I'm trying to do that. As time goes by you start to relate to things that you've made in the past. Things you grappled with previously. You have more ease, more distance from it so you can try things out. Things you may have done as a sketch in the past can become a more grounded attempt, bolder, explicit; things that you did in a drawing very quickly.

PD: I'm always wary of when a painting becomes a type of mannerism. You have to have your trademark. It begins like a sophisticated way of making cakes sometimes! [laughter]

CO: I find it interesting that you can't tell how long something took to make. People will look at something made of dots and say, how long does it take? It doesn't matter. It's not a way of measuring what a painting is.

More recently I've approached painting by trying to keep it as simple as possible, trying to keep forms simple and working in a way that is almost non-painting, as in no-dressings.

Untitled 2007, oil on paper, 22 × 19

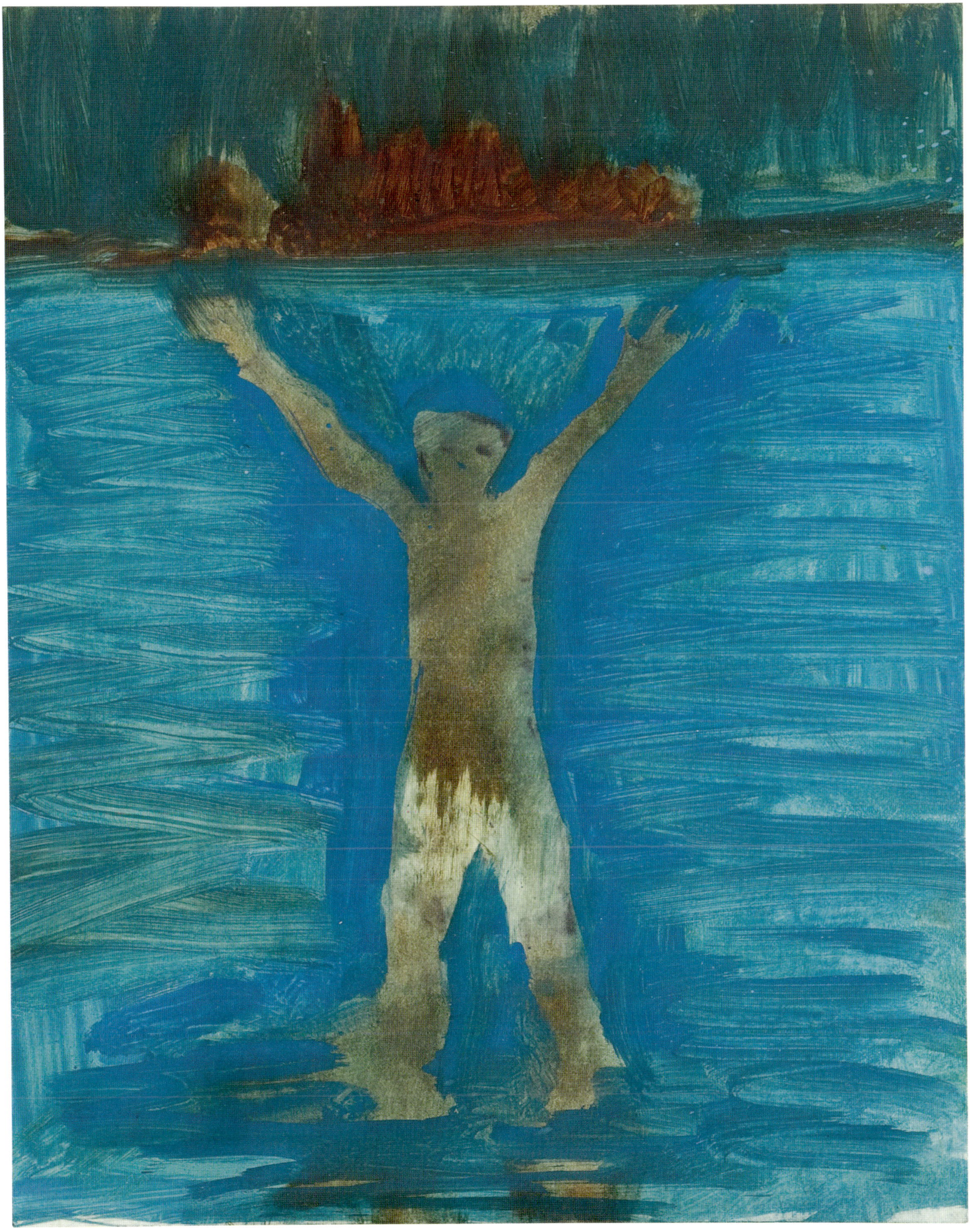

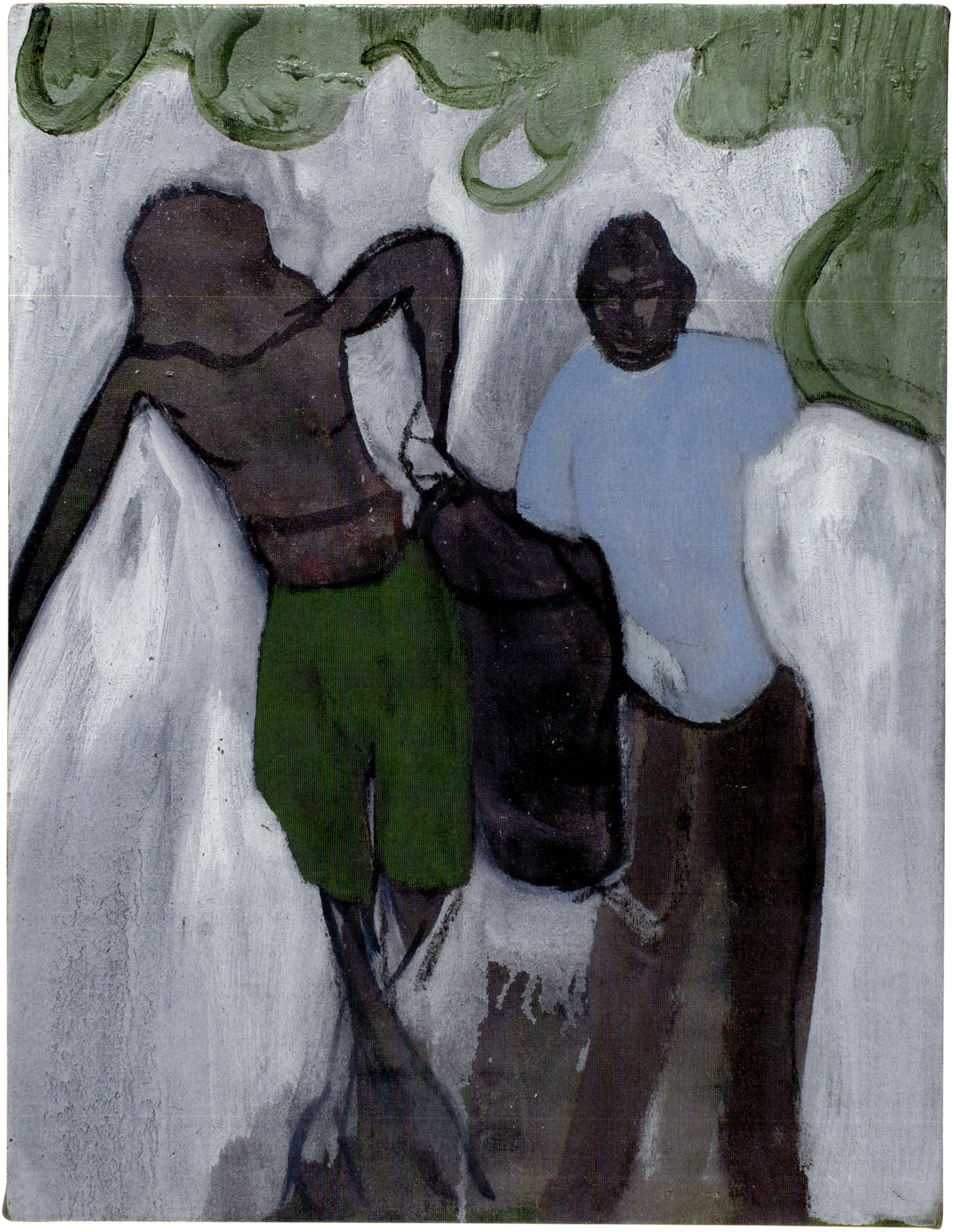

PD: No brushstrokes for you, sir; no fancy stuff.

CO: No pony tricks. [Laughter] It's a pared down way of working, which is incredibly refreshing and highly reflective in that you see yourself and you can't hide behind anything.

PD: The question for a lot of painters is, why can't we just make a painting? You're searching for a way to make pure painting. Painting should evolve into a type of abstraction; it should slowly dissipate into something else through time, through working, seeing things through. It becomes unnecessary to have narrative subjects and that's difficult to come to terms with.

CO: I think there's always going be a driver in my approach to making paintings, which you may not necessarily be able to read. The process is one of distillation, to the point where it's just essence, just itself. Maybe it's ultimate freedom to do whatever you want; not to be held down by a subject.

PD: I have been trying to find a way to interpret some of the things we've seen on the north coast by boat: incredible landscapes and caves and archaic spaces, like natural cathedrals, chasms, strange pelicans, islands covered in their shit.

I'd been trying to make some paintings about this, just from my head without using any photographs; it was too wet to take a camera. I made a painting for SITE Santa Fe, *Untitled*, that's much closer to what I want to achieve. The mood is very simple and strange things happened when rubbing the colour down or trying to correct it. It has representative elements but it's more primal. It's getting away from the photograph, but it's a big jump for me to take.

CO: You've clearly liked seeing the work go in a particular way.

PD: The mood of the painting has always been important, but now I'm trying to get the same mood with a different method.

CO: We've been talking about liberating the work through working. Beginning a painting you have this freedom. Ten years ago we spoke about how the beginnings of some of your work were where the work could end. There was a certain simplicity in how you drew out your paintings.

How did you begin making *Metropolitain (House of Pictures)*?

PD: I was in Chicago for an exhibition and I saw the Daumier painting, *The Print Collector*, a painting of someone looking at prints. I was quite drawn to this male figure looking and the expression on his face. There wasn't much detail; a lot of it had to do with body language. Back in London I made a painting based on the same idea called *House of Pictures.* It was a combination of the Daumier painting and a gallery I'd seen in Vienna called Haus der Bilder that was full of different types of paintings, landscapes, genre scenes, portraits. The Daumier painting reminded me of this shop front in Vienna and provided me with an entry point to this other world. So I tried to piece together my own version. I was also thinking of the Fritz Lang film called *Women in the Window* with Edward G. Robinson where he is transfixed by a portrait of a woman in a gallery window. *Metropolitain (House of Pictures)* was a questioning painting. How does one interpret what you do?

CO: I see that painting as a portrait of the art world; this rugged connoisseur coming to view your work. There's no reflection of the looker in the glass.

PD: In the first painting he's too far away to see a reflection. It was painted like a stage set. I was also thinking of Hopper. Then I went back to the original Daumier and found another way of painting the subject. In my subsequent small versions – this sounds convoluted – the figure has a red clown's nose. Shortly after I arrived in Trinidad I was told about some carnival characters who painted their faces white and their noses and ears bright red to mock the Europeans. So my bohemian Daumier figure of the arts originally had this pronounced clown-red nose. That changed in the bigger painting to something more subtle, less comic.

CO: The figure is much closer in the second *Metropolitain* painting, a large work on paper.

PD: Yes, I put him in a simplified landscape of what I see outside my studio window.

CO: The coat the guy is wearing is a little ragged. Whereas in the Daumier it's the coat of a connoisseur.

PD: I wanted him to be beatnik bourgeois, more of an artist than a collector.

CO: How do you go about making a translation from another person's painting?

PD: I started by making etchings. The medium throws up a lot of surprises. I would make the etching then take photographs of the etching, then blow the photographs up so you could see the breakdown of what the acid had done; the breakdown of the drawing as it were. It would go from there; a mixture of etchings, works on paper, small paintings, and then the bigger painting. I don't know if the figure in the bigger painting was the most successful of the figures?

CO: There are two big paintings: one on paper and a painting on canvas.

PD: The slightly dopey expression on the face of the figure in the large painting on canvas was developed through painting and

Untitled 2007, oil on canvas, 50.5 × 38.5

painting and changing. It was quite strange, like making your own person that was almost life size. I don't normally do the face. It was meant to be slightly pathetic. And it actually is in the end.

CO: In that painting the figure is looking at a painting of yours of a real situation that you and I saw on the beach here in Yara of a man and a pelican. Which painting was made first?

PD: The *Pelican* painting. At one point there were lots of paintings with different imagery and I rubbed them out. The *Pelican* painting is the only one you can still vaguely make out.

CO: There's more than one version of the Pelican painting.

PD: There are two quite different paintings. *Pelican* and *Pelican (Stag)*. With *Pelican (Stag)* I was thinking about confrontation with the subject. There is a startled look on the man's face, and I assume on the face of the viewer as well. *Pelican* is more pastoral. They are reflections on the incident with the pelican that you and I witnessed the first time we came to Trinidad. We saw this guy off a remote beach, bobbing around in his underwear in the sea with a pelican.

At first I thought he was rescuing the pelican, or it had broken its wing. Then it became clear that he was trying to drown it. He came on to the beach, and as he walked along the sand, you could see that he was swinging the pelican around by its neck. The way the pelican was looping and looping he was obviously wringing its neck.

He glared at us as if to say, you shouldn't be watching this. Of course, he was probably getting something to eat. It felt voyeuristic watching him, but also incredibly exciting. It was amazing how he caught the pelican. I don't know if he used a hook, or he lured it, or if it had actually broken its wing. I attempted to make paintings of this from my memory. I don't think we would have taken a photograph of it.

CO: It was too uncomfortable. I had never seen anything like that before. It was also strangely quiet.

We spoke before about how it seems appropriate to take a painting from its start, right through to its finish, and work very simply and very clearly. My observations of how you work, Peter, is that at times it looks like paintings in the studio are just hanging around, almost discarded, as if there are lots of false starts. That state of being left could go on for a long period of time.

PD: Are you saying that my studio is like an elephant's graveyard? [laughter]

CO: It's an artist's Oxfam. [laughter] It is a very particular approach to working because it seems like you tolerate a state where you're not happy with your paintings for a long period of time.

PD: I don't know if that's true. If I'm not happy with a painting I'll get rid of it completely, I'll discard it. The ones that are hanging in the studio for a long time are incomplete. But I still think there's hope for them; there's still something I very much like.

CO: Is that any stage in making?

PD: Usually it's just starting. I really believe that you also have to take paintings from bad stages to get to good stages. But I need the vestiges of paintings around to give me starting points.

CO: What do you mean by starting points?

PD: It's like having a blank canvas, having a starting point. Some things have started, begun.

CO: Like notation.

PD: There's something to add to. Getting rid of things is always a hard thing for me.

CO: I'm interested in the long gestation period where very little is happening. You're walking in and out of the room and not doing anything to the painting.

PD: I would consider that a part of the working. It's not the case for every painting but, over time, it's proven to be the way that I work. The painting is there in my studio and I'm thinking about it every day. I'm just not compelled at that point in time to finish it.

CO: So the action's taking place, when nothing's taking place; that's just as vital a moment.

PD: I don't think that actual time on the canvas is necessarily time well spent.

CO: Or a way of measuring progress.

PD: Or a way of seeing the results. It's not a matter of time spent, it's the importance of the time spent. Some passages in a painting took seconds; others take longer. With others it was just a wash, a combination of moments that speak of making or different places we've been. Is that a good place to end?

CO: Wherever it falls, it falls.

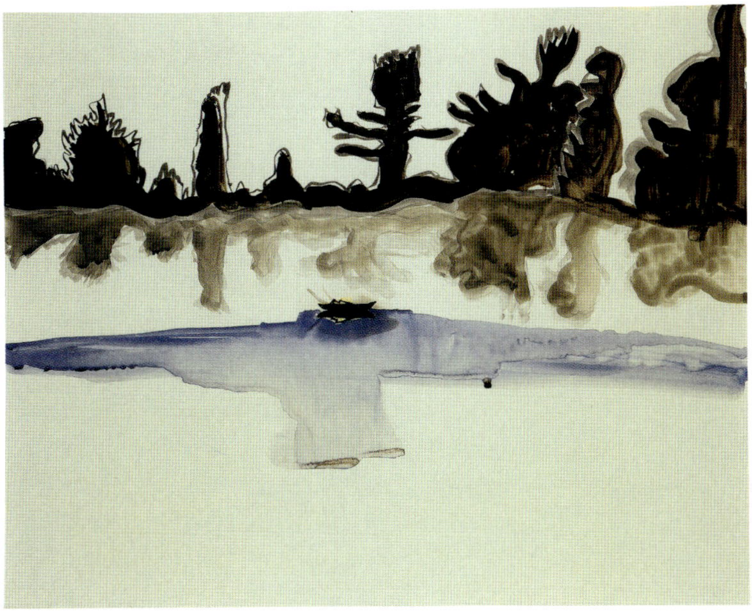

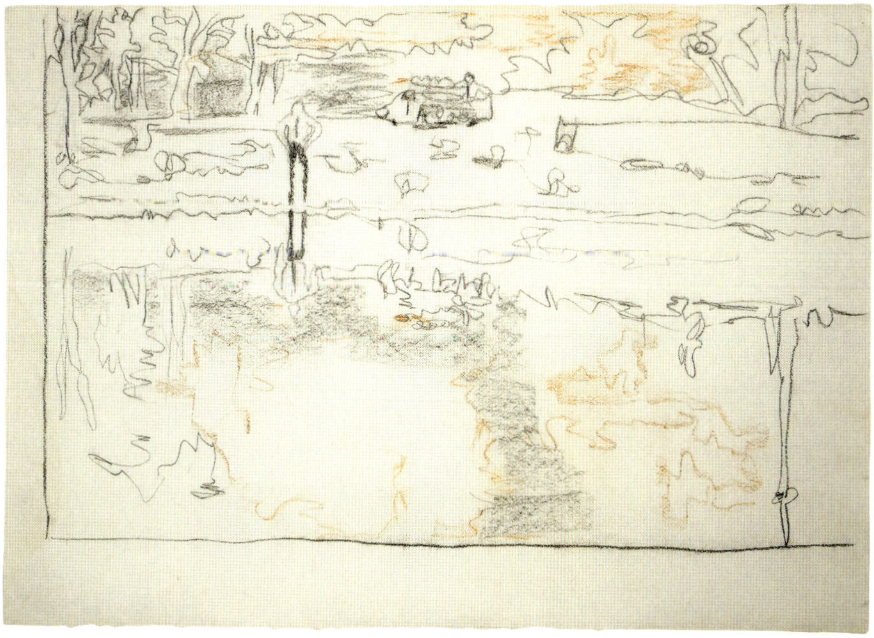

Untitled (Study for Milky Way) 1990, watercolour on paper, 52.1 × 63.5
Swamped 1990, black and red-brown chalk, 57 × 78.8

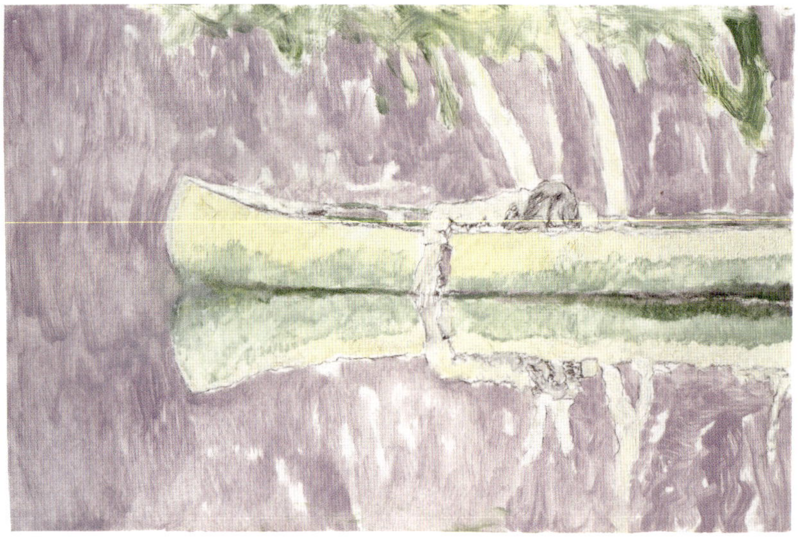

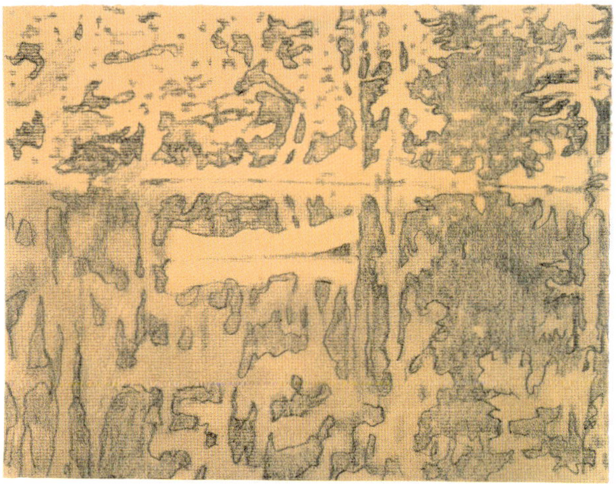

Canoe Lake 1999, watercolour, pencil and oil on paper 38.1 × 55.9
Swamped 1994, pencil on paper, 20.3 × 24.8

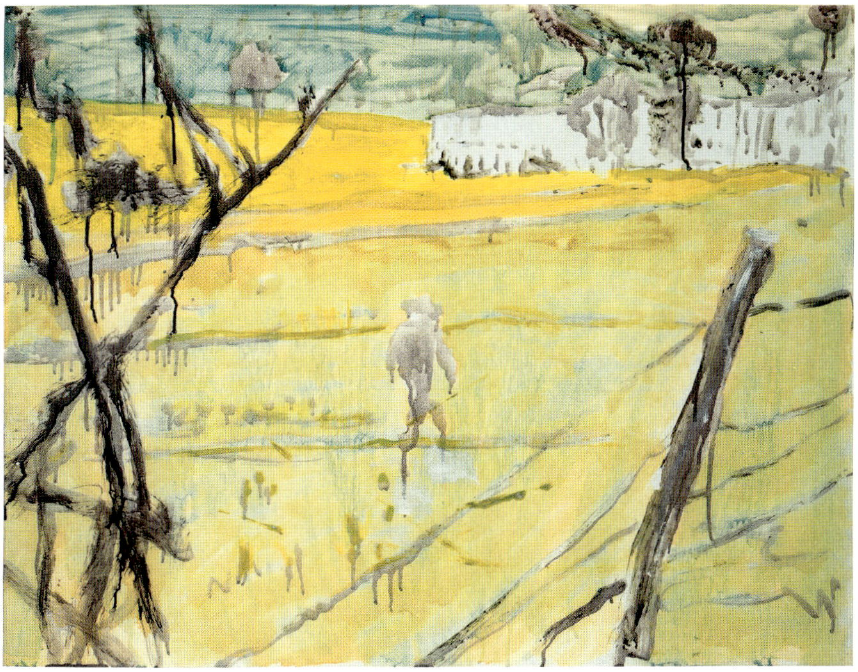

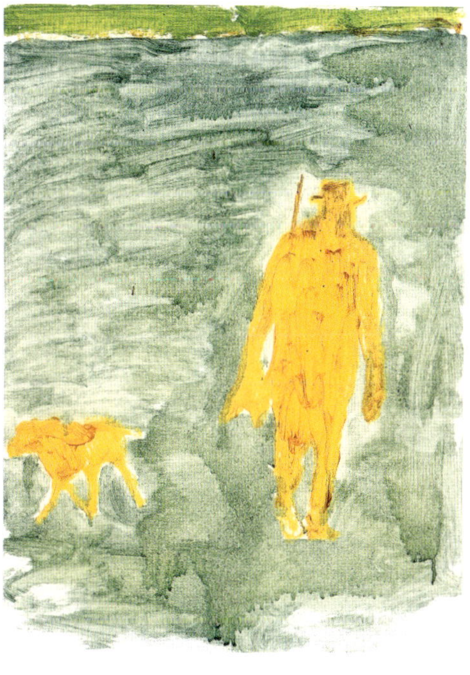

Study for Young Bean Farmer 1991, oil on paper, 57.2 × 72.4
Untitled 1991, oil on paper, 29.9 × 21.6

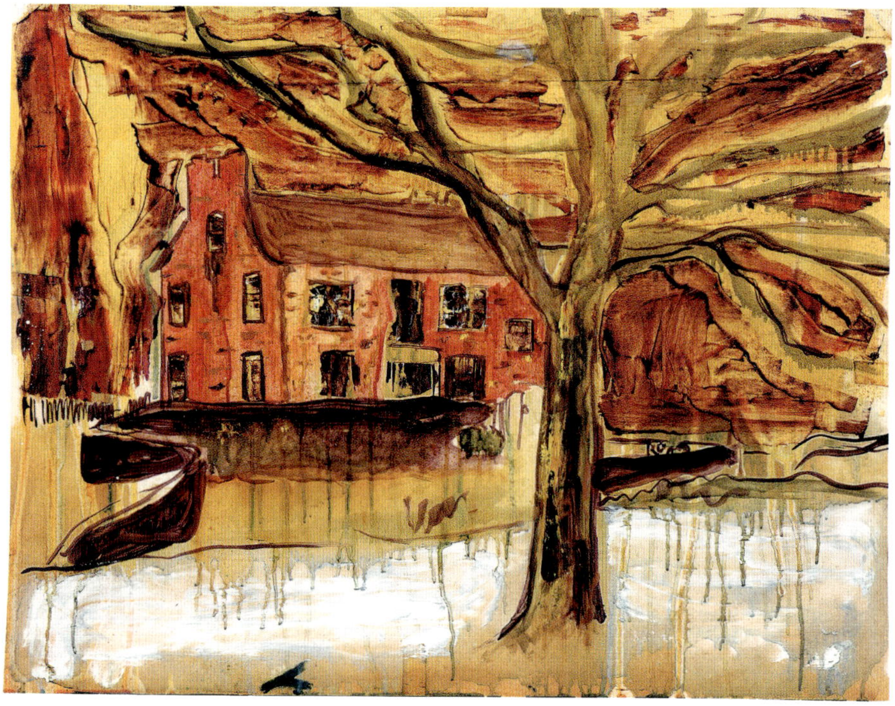

Rosedale 1991, oil on paper, 57.2 × 73.7
Study for Concrete Cabin 1992, mixed media on paper, 57.2 × 72.4
Unité 1992 mixed media on paper, 72.4 × 57.8

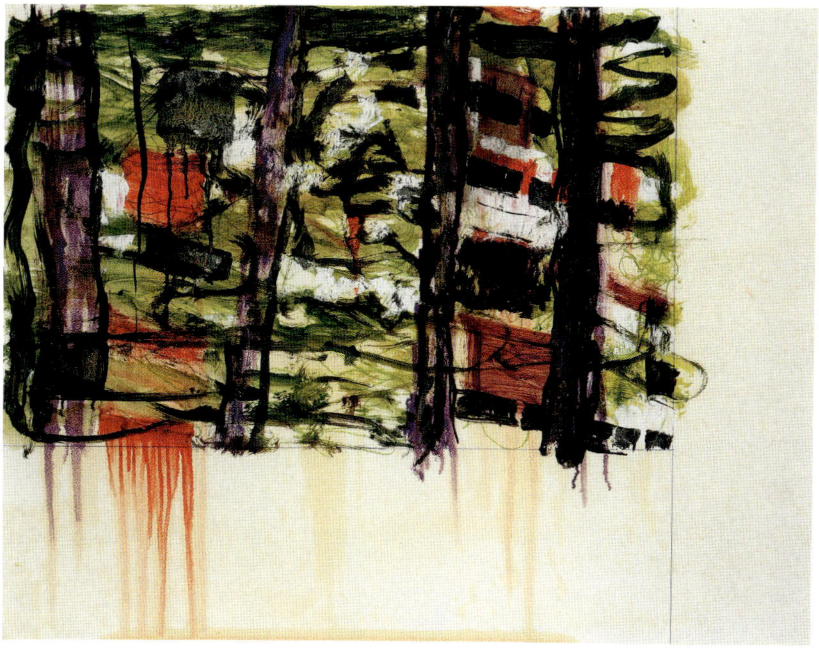

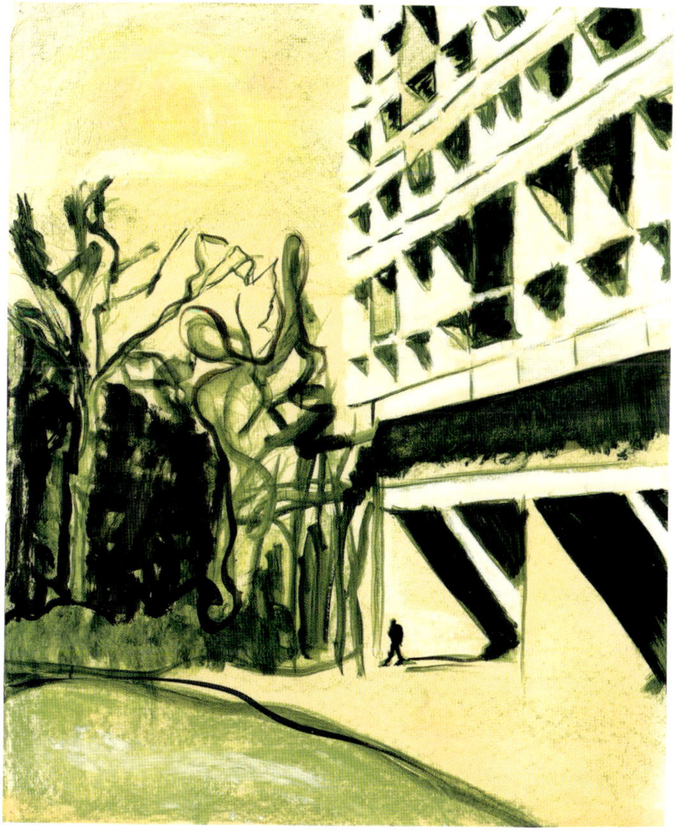

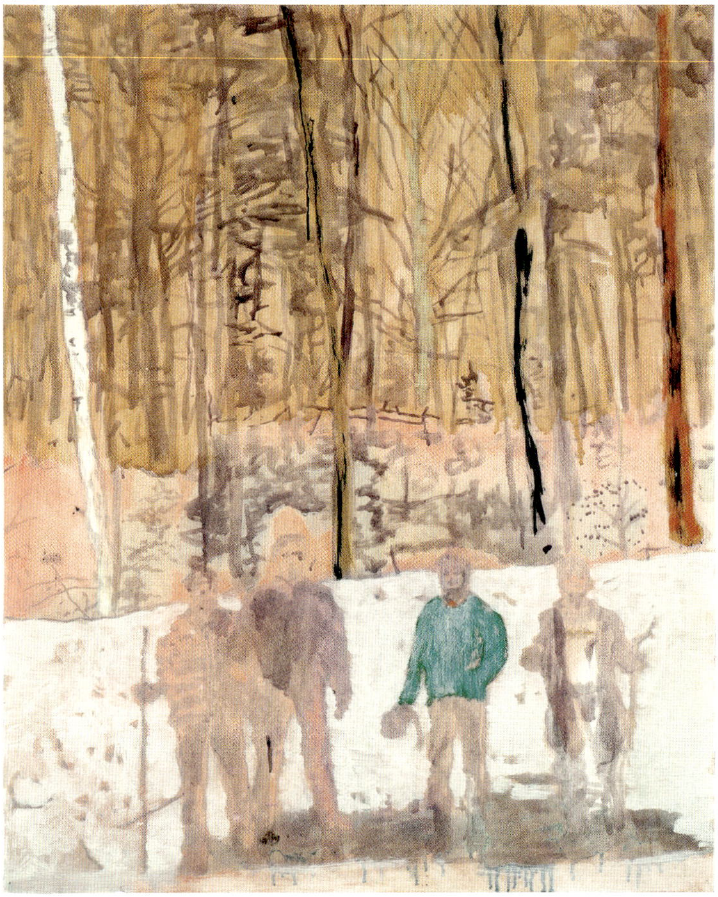

Cobourg 3+1 More 1995, acrylic on paper, 72.4 × 57.8 [not exhibited]

Blotter 1995, acrylic on paper, 135.3 × 27.9

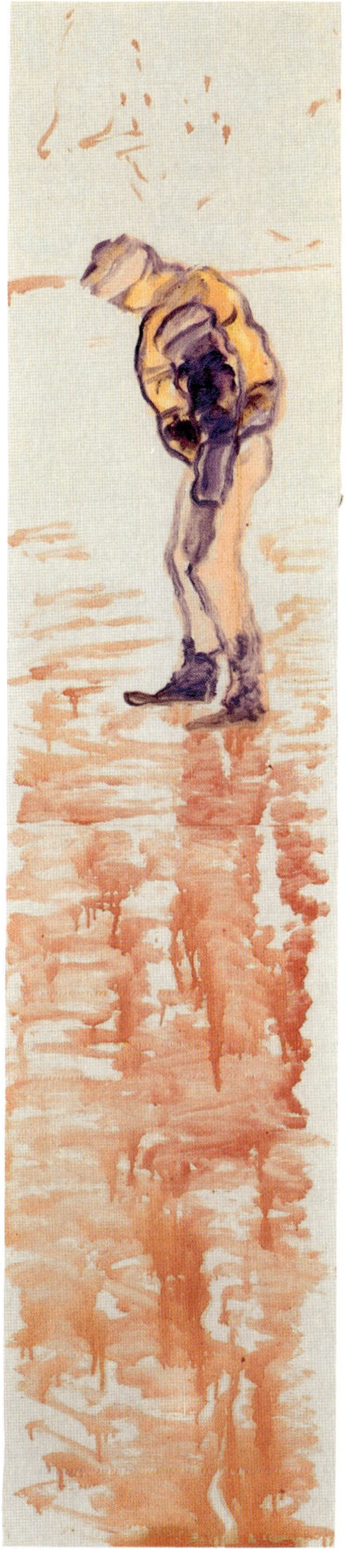

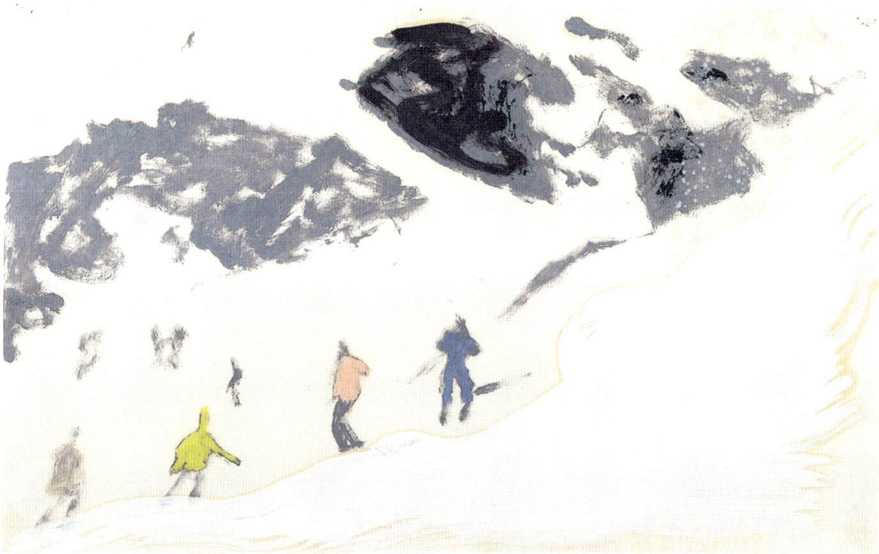

Study for White Creep 1996, oil on paper, 36.8 × 57.8
Untitled (Figure in Green Jacket) 1991, mixed media on paper, 47 × 35.6
Three Bears 1999, ink, sugar and watercolour on paper, 50.8 × 64.8

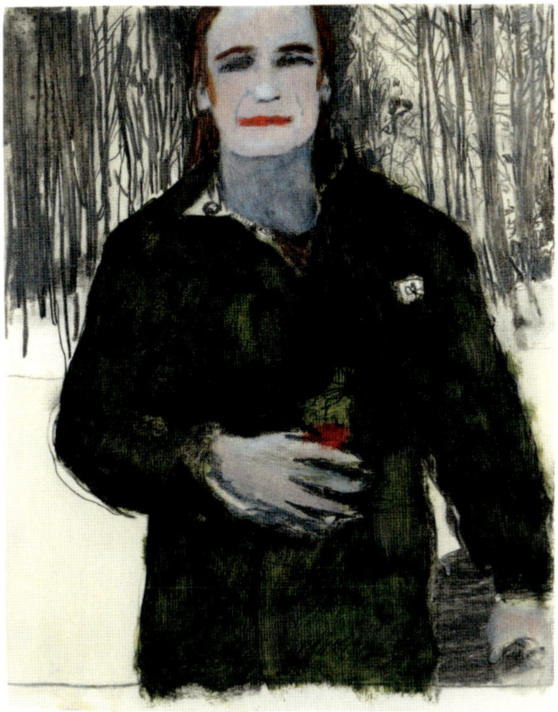

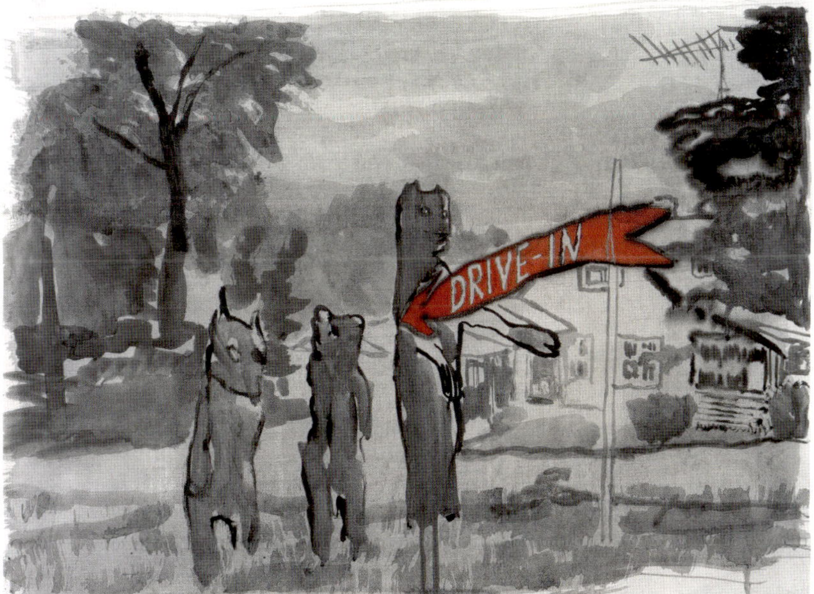
DRIVE-IN

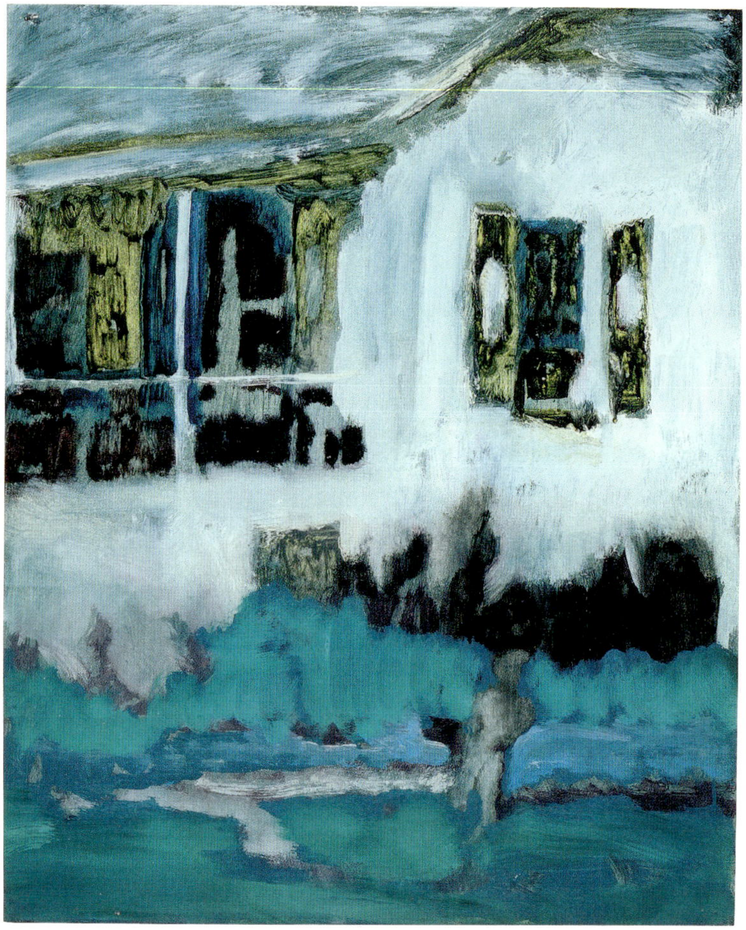

Study for Camp Forestia I 1996, oil on paper, 72.8 × 57.6
Study for The Heart of Old San Juan 1999, acrylic and gouache on brown paper, 100.3 × 69.9

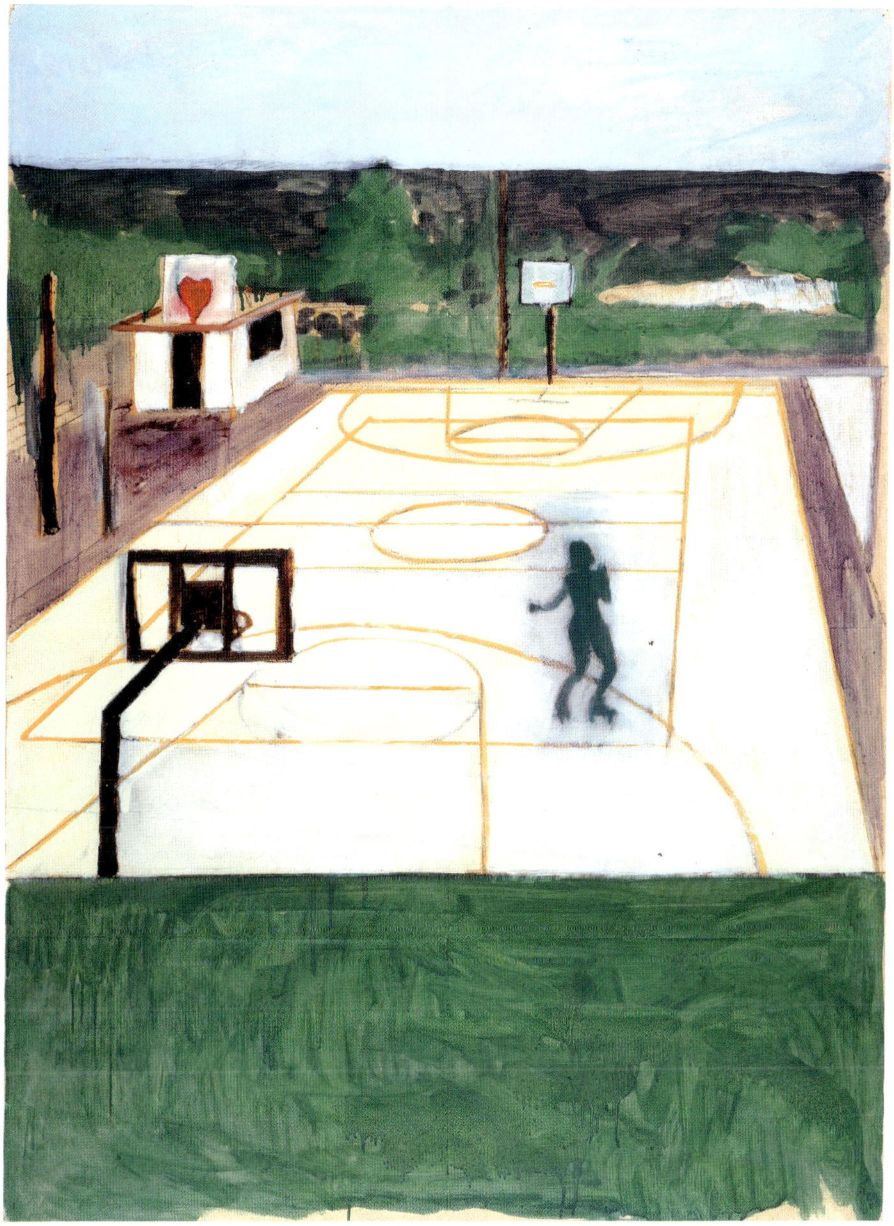

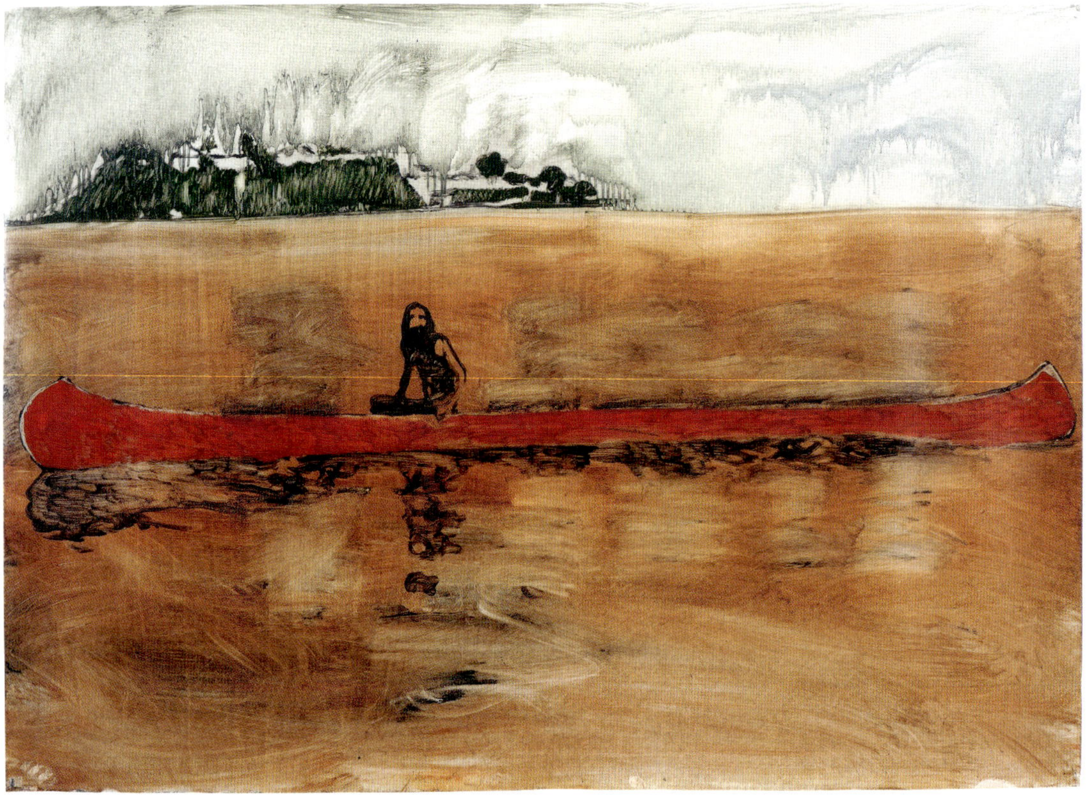

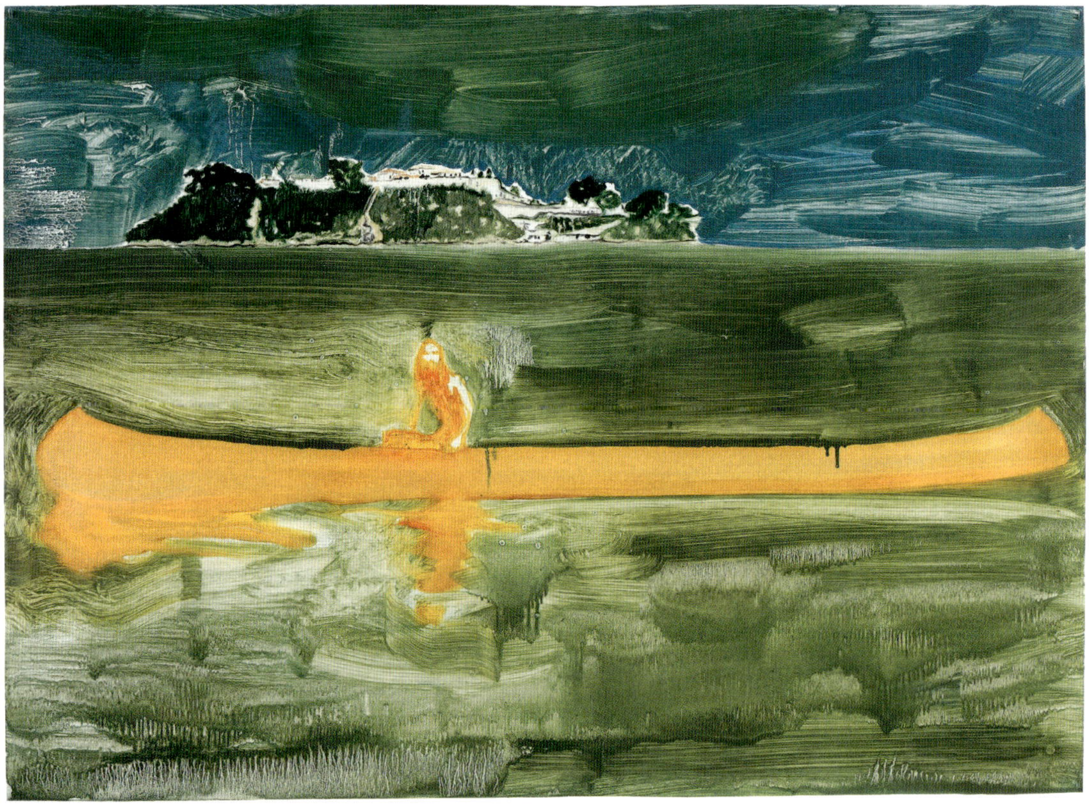

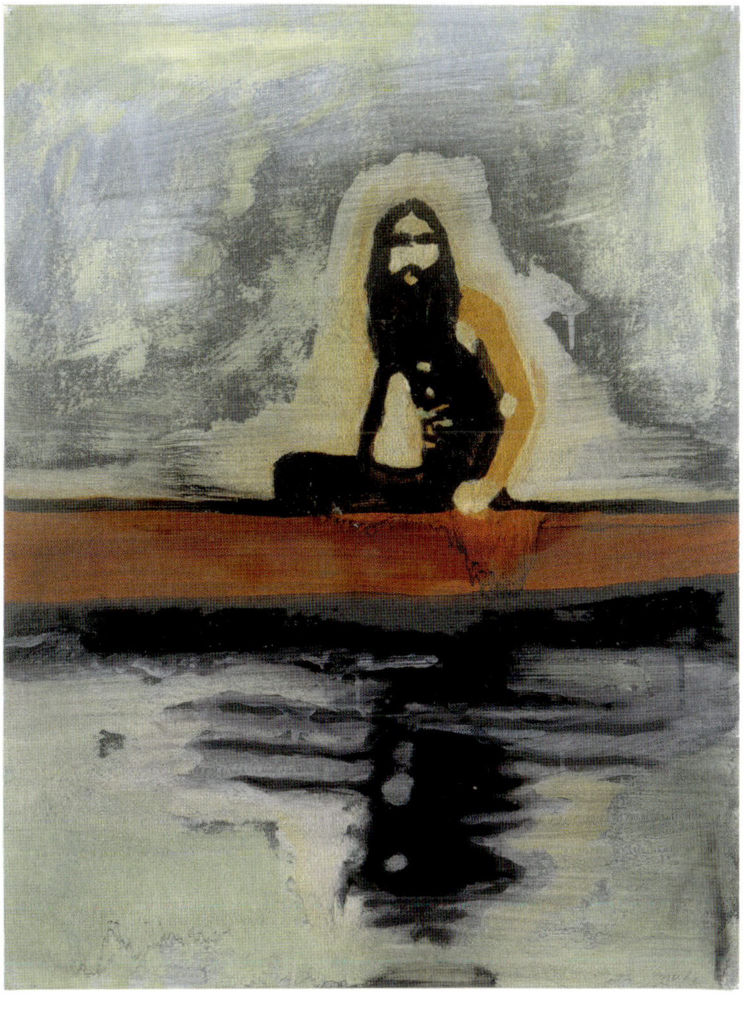

100 Years Ago 2001, oil on paper, 101.6 × 137.2
100 Years Ago 2001, oil on paper, 101.6 × 137.2
100 Years Ago 2002, oil on paper, 75.8 × 55.9

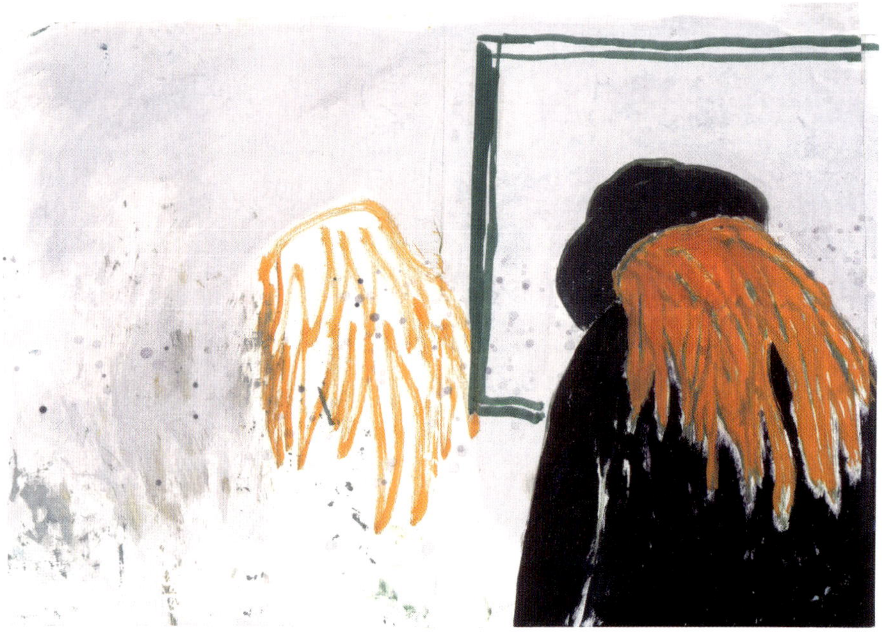

House of Pictures 2001, oil on paper, 41.9 × 59.7
Untitled (Double Portrait) 2002, oil on paper, 63.5 × 52.3 (irregular)
Untitled 2001, watercolour on paper, 34.9 × 24.7

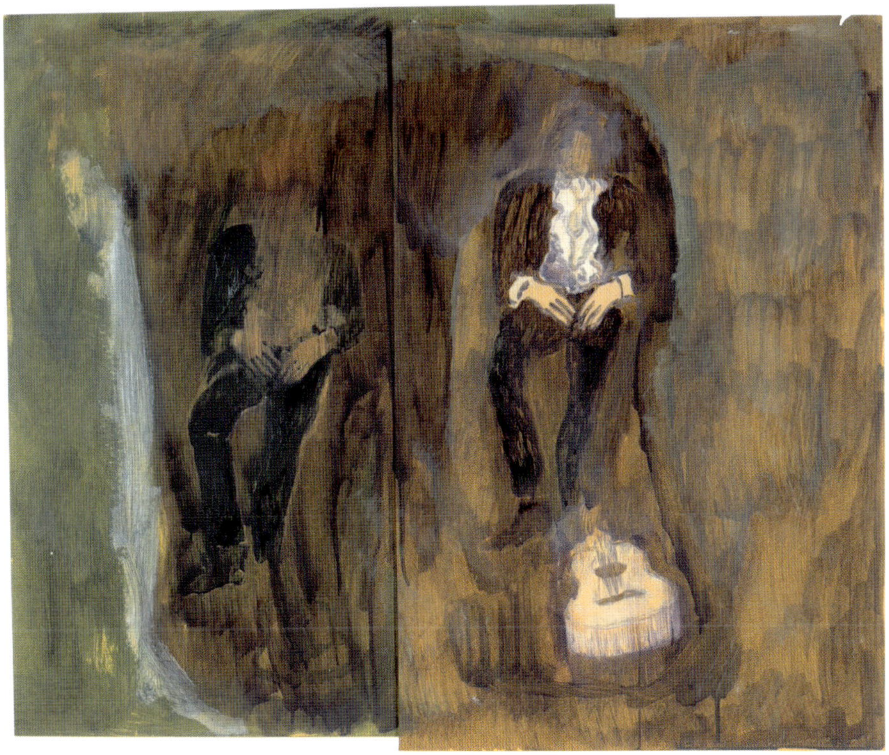

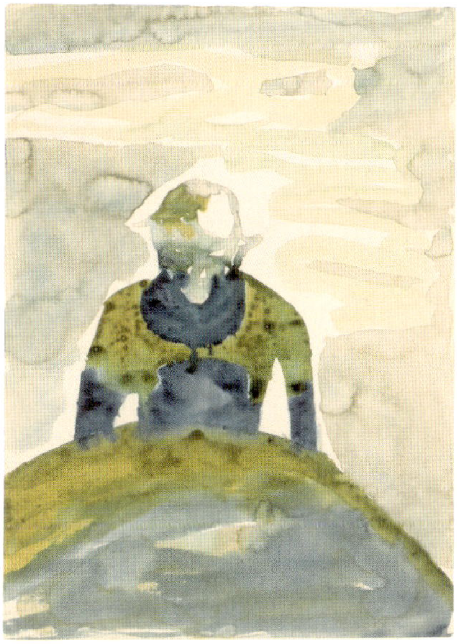

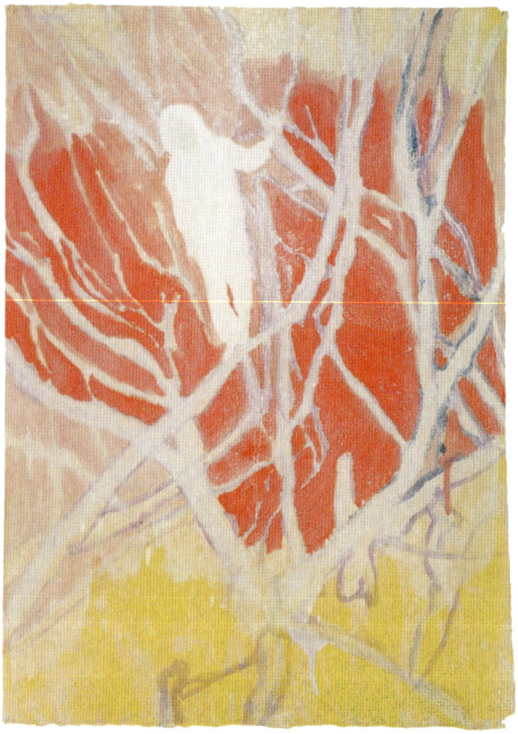

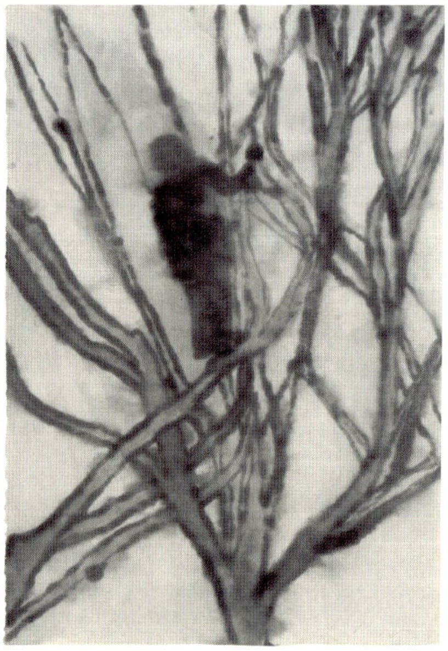

Girl in Tree 2001, oil on paper, 55.9 × 38.7
Untitled 2002, ink on paper, 36.2 × 24.1
Girl in Tree 2001, oil on paper, 63.5 × 52

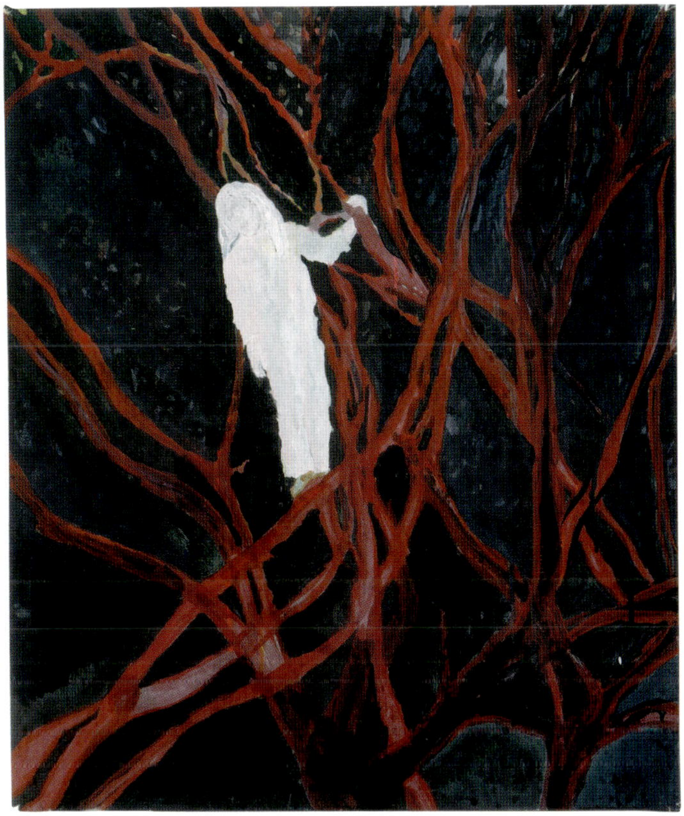

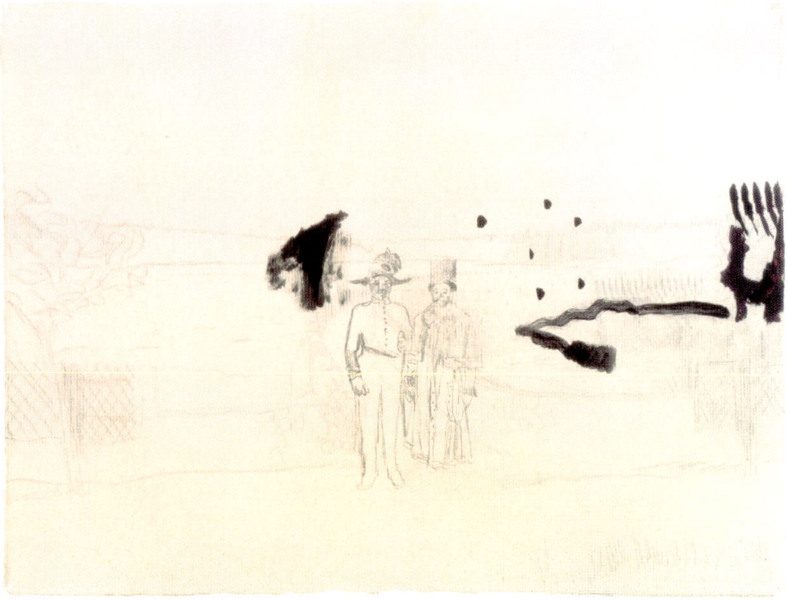

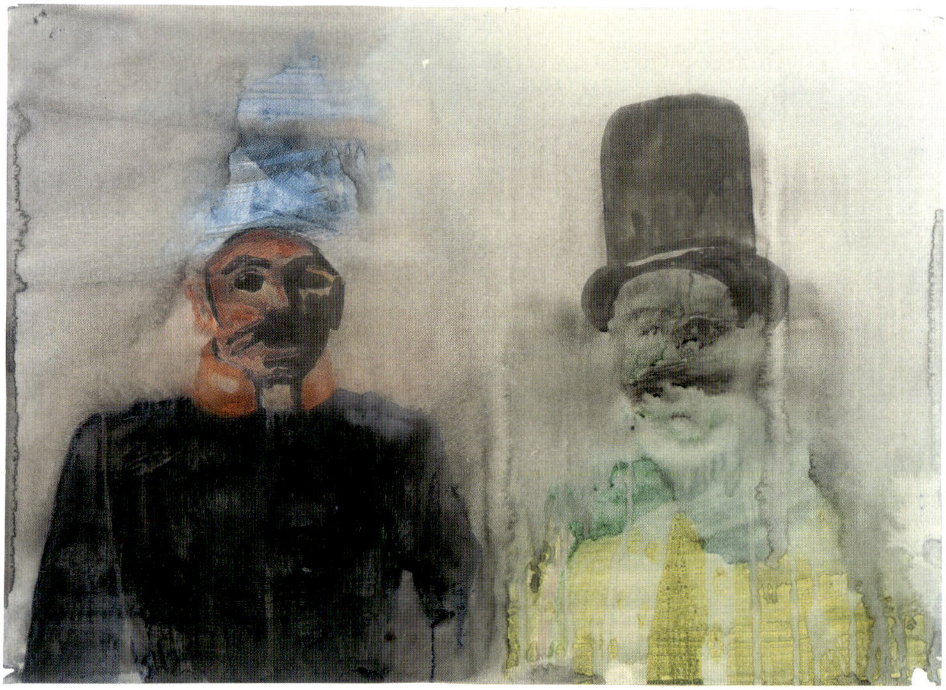

Untitled 2002, pencil and ink on paper, 50.4 × 66
Guest House 3 2002, watercolour on paper, 57.2 × 72.4

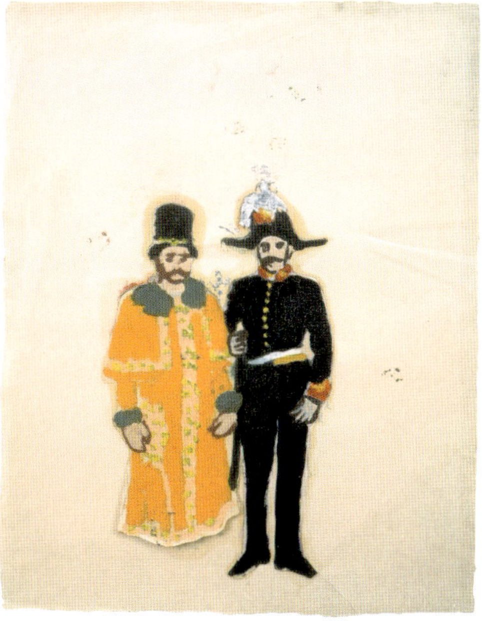

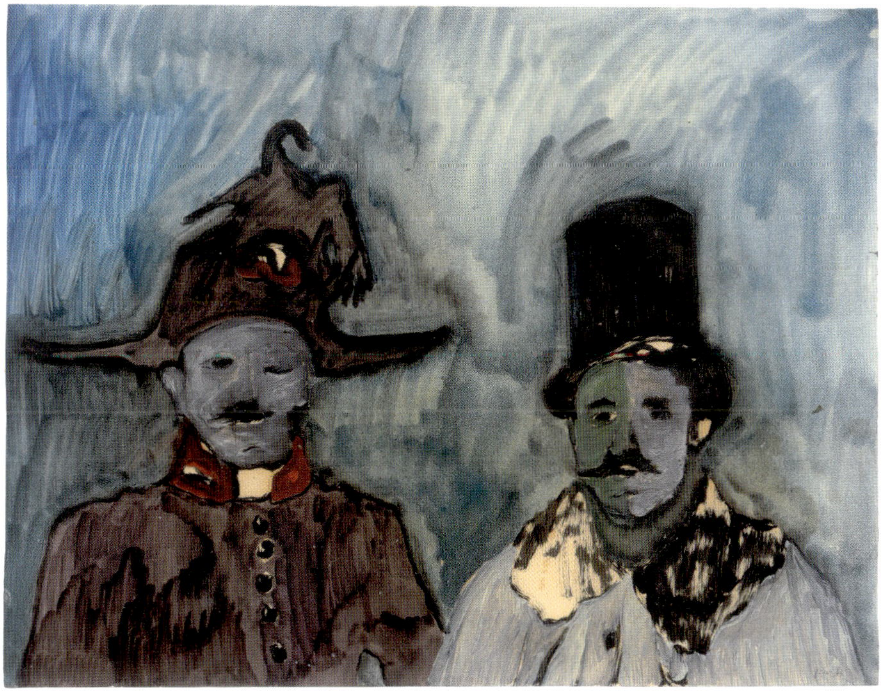

Untitled 2002, oil on cut paper, 64.8 × 50.2
Guest House 1 2002, oil on paper, 55.9 × 76.2

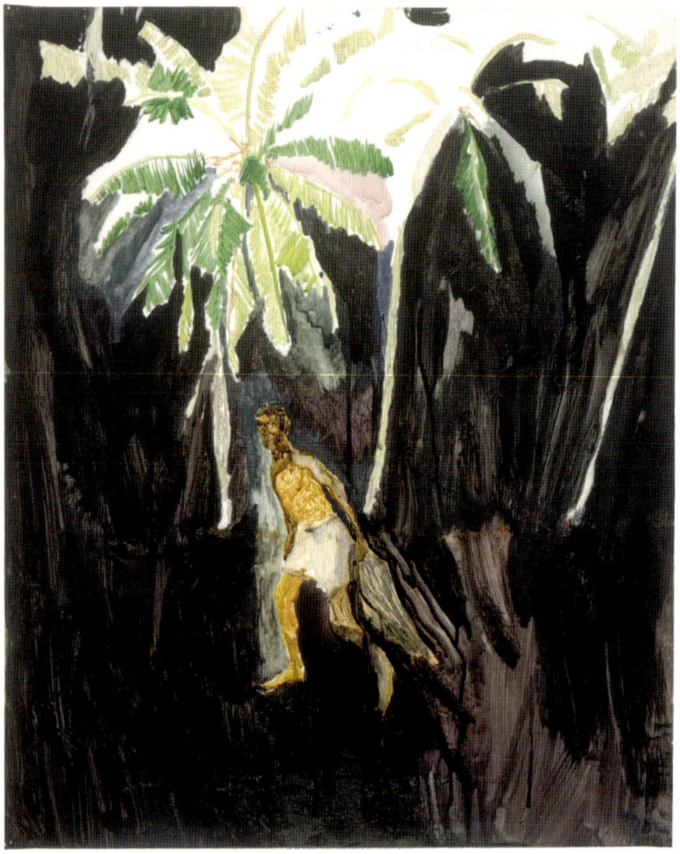

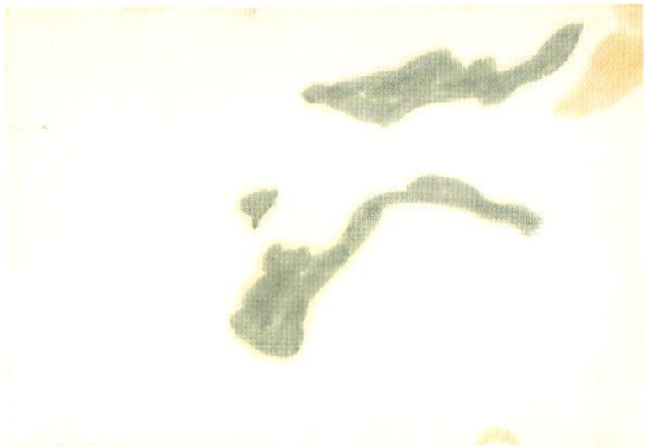

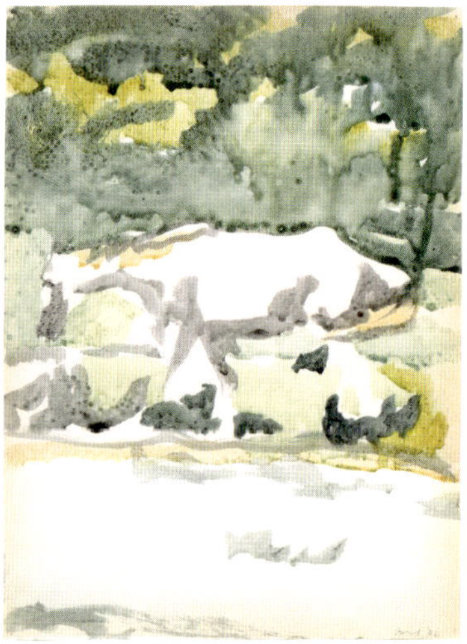

Fisherman 2002, Watercolour and gouache on paper, 72.4 × 57.2
Grande Riviere 2002, oil on paper, 17.8 × 25.4
Grande Riviere 2002, watercolour on paper, 34.9 × 24.8

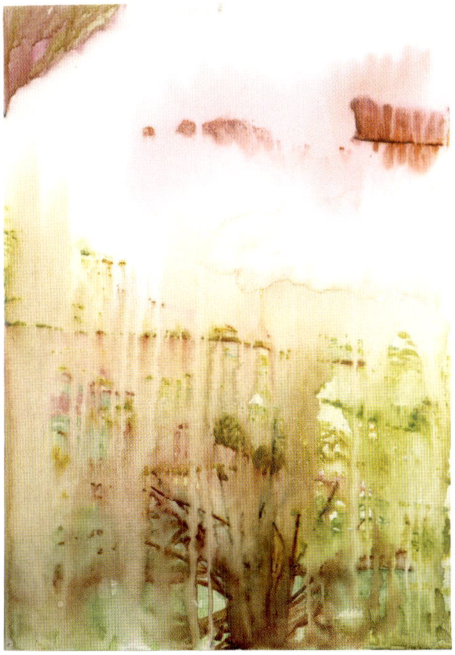

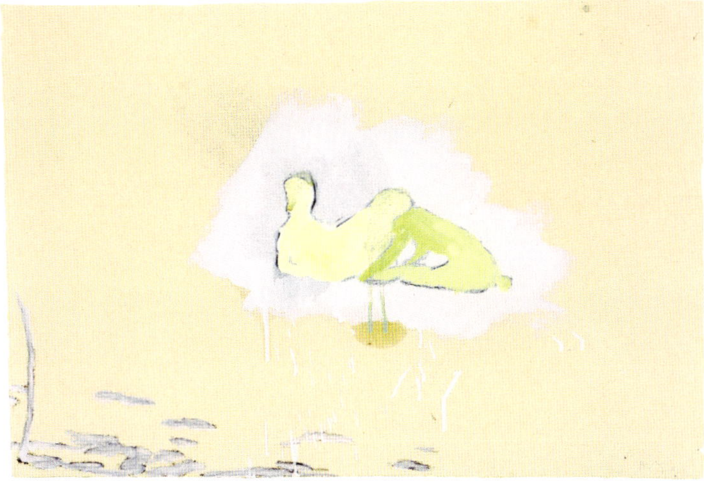

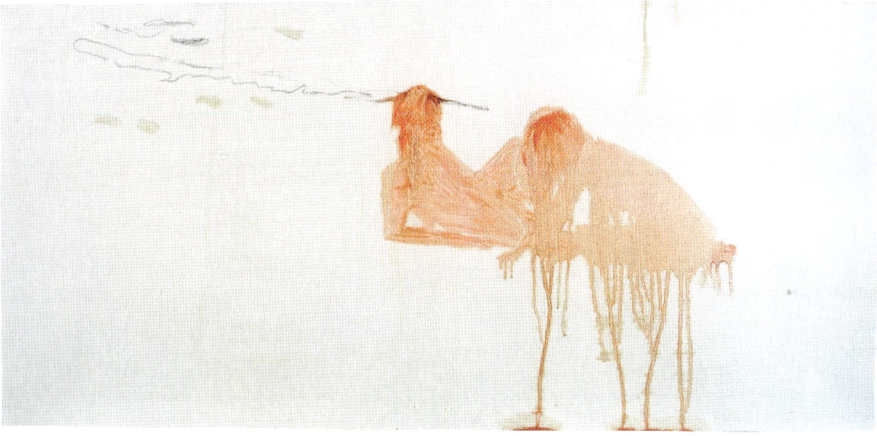

Driftwood (Yara) 2002, watercolour on paper, 55.9 × 35.7
Untitled 2001, oil on paper, 39.4 × 56.5
Untitled 2003, charcoal and oil on paper, 44.5 × 90.2

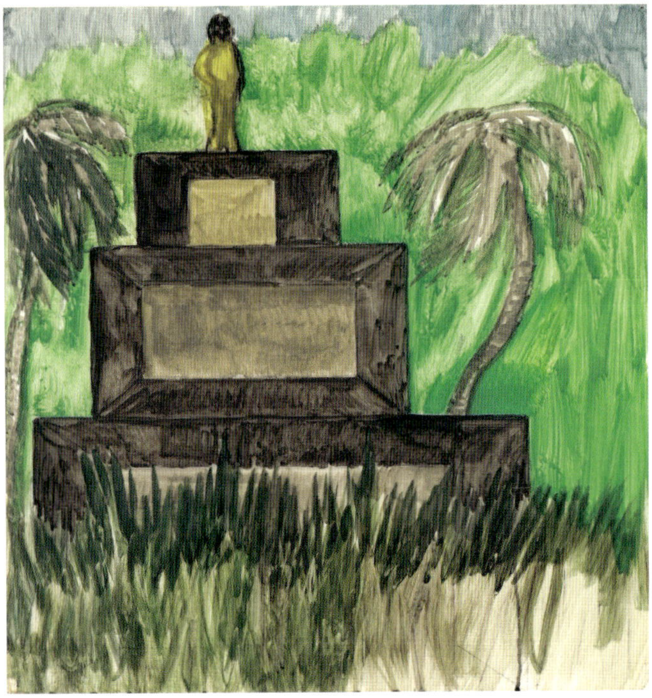

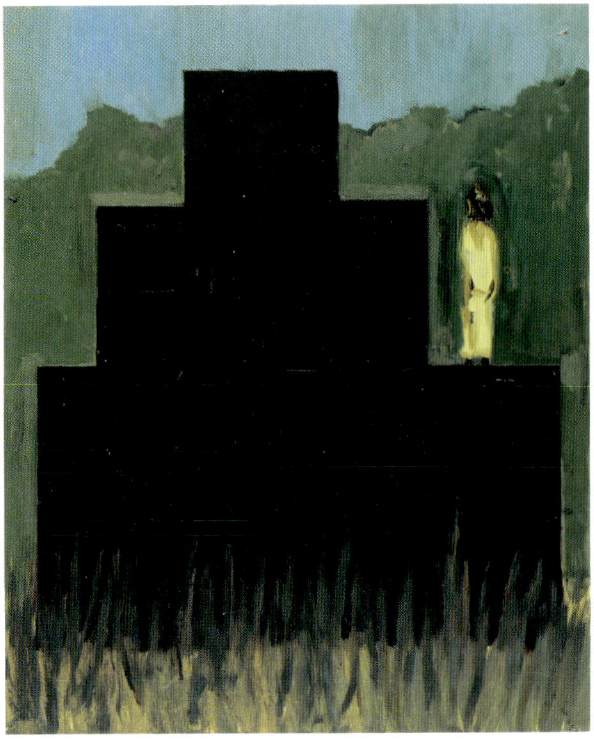

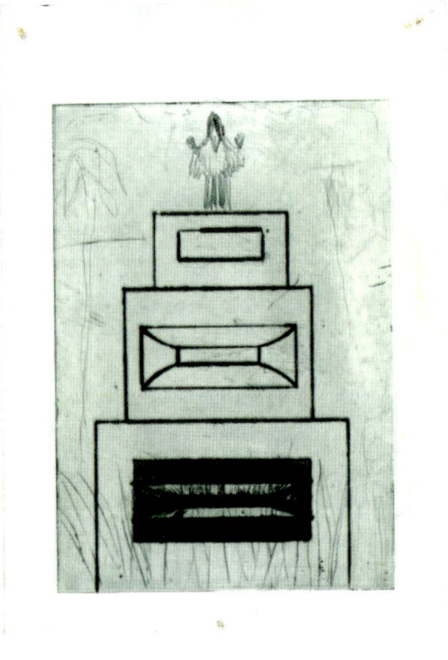

Maracas II 2004, oil on paper, 72.6 × 57.5
Maracas 2004, oil on paper, 72.2 × 57.5
Proofprint for Black Palms 2003, etching on paper, 38.5 × 26.5

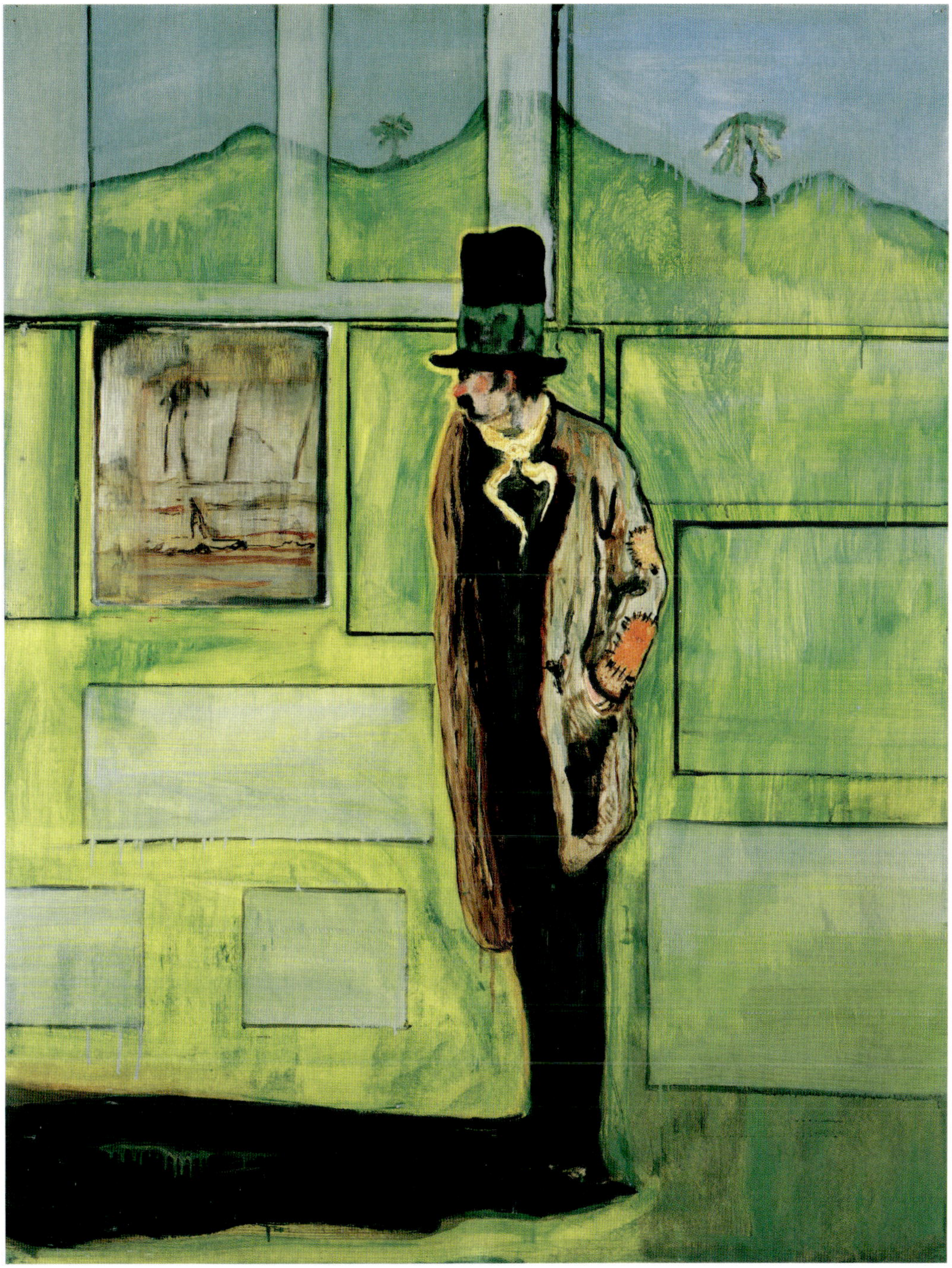

Metropolitain 2003, oil on paper, 137.8 × 101.6

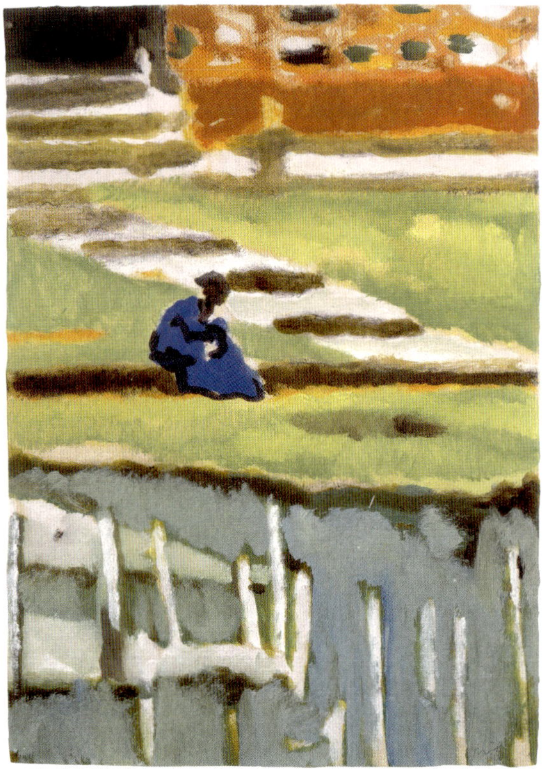

Ooty Boathouse 2002, oil on paper, 56.5 × 39.4
Lapeyrouse Wall 2004, oil on paper, 235 × 128.9

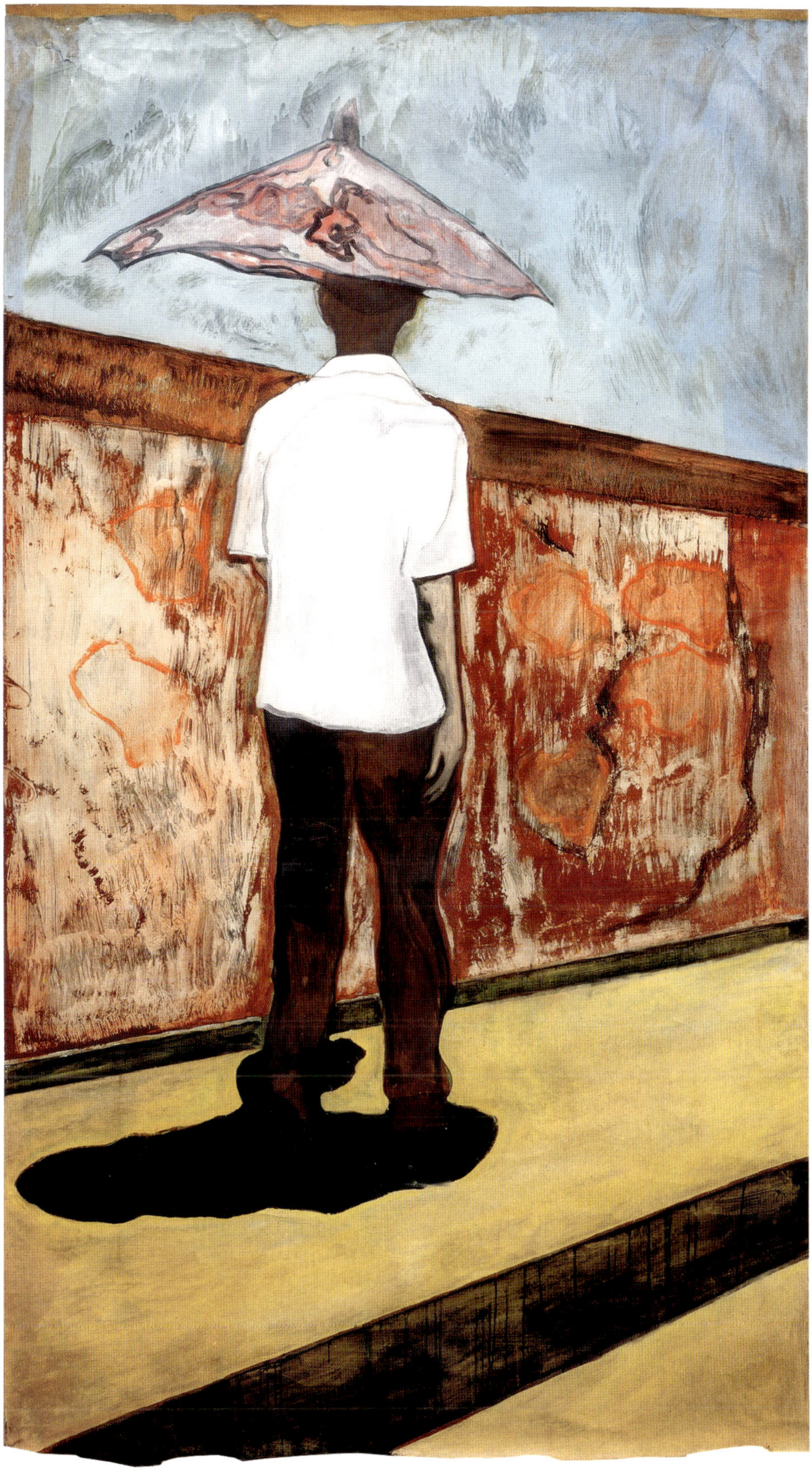

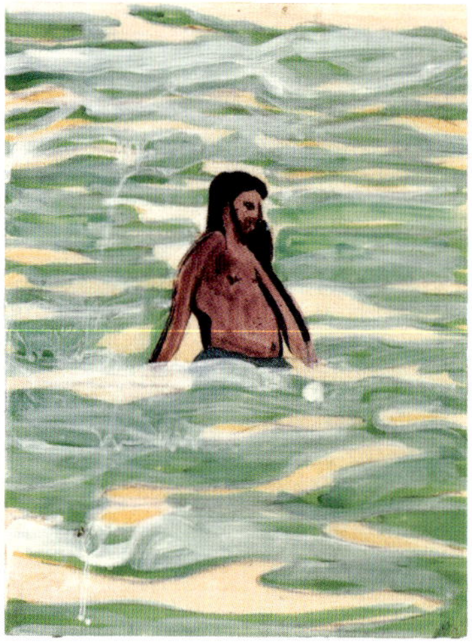

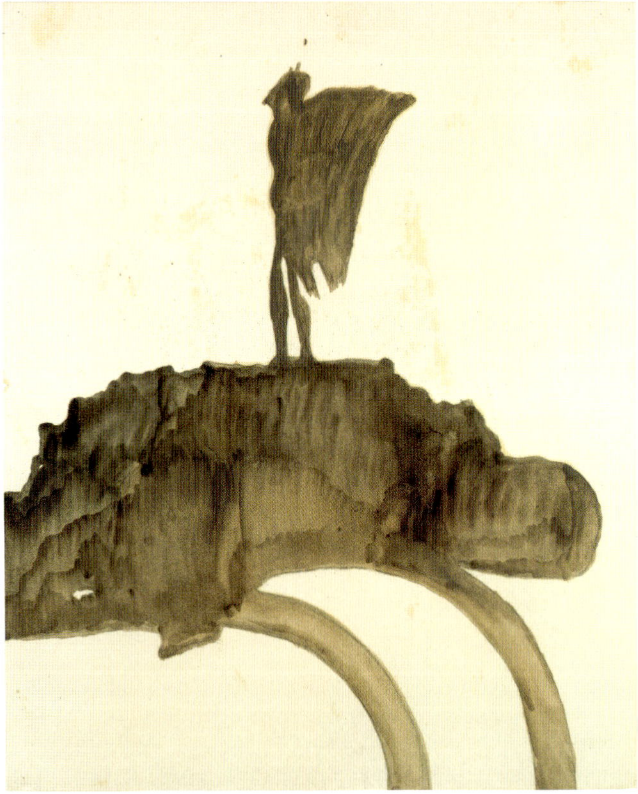

J.M. at Paragon 2003, oil on paper, 35.2 × 25
Man Dressed as Bat 2004, oil on paper, 72.4 × 57.8

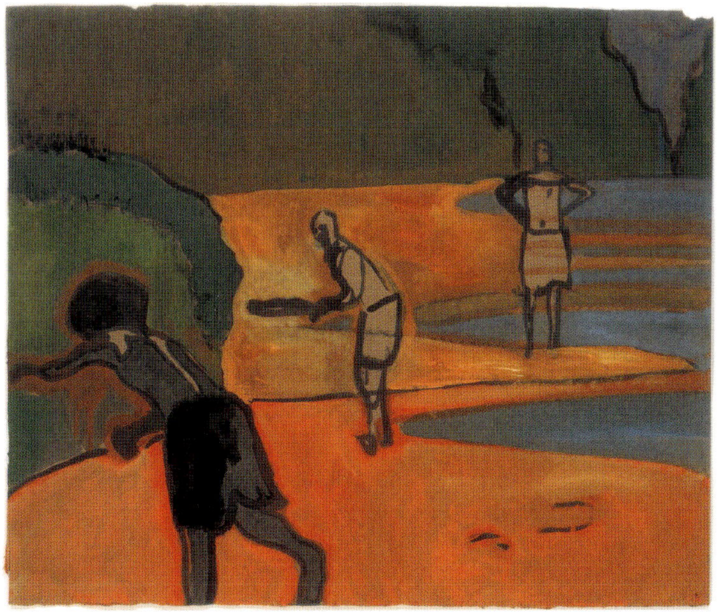

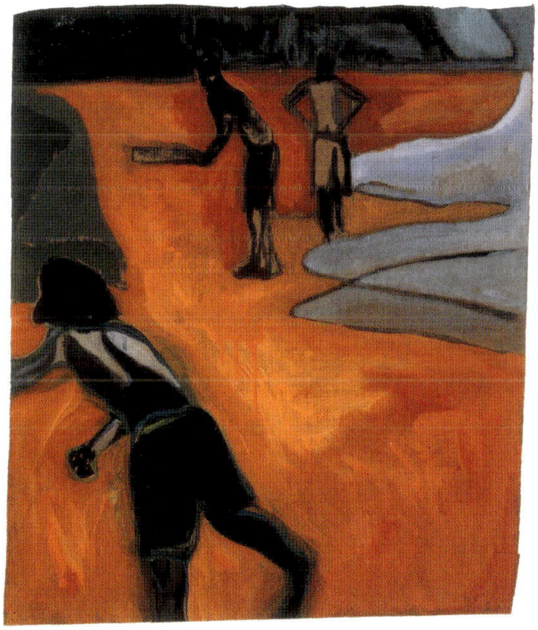

Paragon 2005, oil on paper, 58.2 × 67.4
Paragon 2005, oil on paper, 60.3 × 50.3

Peter Doig Chronology

1959

Born in Edinburgh

1962

Moved to Trinidad

1966

Moved to Canada

1979

Moved to London

1979–1980

Wimbledon School of Art, London

1980–83

St Martins School of Art, London, B.A.

1982

New Contemporaries, Institute of Contemporary Arts, London (group)

Exhibition, St Martins School of Art, London (group)

1983

New Contemporaries, Institute of Contemporary Arts, London (group)

On Parade, St Martins School of Art, London (group)

1984

Urban Mayhem, Metropolitan Gallery, London (solo)

1985

Things as They Are, Riverside Studios, London (group)

1986

Moved to Canada

The Naked City, Air Gallery, London (solo)

1989

Moved to London

Raving Formalists, Galerie Nomad, Montreal (group)

1989–1990

Chelsea School of Art, London, M.A.

1990

Articule Gallery, Montreal, Quebec (solo)

Into the Nineties, Mall Galleries, London (group)

1991

Whitechapel Artist Award, Whitechapel Art Gallery, London (solo)

Barclays Young Artist Award, Serpentine Gallery, London (group)

1992

New Voices, Centre Albert Borschette, Brussels (group)

Inside a Microcosm, Laure Genillard Gallery, London (group)

1993

Twelve Stars, Arts Council Gallery, Belfast, toured to City Art Centre, Edinburgh; Barbican Art Gallery, London (group)

Project Unité Firminy, Firminy-Vert, France (group)

Exhibition 18, John Moore's Prize, Walker Art Gallery, Liverpool (awarded first prize)

1994

Concrete Cabins, Victoria Miro Gallery, London (solo)

Unbound: Possibilities in Painting, Hayward Gallery, London (group)

Gavin Brown's enterprise, New York (group)

Imprint '93, Cabinet Gallery, London (group)

Here and Now, Serpentine Gallery, London (group)

Peter Doig, Gavin Brown's enterprise, New York (solo)

Turner Prize Exhibition, Tate Gallery, London (group)

Group Painting Exhibition, Victoria Miro Gallery, London (group)

Prix Eliette von Karajan: Peter Doig, Max Gandolph-Bibliothek, Salzburg, toured to Herbert von Karajan Centrum, Vienna (solo) (awarded first prize)

Moyra Davey / Peter Doig, Gavin Brown's Enterprise, New York (solo)

1995

Blotter, Contemporary Fine Arts, Berlin (solo)

Zombie Golf, Burbage House, London (group)

1995–2000

Trustee of Tate Gallery, London

1996

Freestyle, Victoria Miro Gallery, London (solo)

Peter Doig, Gavin Brown's enterprise, New York (solo)

Small Paintings, Riding House Editions, London (solo)

Homely, Gesellschaft für Aktuelle Kunst, Bremen (solo)

Drawings from the MAB Library, AC Project Room, New York (group)

Ghislaine Hussenot, Paris (group)

There's not a Painting on the Wall (collaboration with Matthew Higgs), Anthony Wilkinson Fine Art, London (group)

Answered Prayers, with John Currin, Richard Patterson, Raymond Pettibon, Contemporary Fine Arts, Berlin (group)

Belladonna, Institute of Contemporary Arts, London (group)

About Vision: New British Painting in the 1990s, Fruitmarket Gallery, Edinburgh, toured to Museum of Modern Art, Oxford (group)

Faustrecht der Freiheit, Kunstsammlung Gera, Gera, toured to Neues Museum Weserburg, Bremen (group)

1997

Alpenblick, Kunsthalle Wien, Vienna (group)

New Found Landscape, Kerlin Gallery, Dublin (group)

Malerei 4, Galerie Monika Sprüth, Düsseldorf (group)

Package Holiday: New British Art in the Ophiuchus Collection, Hydra Workshop, Greece (group)

About Vision: New British Painting in the 1990s, Christchurch Mansion, Ipswich, toured to Laing Art Gallery, Newcastle (group)

1998

Uk: Maximum Diversity, Gallery Krinzinger im Benger-Areal, Bregenz, and Galerie Krinzinger im Semperdepot, Vienna (group)

Peter Doig Blizzard seventy-seven, Kunsthalle Kiel, Kiel, toured to Kunsthalle Nürnberg, Nuremberg; Whitechapel Art Gallery, London (solo)

Peter Doig and Udomsak Krisanamis, Arnolfini Gallery, Bristol, toured to Fruitmarket Gallery, Edinburgh (group)

Buffalo Station, Victoria Miro Gallery, London (solo)

Sunday, Cabinet Gallery, London (group)

1999

Country Rock, Contemporary Fine Arts, Berlin (solo)

Version, Kunsthaus Glarus, Switzerland (solo)

Wing Mirror, Gavin Brown's enterprise, New York (solo)

From A to B and Back Again, Royal College of Art, London (group)

Contemplating Pollock, Victoria Miro Gallery, London (group)

Matthew Higgs, Anthony Wilkinson Gallery, London (group)

Version (Drawings) in Rirkrit Tiravanija's apartment, Gavin Brown's enterprise, New York (solo)

River Deep Mountain High, Gallery Westland Place, London, toured to The Cooper Gallery, Dundee (group)

Group Show, Bonakdar Jancou Gallery, New York (group)

Examining Pictures, Whitechapel Art Gallery London, toured to Museum of Contemporary Art, Chicago, Hammer Museum, Los Angeles (group)

2000

Echo-lake, MATRIX, Berkeley Art Museum at University of California, toured to Museum of Contemporary Art, Miami; Saint Louis Art Museum, Missouri (solo)

Almost Grown, The Douglas Hyde Gallery, Dublin (solo)

Spot on, Victoria Miro Gallery, London (group)

Peter Doig, Michael Raedecker, Raucci / Santamaria Gallery, Naples (group)

Drawings 2000, Barbara Gladstone Gallery, New York (group)

From a Distance: Approaching Landscape, The Institute of Contemporary Art, Boston (group)

Twisted: Urban and Visionary Landscapes in Contemporary Painting, Van Abbemuseum, Eindhoven (group)

2001

Peter Doig, Morris and Helen Belkin Art Gallery, The University of British Columbia, Vancouver, toured to National Gallery of Canada, Ottawa; The Power Plant, Toronto (solo)

Fig.1: 50 Projects in 50 Weeks, multiple venues, London (group)

The Way I See it, Galerie Jennifer Flay, Paris (group)

Camera Works: The Photographic Impulse in Contemporary Art, Marianne Boesky Gallery, New York (group)

Extended Painting, Monica De Cardenas, Milan (group)

Works on Paper: From Acconci to Zittel, Victoria Miro Gallery, London (group)

Work on Paper, The Kerlin Gallery, Dublin (group)

Hier ist dort, Salzburger Kunstverein, Salzburg (group)

EU, Stephen Friedman Gallery, London (group)

About the Bayberry Bush, Parrish Art Museum, Southampton, New York (group)

2002

Moved to Trindad

Peter Doig: The Prints, The Bailey Collection, Toronto (solo)

Peter Doig: Works on Paper, Michael Werner Gallery, New York (solo)

100 Years Ago, Victoria Miro Gallery, London (solo)

The Galleries Show, Royal Academy of Art, London (group)

Art and Mountains: conquistadors of the useless, The Alpine Club, London (group)

Cher peintre: Peintures figuratives depuis l'ultime Picabia, Centre Pompidou, Paris, toured to Kunsthalle Wien, Vienna and Schirn Kunsthalle, Frankfurt (group)

Cavepainting, Santa Monica Museum of Art, California (group)

Premio Biello per L'incisione, Museo del Territorio Biellese, Biello (group)

2003

Peter Doig, The Arts Club of Chicago (solo)

Peter Doig: Painter as Printmaker, James Hyman Fine Art, London (solo)

Charley's Space, Bonnefanten Museum, Maastricht, toured to Carré d'Art Contemporain de Nîmes, Nimes (solo)

Pittura/Painting: From Rauschenberg to Murakami 1964–2003, 50th International Art Exhibition, Musei Civici Veneziani/La Biennale de Venezia, Venice (group)

Days Like These: Tate Triennial Exhibition of Contemporary British Art 2003, Tate Britain, London (group)

Unheimlich, Städtische Galerie Delmenholst, Germany (group)

Happiness, Mori Art Museum, Toyko (group)

2004

Peter Doig - Jochen Klein, Galerie Daniel Buchholz, Cologne (group)

Bearings: Landscapes from the IMMA Collection, Irish Museum of Modern Art, Dublin (group)

Metropolitain, Pinakothek der Moderne, Munich, toured to Kestnergesellschaft, Hanover (solo)

Huts, The Douglas Hyde Gallery, Dublin (group)

Rheingold III, Städtisches Museum Abteiberg, Mönchengladbach (group)

New Blood: New Young Artists, New Acquisitions, Saatchi Gallery, London (group)

Contemporary Painting, Colby College Museum of Art, Maine (group)

The Undiscovered Country, Hammer Museum, Los Angeles (group)

Carnegie International, Carnegie Museum of Art, Pittsburgh (group)

2005

Professor at Düsseldorf State Academy of Art

René Daniels, Peter Doig, Silke Otto-Knapp, Gavin Brown's enterprise, New York (group)

Ideal Worlds: New Romanticism in Contemporary Art, Schirn Kunsthalle, Frankfurt (group)

Looking at Words: The Formal Use of Text in Modern and Contemporary Works on Paper, Andrea Rosen Gallery, New York (group)

Peter Doig: Studiofilmclub, Museum Ludwig, Cologne, toured to Kunsthalle Zürich (solo)

Peter Doig: Works on Paper, Dallas Museum of Art, Dallas, toured to The Gallery at Windsor, Florida; Art Gallery of Ontario, Toronto (solo)

The Triumph of Painting, Part One, Saatchi Gallery, London (group)

Munch Revisited: Edvard Munch und die heutige Kunst, Museum für Kunst und Kulturegesschichte, Dortmund (group)

Geschichtenerzähler, Hamburger Kunsthalle, Hamburg (group)

Wunschwelten, Schirn Kunsthalle, Hamburg (group)

The Big Bang, Centre Pompidou, Paris (group)

Works on Paper: Georg Baselitz, Peter Doig, Jörg Immendorf, Per Kirkeby, Michael Werner Gallery, New York (group)

2006

Peter Doig: Studiofilmclub 2003–2006, Ballroom Marfa, Texas (solo)

Go West Young Man, Museum der bildenden Künste, Leipzig (solo)

Imagination Becomes Reality, Part III: Talking Pictures, Sammlung Goetz, Munich (group)

Tate Triennial 2006: New British Art, Tate Britain, London (group)

Whitney Biennial 2006: Day for Night, Whitney Museum of American Art, New York (group)

Once Upon a Time in the West, Part One, Contemporary Fine Arts, Berlin (group)

Still Points of the Turning World: SITE Santa Fe's 6th International Biennial, SITE Santa Fe, New Mexico (group)

Surprise, Surprise, Institute of Contemporary Arts, London (group)

How to improve the World, 60 Years of British Art, Arts Council Collection, Hayward Gallery, London (group)

Essential Painting, The National Museum of Art, Osaka (group)

In the Alps, Kunsthalle Zürich, Zurich (group)

2007

Very Abstract and Hyper Figurative, Thomas Dane Gallery, London (group)

Der Symbolismus und die Kunst der Gegenwart, Van der Heydt Museum, Wuppertal (group)

The Painting of Modern Life, Hayward Gallery, London (group)

Notes from 'A Suitable Distance'

1. Peter Doig, article on artists' responses to the Cezanne exhibition at the Tate Gallery, *The Times*, 5 February 1996, p.14.
2. See Adrian Searle's account of this period in 'A Kind of Blankness', in Adrian Searle, Kitty Scott and Catherine Grenier, *Peter Doig*, London 2007, pp.60–70.
3. Doig, interview with Karen Wright, 'Keeping it Real', *Modern Painters*, March 2006, p.68.
4. Ibid.
5. Ibid.
6. Ibid.
7. Gareth Jones, 'Weird Places, Strange Folk', *frieze*, issue 6, September–October 1992, p.26.
8. Sigmund Freud, *The 'Uncanny'*, first published 1919, first English translation 1925, modified version republished 1955, reprinted in *The Penguin Freud Library*, vol. 14, *Art and Literature*, pp. 335–376.
9. Ibid, p. 345.
10. Ibid.
11. Ibid, p. 347
12. Paul Bonaventura, 'Peter Doig: A Partial Record', *Parkett*, 67, 2003, p. 54. Bonaventura writes, 'I recall a conversation I once had with Peter in London when he confessed that he's nearly always torn between retaining the motif and undermining it. I start wondering how far he could push the issue of likeness before his paintings begin to fall apart entirely and whether one day he might produce something wholly abstract'.
13. See Richard Shiff's detailed account of this series in his essay for this catalogue.
14. Doig, *The Times*, 5 February 1996, p.14.
15. Doig, statement in Paul Bonaventura, 'Peter Doig: A Hunter in the Snow', *Artefactum* issue 9, 1994, p.13.
16. Doig in Jones 1992 p. 26.
17. Reported in Bonaventura 2003, p.57.
18. Adrian Searle, 'The Twilight Zonc', Independent, 21 October 1994.
19. Doig, 'Kitty Scott in conversation with Peter Doig' in Searle, Scott and Grenier 2007, p.14.
20. Freud 1919, p. 356.
21. Doig, unedited transcript of a conversation between Peter Doig and Chris Ofili, 2007.
22. Doig, ibid.
23. Freud 1919, p. 367.
24. Doig has only once shown his work in Trinidad, in a joint exhibition in 2006 with his friend, the artist, Chris Ofili, who also lives there. The show was appropriately titled 'A Suitable Distance' and this seemed a most apt title for this essay too.
25. Peter Doig, unedited transcript, 2007.
26. Ibid.
27. Ibid.
28. Freud 1919, p.345.

Notes from 'Incidents'

1. Peter Doig, statement in Paul Bonaventura, 'Peter Doig: A Hunter in the Snow', *Artefactum* 9 (1994), p.12. I thank Peter Doig for generously replying to numerous inquiries regarding his artistic intentions and studio practices. When not attributed by direct quotation, references to his opinions derive from the author's conversations with the artist, conducted between June and September 2007. I am grateful to Gordon VeneKlasen, Jason Duval, Justine Birbil, and Kelly Sturhahn at the Michael Werner Gallery, New York, and Glenn Scott Wright at the Victoria Miro Gallery, London, for facilitating my research; and I thank those who gave me access to Doig's works in their collections: Robert and Anna Marie Shapiro, Marty and Rebecca Eisenberg, Trevor Home and Susan Morris, and Charles Booth-Clibborn. Caitlin Haskell contributed both research and independent thought to this essay.
2. The notion is Bergsonian: 'You define the present in an arbitrary manner as *that which is*, whereas the present is simply *what is happening [ce qui se fait]*'; Henri Bergson, *Matter and Memory*, trans. Nancy Margaret Paul and W. Scott Palmer, London 1911 (1896), p.193 (original emphasis; translation modified).
3. Doig, statement to the author, 28 August 2007 (Doig's emphasis).
4. Doig's contemporary Daniel Richter captures something of Doig's personality – his combination of probing curiosity, introspection, equanimity and capacity to withhold moral judgement – when he states: 'I am a more anxious artist. Peter is a hippie' (Daniel Richter, statement in Kitty Scott, 'Daniel Richter's A to Z: An Incomplete Glossary', in Christoph Heinrich, ed., *Daniel Richter: Die Palette 1995–2007*, Cologne 2007, p.171.
5. Doig, statement in 'Kitty Scott in conversation with Peter Doig', in Adrian Searle, Kitty Scott and Catherine Grenier, *Peter Doig*, London 2007, p.16; statement to the author, 25 August 2007 (referring to the Briey series of paintings). See also Doig, quoted in Sarah Milroy, 'The Big One that Got Away', *The Globe and Mail* (Toronto), 17 December 2001, R1: 'A lot of [British] artists were having their work made for them. I wanted to make something clunky and handmade.'
6. Doig, statement in 'Peter Doig: Twenty Questions', ed. Matthew Higgs, in Kitty Scott, *Peter Doig* , Belkin Art Gallery, University of British Columbia, Vancouver 2001, p.17.
7. Doig, unedited transcript of a conversation between Peter Doig and Chris Ofili, 2007.
8. 'I travel around and take thousands of slides': Doig, statement in 'I've never been canoeing on a toxic swamp (A conversation between Peter Doig and Adrian Searle)', *Peter Doig: Blotter* , Contemporary Fine Arts, Berlin, 1995, p.12.
9. Doig, 'Kitty Scott in conversation with Peter Doig', p.14.
10. For example, washes of white and pulsating contrasts of orange and green in Doig's *Green Tree* 1998 (collection Thomas Dane, London) evoke – but do not strictly imitate – various kinds of photographic colour distortion, including solarisation and lens flare.
11. Doig, 'Kitty Scott in conversation with Peter Doig', p.16.
12. The title alludes to that of an instrumental 'house' recording that Doig heard at the time, 'The Jack that House Built' (1987), which transposes the refrain of a familiar nursery rhyme. House is a type of music and 'jack' is slang for money, but this connection may not be relevant. Because the location of the house Doig painted was Quebec, he replaced 'Jack' with 'Jacques'.
13. Doig, 'Kitty Scott in conversation with Peter Doig', p.16. The allusion to Jack Palance may have come to mind because of the incidental association of 'Jack' with 'Jacques'.
14. The source is a letter by Charles Mair to the *Toronto Globe* in 1869, as quoted in Ken Dryden and Roy MacGregor, *Home Game: Hockey and Life in Canada*, Toronto 1989, p.19. In *The House that Jacques Built*, the location of the house within the canvas would correspond to the human zone, the reduced realm of the grasshopper.
15. Doig, statement to the author, 25 July 2007; see the related statement in Bonaventura, 'Peter Doig: A Hunter in the Snow', p.13.
16. Doig, statement to the author, 2 September 2007.
17. Doig, statement to the author, 13 August 2007.
18. The term 'uncanny' approximates the effect: at once familiar and unfamiliar, for which the more fitting term would be the German *unheimlich* (Un-home-like,lacking a proper place, but also not hidden and therefore familiar). The English version of the concept has been so casually used as to have degenerated into cliché. Doig's art is too peculiar to be encompassed by a shortcutting cliché – too uncanny to be designated 'uncanny' without the substantial analysis that Judith Nesbitt provides in her essay for this catalogue.
19. Doig, in Bonaventura, 'Peter Doig: A Hunter in the Snow', p.12.
20. Doig, statement to the author, 25 August 2007.
21. Matthew Higgs has made a curious parallel: Doig collects recordings of popular music and appreciates their packaging, which often depicts the members of the band. In the 1960s, bands, especially rock groups, began to dispense with uniforms and a coordinated physical appearance. The extreme variation in dress adopted by the members of these groups loosely resembles the dissociative variation that Doig builds into a canvas. See Matthew Higgs, 'Peter Doig's Record Collection', *Peter Doig Blizzard seventy-seven* Kunsthalle zu Kiel, 1998, pp.139–51.
22. On the color of snow, see Doig's comments in 'Peter Doig: Twenty Questions', in Scott, *Peter Doig*, p.17.
23. Doig's words, in a somewhat different context; statement to the author, 31 August 2007.
24. Bergson, *Matter and Memory*, p.173.
25. Doig, in Bonaventura, 'Peter Doig: A Hunter in the Snow', p.13.
26. Matthew Collings, 'Miasma versus Soufflé,' *Modern Painters*, Summer 2002, p.21.
27. 'The hydrant I painted incredibly fast—maybe ten minutes': Doig, statement to the author, 12 August 2007.
28. *Lapeyrouse Wall* 'possesses a type of realism that I never thought I would enter into, something that looks Edward Hopper-like in parts': Doig, 'Kitty Scott in conversation with Peter Doig', p.30. Note that Doig

uses 'realism' to refer to his style of rendering, as opposed to a fidelity to appearances.
29. Doig, quoted in Gareth Jones, 'Weird Places, Strange Folk', *Frieze*, October 1992, p.27.
30. Doig refers to elements of 'unrealised potential' within early modernist representational painting; conversation with the author, 1 June 2007.
31. For his exhibition catalogue *Peter Doig Blizzard seventy-seven*, Doig included a detail of the Bruegel painting in an unpaginated front section. He has stated on a number of occasions that his interest in snow extends to the electronic kind. On electronic snow, as well as photographic blur and filmic flicker, see Richard Shiff, 'Something Is Happening', *Art History* 28 (November 2005): pp.752–82, esp. pp.768–73.
32. Doig, statement in Leo Edelstein, 'Peter Doig: Losing Oneself in the Looking', *Flash Art* 31 (May–June 1998): p.86. It could be argued that the particles of snow in Bruegel's painting are more varied in size than they are similar. One of the beauties of snow is its perceptual formlessness: as with the 'snow' on the video monitor, each viewer is free to structure his or her view of it.
33. Doig, statement to the author, 25 August 2007.
34. Doig, in Bonaventura, 'Peter Doig: A Hunter in the Snow', p.13.
35. Doig remarks that at one stage he found this painting 'way too sweet. I remember having it hanging quite high up on my studio wall and lobbing white paint at it straight from the tube. I might have scraped it off – or thrown the painting away – but was surprised by, and very much liked, the way it seemed to push the image back and change the feel of the painting at the same time' (statement to the author, 31 August 2007).
36. Doig, in Bonaventura, 'Peter Doig: A Hunter in the Snow', p.14. Here, Doig drew an analogy between the use of hallucinogens and the experience of painting as means to leave the ordinary behind.
37. Doig, in conversation with Chris Ofili, August 2007.
38. 'Peter didn't watch the film with the intention of making a painting. It was when his snapshots [of a video projection of the film] came back from the processors that he suddenly saw their potential'; Paul Bonaventura, 'Peter Doig: A Partial Record', *Parkett* 67 (2003), p.56.
39. Doig, in conversation with Adrian Searle, *Peter Doig: Blotter*, p.14. Searle suggested the title *Lunker*, which refers to a large fish, usually a large bass. Searle also alluded to the Captain Beefheart album *Trout Mask Replica* (1969), perhaps recalling it because of an image of a fish (or man-fish) on its cover, but also because of Doig-like visual effects in the photography included in its design.
40. Doig, statement to the author, 2 September 2007.
41. Marcel Proust, 'Within a Budding Grove', *Remembrance of Things Past*, trans. C.K. Scott Moncrieff, 2 vols, New York 1934, vol. 1 p. 488.
42. Doig, in conversation with Adrian Searle, p.14.
43. Doig, statement to the author, 2 September 2007.
44. Daniel Richter, 'Dots on Doig', *Afterall*, no. 2, 2000, p.95.
45. Doig, in Bonaventura, 'Peter Doig: A Hunter in the Snow', p.12.
46. Doig, in conversation with Adrian Searle, p.10.
47. Doig, in Edelstein, 'Peter Doig: Losing Oneself in the Looking', p.86. See also, Doig, in Bonaventura, 'Peter Doig: A Hunter in the Snow', p.14.
48. At the time that Doig painted *Echo Lake*, he was thinking of the gesture of the female figure in Munch's *Ashes* 1894 (National Gallery, Oslo); it resembles the policeman's gesture, although in a different emotional context. The physical setting is also analogous: Munch's figure stands facing outwards from a rocky shore with a wall of trees behind. Munch often ringed forms with primary and secondary colours in a way not very different from Doig.
49. Perhaps Doig would dispute my sense of the distribution of visual features in *Lapeyrouse Wall* as remnants of a snow-screen effect. In 2001, he referred to his 'paintings with a proliferation of matter on the surface of the canvas', remarking that he 'had wanted to get away from that device of always "looking through", whether it be trees, branches, or snow – into the painting. It could have become manneristic.' Doig, statement in Scott, *Peter Doig*, p.17.
50. Doig, statement to the author, 2 September 2007; see also Doig, statement in 'Keeping It Right: Interview by Karen Wright', *Modern Painters*, March 2006, p.73.
51. 'Pelican' refers to the story involving the bird; 'Stag' is the name of a popular Trinidad beer, advertised as a 'man's beer.'
52. Ofili, in conversation with Peter Doig, August 2007.
53. Doig, statement in Scott, *Peter Doig*, p.21.
54. 'It was the somewhat solid rendering of light in [Matisse's] painting in the unlikely wooded setting that I found inspiring'; Doig, statement to the author, 31 August 2007. Doig saw this work at the Tate Modern exhibition of Matisse and Picasso in 2002.
55. Doig, in Edelstein, 'Peter Doig: Losing Oneself in the Looking', p.84. Doig was recalling having once had to walk a distance along a dark, deserted highway.
56. Doig, statement to the author, 25 August 2007; Doig was comparing his emotional response to images of Le Corbusier's Unité d'Habitation at Briey, France, and buildings on the island city of Suakin, Sudan, which appear in his *Bomb Island* 1991 (see p.54): 'It had been bombed many times and looked to be an "isle of the dead", its buildings like little skulls. Somehow this tied in with the image of the Corbusier building (for me).' See also Johanne Sloan, 'Hallucinating Landscape, Canadian-Style', in Scott, *Peter Doig*, p.12.
57. On the unfortunate history of the building at Briey, see Jacques Sbriglio, *Le Corbusier: The Unité d'Habitation in Marseilles*, trans. Sarah Parsons, Basel 2004, pp.211–18. Both the political Left and the political Right love to hate the Unité building type, regarding it as a failed utopian effort to design housing for the working class. The Left considers the project an elitist imposition of aesthetic form on social groups who should not be compelled to accept it. The Right views it as a morally bankrupt welfare project compounded by the sins of avant-garde art: 'communal lodging off in the wilderness [for] migrant workers, Italians or Portuguese or North Africans, for whom planning theories did not exist' (anonymous, 'Ruin', *National Review*, 13 July 1984, p.40.
58. 'I did a lot of physical work in the actual building – stripping wood, stripping concrete of years of paint'; Doig, statement to the author, 14 August 2007.
59. The title *Concrete Cabin* has at least a twofold reference: the Unité is a dwelling in the midst of woods or wilderness, the entire structure becoming like a cabin; in addition, its individual 'apartments are quite small and cabin-like – like stacked cabins' (Doig, statement to the author, 2 September 2007). As a transitive verb, 'cabin' refers to partitioning into small apartments.
60. Doig, statement to the author, 24 July 2007.
61. Doig, statement to the author, 28 August 2007.
62. Doig, statement to the author, 24 July 2007.
63. Ibid (emphasis added).
64. Doig, statement to the author, 28 August 2007.
65. Doig, statement in 'Kitty Scott in conversation with Peter Doig', p.16; statement to the author, 25 August 2007.
66. Doig's video and photographic work was in colour. He converted the images to black and white specifically for the photocopy book.
67. Doig, statement in Bonaventura, 'Peter Doig: A Hunter in the Snow', p.15.
68. Ibid.
69. Ibid, p.12.

List of Exhibited Works

Paintings

Hitch Hiker 1989–90
Oil on postal bags, 152 × 226 cm
Courtesy the artist
(p.45)

Milky Way 1989–90
Oil on canvas, 152 × 203.5 cm
Courtesy the artist
(p.47)

Art School 1990
Oil on canvas, 58.5 × 86.5 cm
Courtesy the artist
(p.46)

Baked 1990
Oil on canvas, 182 × 235 cm
Carlos and Rosa de la Cruz Collection
(p.48)

Swamped 1990
Oil on canvas, 197 × 241 cm
Private Collection
(p.51)

Bomb Island 1991
Oil on canvas, 200 × 300 cm
The Speyer Family Collection, New York
(p.54)

Young Bean Farmer 1991
Oil on canvas, 186 × 199 cm
Collection of Victoria and Warren Miro
(p.57)

Concrete Cabin 1991–2
Oil on canvas, 200 × 240 cm
Leicester Arts and Museums Service
(p.60)

Concrete Cabin II 1992
Oil on canvas, 200 × 275 cm
Collection of Victoria and Warren Miro
(p.61)

The House that Jacques Built 1992
Oil on canvas, 200 × 250 cm
Collection Tel Aviv Museum of Art. Gift of the British Friends of the Art Museums of Israel, Young Friends Committee, 1995
(p.49)

Blotter 1993
Oil on canvas, 249 × 199 cm
National Museums Liverpool, Walker Art Gallery
(p.66)

Pond Life 1993
Oil on canvas, 185 × 240 cm
Private Collection
(p.75)

Window Pane 1993
Oil on canvas, 250 × 200 cm
Collection of Victoria and Warren Miro
(p.67)

Cabin Essence 1993–4
Oil on canvas, 230 × 360 cm
Private Collection
(p.58)

Boiler House 1994
Oil on canvas, 200 × 275 cm
Collection of Ken and Judy Siebel; promised gift to the San Francisco Museum of Modern Art
(p.65)

Briey (Concrete Cabin) 1994–6
Oil on canvas, 275 × 200 cm
Courtesy Michael Werner Gallery, New York and Cologne
(p.62)

Cobourg 3+1 more 1994
Oil on canvas, 200 × 250 cm
Provinzial Rheinland Versicherung Düsseldorf
(p.72)

Corn Cob 1994
Oil on canvas, 121.9 × 152.4 cm
Los Angeles County Museum of Art, Gift of Peter Norton
(p.56)

Jetty 1994
Oil on canvas, 200 × 248 cm
Mimi and César Reyes Collection, Puerto Rico
(p.52)

Pine Houses (Rooms for Rent) 1994
Oil on canvas, 200 × 253 cm
Jennifer B. Stockman
(p.53)

Ski Jacket 1994
Oil on canvas, 295 × 190 cm (left)
295.3 × 160.4 cm (right)
Tate. Purchased with assistance from Evelyn, Lady Downshire's Trust Fund 1995
(p.70)

Red House 1995–6
Oil on canvas, 200 × 275 cm
Olbricht Collection
(p.77)

Reflection (What does your soul look like) 1996
Oil on canvas, 295 × 200 cm
Mima and César Reyes Collection, Puerto Rico
(p.69)

Canoe Lake 1997–8
Oil on canvas, 200 × 300 cm
Yageo Foundation Collection, Taiwan
(p.78)

Figure in Mountain Landscape 1997–8
Oil on canvas, 289 × 199.5 cm
Pinchuk Art Centre, Kiev
(p.73)

Country Rock 1998–9
Oil on canvas, 202 × 300 cm
Ole Faarup Collection, Copenhagen
(p.84 and cover)

Echo Lake 1998
Oil on canvas, 230.5 × 360.5 cm
Tate. Presented by the Trustees in honour of Sir Dennis and Lady Stevenson (later Lord and Lady Stevenson of Coddenham), to mark his period as Chairman 1989–98, 1998
(p.80)

Briey (Interior) 1999
Oil on canvas, 250 × 196 cm
Private Collection, Courtesy Michael Werner Gallery, New York and Cologne
(p.63)

The Heart of Old San Juan 1999
Oil on canvas, 250 × 195.5 cm
Private Collection
(p.97)

Gasthof zur Muldentalsperre 2000–2
Oil on canvas, 196 × 296 cm
Collection of Nancy Lauter McDougal and Alfred L. McDougal, partial and promised gift to The Art Institute of Chicago
(p.88)

100 Years Ago (Carrera) 2001
Oil on canvas, 229 × 358.5 cm
Centre Pompidou, Paris. Musée national d'art moderne – Centre de création industrielle. Purchased 2002
(p.82)

Girl in White with Trees 2001–2
Oil on canvas, 300 × 200 cm
Bonnefantenmuseum Maastricht
(p.95)

Grand Riviere 2001–2
Oil on canvas, 228.8 × 358.4 cm
National Gallery of Canada, Ottawa. Purchased 2003
(p.86)

Stag 2002–5
Oil on canvas, 250 × 200 cm
Martin and Rebecca Eisenberg
(p.92)

J.M. at Paragon 2004
Oil on canvas, 275 × 200 cm
Goetz Collection
(p.96)

Metropolitain (House of Pictures) 2004
Oil on canvas, 275.3 × 200 cm
Pinakothek der Moderne, Munich
Erworben von PIN. Freunde der Pinakothek der Moderne für die Sammlung Moderne Kunst
(p.91)

Black Curtain (Towards Monkey Island) 2004
Oil on linen, 200 × 275 cm
Mima and César Reyes Collection, Puerto Rico
(p.94)

Lapeyrouse Wall 2004
Oil on canvas, 200 × 250.5 cm
Private Collection; fractional and promised gift to The Museum of Modern Art, New York in honour of Kynaston McShine
(p.90)

Pelican 2004
Oil on canvas, 275 × 200 cm
Private Collection, Munich
(p.93)

Music of the Future 2002–7
Oil on linen, 200 × 300 cm
Courtesy the artist
(p.98)

Figures in Red Boat 2005–7
Oil on linen, 250 × 200 cm
Courtesy the artist
(p.101)

Untitled 2006
Oil and pastel on linen
300 × 350 cm
Courtesy the artist
(p.102)

Pelican Island 2006
Oil on canvas, 120 × 70 cm
Private Collection
(p.104)

Man Dressed as Bat 2007
Oil on linen, 300 × 350 cm
Courtesy the artist
(p.106)

Untitled (Jungle Painting) 2007
Oil on linen, 275 × 200 cm
Courtesy the artist
(p.105)

Small paintings

Ski Jacket 1993
Oil on canvas, 51 × 46 cm
Rosa de la Cruz Bonfiglio
(p.109)

Snowballed Boy 1995
Oil on wood, 60.5 × 40 cm
From the Donald R. Sobey Collection
(p.109)

Girl on Skis 1997
Oil on canvas, 30.3 × 40.6 cm
Southampton City Art Gallery
(p.109)

Friday 13th 1999
Oil on linen, 35.6 × 27.9 cm
Private Collector, Coral Gables, Florida USA
(p.109)

Pinto 2000
Oil on linen, 49 × 69 cm
Collection Carolyn and Leslie Goldbart
(p.109)

Cemetery Wall 2003
Oil on canvas, 36 × 46 cm
Courtesy the artist
(p.110)

Lapeyrouse P.O.S. Pink Umbrella 2003
Oil on canvas, 41 × 32 cm
Contemporary Fine Arts, Berlin
(p.110)

Black Palm 2004
Oil on canvas, 41 × 31.3 cm
Collection of Daniel Buchholz and Christopher Müller, Cologne
(p.111)

Lapeyrouse Umbrella 2004
Oil on canvas, 31.3 × 41 cm
Private Collection, Munich, Courtesy CFA, Berlin
(p.110)

Man Dressed as Bat (Embah) 2004
Oil on canvas, 23 × 17 cm
Courtesy Michael Werner Gallery, New York and Cologne
(p.111)

Purple Jesus (Black Rainbow) 2004
Oil on canvas, 120 × 70 cm
Private Collection
(p.112)

Untitled (Paramin) 2004
Oil on linen, 58.2 × 42.9 cm
Courtesy the artist
(p.111)

Works on paper

Swamped 1990
Black and red-brown chalk
57 × 78.8 cm
The British Museum, London
(p.123)

Untitled (Study for Milky Way) 1990
Watercolour on paper
52.1 × 63.5 cm
Private Collection, Germany
(p.123)

Rosedale 1991
Oil on paper, 57.2 × 73.7 cm
Mima and César Reyes Collection, Puerto Rico
(p.126)

Study for Young Bean Farmer 1991
Oil on paper, 57.2 × 72.4 cm
Mima and César Reyes Collection, Puerto Rico
(p.125)

Untitled 1991
Oil on paper, 29.9 × 21.6 cm
Private Collection, Courtesy Michael Werner Gallery, New York and Cologne
(p.125)

Untitled (Figure in Green Jacket) 1991
Mixed media on paper
47 × 35.6 cm
Private Collection, Germany
(p.130)

Study for Concrete Cabin 1992
Mixed media on paper, 57.2 × 72.4 cm
Private Collection, Germany
(p.127)

Unité 1992
Mixed media on paper, 72.4 × 57.8 cm
Collection of Stanley and Gail Hollander, Los Angeles
(p.127)

Swamped 1994
Pencil on paper, 20.3 × 24.8 cm
Private Collection, Courtesy Michael Werner Gallery, New York and Cologne
(p.124)

Blotter 1995
Acrylic on paper, 135.3 × 27.9 cm
Collection Manfred P. Herrmann, Berlin
(p.129)

Cobourg 3+1 More 1995
Acrylic on paper, 72.4 × 57.8 cm
[Not exhibited]
(p.128)

Study for Camp Forestia I 1996
Oil on paper, 72.8 × 57.6 cm
Collection Bremer Landesbank
(p.132)

Study for White Creep 1996
Oil on paper, 36.8 × 57.8 cm
Private Collection, Bremen
(p.130)

Canoe Lake 1999
Watercolour, pencil and oil on paper, 38.1 × 55.9 cm
Rubell Family Collection, Miami
(p.124)

Study for The Heart of Old San Juan 1999
Acrylic and gouache on brown paper, 100.3 × 69.9 cm
Private Collection
(p.133)

Three Bears 1999
Ink, sugar and watercolour on paper, 50.8 × 64.8 cm
Mr and Mrs W. Gaylen Weston
(p.131)

100 Years Ago 2001
Oil on paper, 101.6 × 137.2 cm
Collection of Matt Aberle, Los Angeles
(p.134)

100 Years Ago 2001
Oil on paper, 101.6 × 137.2 cm
Martin and Rebecca Eisenberg
(p.134)

Girl in Tree 2001
Oil on paper, 55.9 × 38.7 cm
Private Collection, Courtesy Michael Werner Gallery, New York and Cologne
(p.138)

Girl in Tree 2001
Gouache and watercolour on paper, 63.5 × 52.1 cm
Jennifer B. Stockman
(p.139)

House of Pictures 2001
Oil on paper, 41.9 × 59.7 cm
Laura and Marshall Front Collection
(p.136)

Untitled 2001
Watercolour on paper
34.9 × 24.7 cm
Collection of Melva Bucksbaum and Raymond Learsy
(p.137)

Untitled 2001
Oil on paper, 39.4 × 56.5 cm
The Dicke Collection
(p.143)

100 Years Ago 2002
Oil on paper, 75.8 × 55.9 cm
The Museum of Modern Art, New York. Fractional and promised gift of Martin and Rebecca Eisenberg
(p.135)

Driftwood (Yara) 2002
Watercolour on paper
55.9 × 35.7 cm
Collection of Allison and Edward Shearmur, Los Angeles, California
(p.143)

Fisherman 2002
Watercolour and gouache on paper, 72.4 × 57.2 cm
Collection of Beth Swofford
(p.142)

Grande Riviere 2002
Watercolour on paper
34.9 × 24.8 cm
Corinne Flick, London
(p.142)

Grande Riviere 2002
Oil on paper, 17.8 × 25.4 cm
Annabelle Selldorf
(p.142)

Guest House 1 2002
Oil on paper, 55.9 × 76.2 cm
Courtesy Michael Werner Gallery, New York and Cologne
(p.141)

Guest House 3 2002
Watercolour on paper
57.2 × 72.4 cm
The Art Institute of Chicago, Margaret Fisher Endowment
(p.140)

Ooty Boathouse 2002
Oil on paper, 56.5 × 39.4 cm
Private Collection, Courtesy Michael Werner Gallery, New York and Cologne
(p.146)

Untitled 2002
Pencil and ink on paper
50.4 × 66 cm
The Museum of Modern Art, New York. Purchased with funds provided by The Buddy Taub Foundation, Dennis A. Roach, Director, 2003
(p.140)

Untitled 2002
Ink on paper, 36.2 × 24.1 cm
Private Collection, Courtesy Michael Werner Gallery, New York and Cologne
(p.138)

Untitled 2002
Oil on cut paper, 64.8 × 50.2 cm
Private Collection, Dallas, Texas.
(p.141)

Untitled (Double Portrait) 2002
Oil on paper
63.5 × 52.3 cm (irregular)
National Gallery of Canada, Ottawa. Purchased 2003
(p.136)

J.M. at Paragon 2003
Oil on paper, 35.2 × 25 cm
Collection of Jonathan Meese
(p.148)

Metropolitain 2003
Oil on paper, 137.8 × 101.6 cm
Private Collection
(p.145)

Proofprint for Black Palms 2003
Etching on paper, 38.5 × 26.5 cm
Courtesy the artist
(p.144)

Untitled 2003
Charcoal and oil on paper
44.5 × 90.2 cm
Collection of Rosette Delug
(p.143)

Lapreyrouse Wall 2004
Oil on paper, 235 × 128.9 cm
The Museum of Modern Art, New York. Fractional and promised gift of David Teiger in honour of Gary Garrels, 2005
(p.147)

Man Dressed as Bat 2004
Oil on paper, 72.4 × 57.8 cm
Courtesy Michael Werner Gallery, New York and Cologne
(p.148)

Maracas 2004
Oil on paper, 72.2 × 57.5 cm
Deutsche Bank Art Collection
(p.144)

Maracas II 2004
Oil on paper, 72.6 × 57.5 cm
Deutsche Bank Art Collection
(p.144)

Paragon 2005
Oil on paper, 60.3 × 50.3 cm
The Rachofsky Collection
(p.149)

Paragon 2005
Oil on paper, 58.2 × 67.4 cm
Sharon and Michael Young
(p.149)

Untitled 2007
Oil on card, 56 × 36 cm
Courtesy the artist
(p.115)

Untitled 2007
Oil on paper, 51 × 40 cm
Courtesy the artist
(p.116)

Untitled 2007
Oil on paper, 22 × 19 cm
Courtesy the artist
(p.119)

Untitled 2007
Oil on canvas, 50.5 × 38.5 cm
Courtesy the artist
(p.120)

Lenders

Public Collections

The Art Institute of Chicago
The British Museum, London
Provinzial Rheinland Versicherung Düsseldorf
Leicester Arts and Museums Service
National Museum's Liverpool
Los Angeles County Museum of Art
Bonnefantenmuseum, Maastricht
Pinakothek der Moderne, Munich
The Museum of Modern Art, New York
National Gallery of Canada, Ottawa
Centre Pompidou, Paris. Musée national d'art moderne – Centre de création industrielle
San Francisco Museum of Modern Art
Southampton City Art Gallery
Tate, London
Tel Aviv Museum of Art

Private Collections

Matt Aberle, Los Angeles
The artist
Bremer Landesbank
Daniel Buchholz and Christopher Müller, Cologne
Melva Bucksbaum and Raymond Learsy
Contemporary Fine Arts, Berlin
Carlos and Rosa de la Cruz Collection
Rosa de la Cruz Bonfiglio
Rosette Delug
Deutsche Bank Art Collection
The Dicke Collection
Martin and Rebecca Eisenberg
Ole Faarup Collection, Copenhagen
Corinne Flick, London
Laura and Marshall Front Collection
Goetz Collection
Carolyn and Leslie Goldbart
Manfred P. Herrmann, Berlin
Stanley and Gail Hollander, Los Angeles
Nancy Lauter McDougal and Alfred L. McDougal
Jonathan Meese
Victoria and Warren Miro
Olbricht Collection
Pinchuk Art Centre, Kiev
Private Collection, Bremen
Private Collection, Coral Gables, Florida
Private Collection, Dallas, Texas
Private Collection, Germany
Private Collection, Munich,
Courtesy Contemporary Fine Arts, Berlin
Private Collection,
Courtesy Michael Werner Gallery, New York and Cologne
The Rachofsky Collection
Mima and César Reyes Collection, Puerto Rico
Rubell Family Collection, Miami
Annabelle Selldorf
Allison and Edward Shearmur, Los Angeles, California
Ken and Judy Siebel
Donald R. Sobey Collection
The Speyer Family Collection
Beth Swofford
David Teiger
Mr and Mrs W. Gaylen Weston
Michael Werner Gallery, New York and Cologne
Yageo Foundation Collection, Taiwan
Sharon and Michael Young
And other private lenders who wish to remain anonymous

Photographic and Copyright Credits

Courtesy of the artist p.27, p.98, p.101, p.105, p.106
Courtesy of the artist and Imprint 93 p.40
Courtesy of the artist and Victoria Miro Gallery, London p.10, p.13, p.14, p.15, p.16, p.17, p.45, p.47, p.48, p.49, p.52, p.54, p.57, p.58, p.61, p.63, p.65, p.66, p.67, p.69, p.72, p.73, p.75, p.77, p.78, p.97, p.82, p.84, p.86, p.88, p.92, p.95, p.96, p.108, p.109, p.111, p.112, p.115, p.117, p.119, p.120
Courtesy Contemporary Fine Arts, Berlin p.10, p.17, p.19, p.90, p.91, p.93, p.110
Courtesy Galerie Daniel Buchholz, Cologne p.11
Courtesy Gavin Brown's enterprise, New York p.13, p.153
Collection Oskar Reinhart "Am Römerholz", Winterthur, Switzerland p.30
New Walk Museum & Art Gallery p.60
Photo Courtesy Michael Werner Gallery, New York and Cologne p.23, p.35, p.36, p.42, p.46, p.62, p.94, p.102, p.104, p.123, p.130, p.135, p.136, p.138, p.140, p.141, p.142, p.143, p.146, p.148, p.149
Private Collection, on extended loan to the Courtauld Institute of Art Gallery, London p.39
Tate p. 15, 33, 15, 70, 80

All works by Peter Doig © the artist
© ARS, NY and DACS, London 2008 p.24
Photo © Jochen Littkemann p.10, p.17, p.19, p.36 p.45, 52, p.57, p.65, p.67, p.69, p.75, p.77, p.78, p.84 (and cover), p.90, p.91, p.93, p.108, p.148 p.110
© 2006 Museum Associates/LACMA p.16, p.56
© Andrew Phelps p.88
© Jurgen Schmidt, Cologne p.111
© Sheldon Memorial Art Gallery p.24
© Succession H Matisse/DACS 2007 p.36
©Tate Photography p.115, p.117, p.119, p.120